Visual Cognition

A **COGNITION** Special Issue

First Published as a Special Issue of *Cognition*, Jacques Mehler, Editor

Visual Cognition, Steven Pinker, Guest Editor

Visual Cognition

edited by
Steven Pinker

A Bradford Book
The MIT Press
Cambridge, Massachusetts
London, England

Second printing, 1986
First MIT Press edition, 1985

Reprinted from *Cognition: International Journal of Cognitive Psychology,* volume 18 (ISSN: 0010-0277). The MIT Press has exclusive license to sell this English-language book edition throughout the world.

Printed and bound in the United States of America

Library of Congress Cataloging in Publication Data

Main entry under title:

Visual cognition.

 (Computational models of cognition and perception)
 "A Bradford book."
 "Reprinted from Cognition:international journal of cognitive psychology, volume 18"—T.p. verso.
 Bibliography: p.
 Includes index.
 1. Visual perception. 2. Cognition. I. Pinker, Steven, 1954–   . II. Series.
 BF241.V564 1985   153.7   85-24155
 ISBN 0-262-16103-6

Contents

Preface

This collection of original research papers on visual cognition first appeared as a special issue of *Cognition: International Journal of Cognitive Science*. The study of visual cognition has seen enormous progress in the past decade, bringing important advances in our understanding of shape perception, visual imagery, and mental maps. Many of these discoveries are the result of converging investigations in different areas, such as cognitive and perceptual psychology, artificial intelligence, and neuropsychology. This volume is intended to highlight a sample of work at the cutting edge of this research area for the benefit of students and researchers in a variety of disciplines. The tutorial introduction that begins the volume is designed to help the nonspecialist reader bridge the gap between the contemporary research reported here and earlier textbook introductions or literature reviews.

Many people deserve thanks for their roles in putting together this volume: Jacques Mehler, Editor of *Cognition*; Susana Franck, Editorial Associate of *Cognition*; Henry Stanton and Elizabeth Stanton, Editors of Bradford Books; Kathleen Murphy, Administrative Secretary, Department of Psychology, MIT; Loren Ann Frost, who compiled the index; and the ad hoc *Cognition* referees who reviewed manuscripts for the special issue. I am also grateful to Nancy Etcoff, Stephen Kosslyn, and Laurence Parsons for their advice and encouragement.

Preparation of this volume was supported by NSF grants BNS 82-16546 and BNS 82-19450, by NIH grant 1RO1 HD 18381, and by the MIT Center for Cognitive Science under a grant from the A. P. Sloan Foundation.

Visual Cognition

Visual cognition: An introduction*

STEVEN PINKER

Massachusetts Institute of Technology

Abstract

This article is a tutorial overview of a sample of central issues in visual cognition, focusing on the recognition of shapes and the representation of objects and spatial relations in perception and imagery. Brief reviews of the state of the art are presented, followed by more extensive presentations of contemporary theories, findings, and open issues. I discuss various theories of shape recognition, such as template, feature, Fourier, structural description, Marr–Nishihara, and massively parallel models, and issues such as the reference frames, primitives, top-down processing, and computational architectures used in spatial cognition. This is followed by a discussion of mental imagery, including conceptual issues in imagery research, theories of imagery, imagery and perception, image transformations, computational complexities of image processing, neuropsychological issues, and possible functions of imagery. Connections between theories of recognition and of imagery, and the relevance of the papers contained in this issue to the topics discussed, are emphasized throughout.

Recognizing and reasoning about the visual environment is something that people do extraordinarily well; it is often said that in these abilities an average three-year old makes the most sophisticated computer vision system look embarrassingly inept. Our hominid ancestors fabricated and used tools for millions of years before our species emerged, and the selection pressures brought about by tool use may have resulted in the development of sophisticated faculties allowing us to recognize objects and their physical properties, to bring complex knowledge to bear on familiar objects and scenes, to

Preparation of this paper was supported by NSF grants BNS 82-16546 and 82-09540, by NIH grant 1R01HD18381-01, and by a grant from the Sloan Foundation awarded to the MIT Center for Cognitive Science. I thank Donald Hoffman, Stephen Kosslyn, Jacques Mehler, Larry Parsons, Whitman Richards, and Ed Smith for their detailed comments on an earlier draft, and Kathleen Murphy and Rosemary Krawczyk for assistance in preparing the manuscript. Reprint requests should be sent to Steven Pinker, Psychology Department, M.I.T., E10-018, Cambridge, MA 02139, U.S.A.

negotiate environments skillfully, and to reason about the possible physical interactions among objects present and absent. Thus visual cognition, no less than language or logic, may be a talent that is central to our understanding of human intelligence (Jackendoff, 1983; Johnson-Laird, 1983; Shepard and Cooper, 1982).

Within the last 10 years there has been a great increase in our understanding of visual cognitive abilities. We have seen not only new empirical demonstrations, but also genuinely new theoretical proposals and a new degree of explicitness and sophistication brought about by the use of computational modeling of visual and memory processes. Visual cognition, however, occupies a curious place within cognitive psychology and within the cognitive psychology curriculum. Virtually without exception, the material on shape recognition found in introductory textbooks in cognitive psychology would be entirely familiar to a researcher or graduate student of 20 or 25 years ago. Moreover, the theoretical discussions of visual imagery are cast in the same loose metaphorical vocabulary that had earned the concept a bad name in psychology and philosophy for much of this century. I also have the impression that much of the writing pertaining to visual cognition among researchers who are not directly in this area, for example, in neuropsychology, individual differences research, developmental psychology, psychophysics, and information processing psychology, is informed by the somewhat antiquated and imprecise discussions of visual cognition found in the textbooks.

The purpose of this special issue of *Cognition* is to highlight a sample of theoretical and empirical work that is on the cutting edge of research on visual cognition. The papers in this issue, though by no means a representative sample, illustrate some of the questions, techniques, and types of theory that characterize the modern study of visual cognition. The purpose of this introductory paper is to introduce students and researchers in neighboring disciplines to a selection of issues and theories in the study of visual cognition that provide a backdrop to the particular papers contained herein. It is meant to bridge the gap between the discussions of visual cognition found in textbooks and the level of discussion found in contemporary work.

Visual cognition can be conveniently divided into two subtopics. The first is the representation of information concerning the visual world currently before a person. When we behave in certain ways or change our knowledge about the world in response to visual input, what guides our behavior or thought is rarely some simple physical property of the input such as overall brightness or contrast. Rather, vision guides us because it lets us know that we are in the presence of a particular configuration of three-dimensional shapes and particular objects and scenes that we know to have predictable properties. 'Visual recognition' is the process that allows us to determine on the basis of retinal input that particular shapes, configurations of shapes, objects, scenes, and their properties are before us.

The second subtopic is the process of remembering or reasoning about shapes or objects that are not currently before us but must be retrieved from memory or constructed from a description. This is usually associated with the topic of 'visual imagery'. This tutorial paper is divided into two major sections, devoted to the representation and recognition of shape, and to visual imagery. Each section is in turn subdivided into sections discussing the background to each topic, some theories on the relevant processes, and some of the more important open issues that will be foci of research during the coming years.

Visual recognition

Shape recognition is a difficult problem because the immediate input to the visual system (the spatial distribution of intensity and wavelength across the retinas—hereafter, the "retinal array") is related to particular objects in highly variable ways. The retinal image projected by an object—say, a notebook—is displaced, dilated or contracted, or rotated on the retina when we move our eyes, ourselves, or the book; if the motion has a component in depth, then the retinal shape of the image changes and parts disappear and emerge as well. If we are not focusing on the book or looking directly at it, the edges of the retinal image become blurred and many of its finer details are lost. If the book is in a complex visual context, parts may be occluded, and the edges of the book may not be physically distinguishable from the edges and surface details of surrounding objects, nor from the scratches, surface markings, shadows, and reflections on the book itself.

Most theories of shape recognition deal with the indirect and ambiguous mapping between object and retinal image in the following way. In long-term memory there is a set of representations of objects that have associated with them information about their shapes. The information does not consist of a replica of a pattern of retinal stimulation, but a canonical representation of the object's shape that captures some invariant properties of the object in all its guises. During recognition, the retinal image is converted into the same format as is used in long-term memory, and the memory representation that matches the input the closest is selected. Different theories of shape recognition make different assumptions about the long-term *memory representations* involved, in particular, how many representations a single object will have, which class of objects will be mapped onto a single representation, and what the format of the representation is (i.e. which primitive symbols can be found in a representation, and what kinds of relations among them can be specified). They will differ in regards to which sports of *preprocessing* are done to the retinal image (e.g., filtering, contrast enhancement, detection of edges) prior to matching, and in terms of how the retinal input or memory representations are *transformed* to bring them into closer correspondence. And they differ in terms of the metric of *goodness of fit* that determines which memory representation fits the input best when none of them fits it exactly.

Traditional theories of shape recognition

Cognitive psychology textbooks almost invariably describe the same three or so models in their chapters on pattern recognition. Each of these models is fundamentally inadequate. However, they are not always inadequate in the ways the textbooks describe, and at times they *are* inadequate in ways that the textbooks do not point out. An excellent introduction to three of these models—templates, features, and structural descriptions—can be found in Lindsay and Norman (1977); introductions to Fourier analysis in vision, which forms the basis of the fourth model, can be found in Cornsweet (1980) and Weisstein (1980). In this section I will review these models extremely briefly, and concentrate on exactly why they do not work, because a catalogue of their deficits sets the stage for a discussion of contemporary theories and issues in shape recognition.

Template matching
This is the simplest class of models for pattern recognition. The long term memory representation of a shape is a replica of a pattern of retinal stimulation projected by that shape. The input array would be simultaneously superimposed with all the templates in memory, and the one with the closest above-threshold match (e.g., the largest ratio of matching to nonmatching points in corresponding locations in the input array) would indicate the pattern that is present.

Usually this model is presented not as a serious theory of shape recognition, but as a straw man whose destruction illustrates the inherent difficulty of the shape recognition process. The problems are legion: partial matches could yield false alarms (e.g., a 'P' in an 'R' template); changes in distance, location, and orientation of a familiar object will cause this model to fail to detect it, as will occlusion of part of the pattern, a depiction of it with wiggly or cross-hatched lines instead of straight ones, strong shadows, and many other distortions that we as perceivers take in stride.

There are, nonetheless, ways of patching template models. For example, multiple templates of a pattern, corresponding to each of its possible displace-ments, rotations, sizes, and combinations thereof, could be stored. Or, the input pattern could be rotated, displaced, and scaled to a canonical set of values before matching against the templates. The textbooks usually dismiss these possibilities: it is said that the product of all combinations of transforma-tions and shapes would require more templates than the brain could store, and that in advance of recognizing a pattern, one cannot in general determine which transformations should be applied to the input. However, it is easy to show that these dismissals are made too quickly. For example, Arnold Trehub (1977) has devised a neural model of recognition and imagery, based on templates, that addresses these problems (this is an example of a 'massively parallel' model of recognition, a class of models I will return to later). Con-tour extraction preprocesses feed the matching process with an array of sym-bols indicating the presence of edges, rather than with a raw array of intensity levels. Each template could be stored in a single cell, rather than in a space-consuming replica of the entire retina: such a cell would synapse with many retinal inputs, and the shape would be encoded in the pattern of strengths of those synapses. The input could be matched in parallel against all the stored memory templates, which would mutually inhibit one another so that partial matches such as 'P' for 'R' would be eliminated by being inhibited by better matches. Simple neural networks could center the input pattern and quickly generate rotated and scaled versions of it at a variety of sizes and orientations, or at a canonical size and orientation (e.g., with the shape's axis of elongation vertical); these transformed patterns could be matched in parallel against the stored templates.

Nonetheless, there are reasons to doubt that even the most sophisticated versions of template models would work when faced with realistic visual inputs. First, it is unlikely that template models can deal adequately with the third dimension. Rotations about any axis other than the line of sight cause distortions in the projected shape of an object that cannot be inverted by any simple operation on retina-like arrays. For example, an arbitrary edge might move a large or a small amount across the array depending on the axis and phase of rotation and the depth from the viewer. 3-D rotation causes some surfaces to disappear entirely and new ones to come into view. These prob-lems occur even if one assumes that the arrays are constructed subsequent to stereopsis and hence are three-dimensional (for example, rear surfaces are still not represented, there are a bewildering number of possible directions of translation and axes of rotation, each requiring a different type of retinal transformation).

Second, template models work only for isolated objects, such as a letter presented at the center of a blank piece of paper: the process would get nowhere if it operated, say, on three-fifths of a book plus a bit of the edge of the table that it is lying on plus the bookmark in the book plus the end of the pencil near it, or other collections of contours that might be found in a circumscribed region of the retina. One could posit some figure–ground segregation preprocess occurring before template matching, but this has problems of its own. Not only would such a process be highly complex (for example, it would have to distinguish intensity changes in the image resulting from differences in depth and material from those resulting from differences in orientation, pigmentation, shadows, surface scratches, and specular (glossy) reflections), but it probably interacts with the recognition process and hence could not precede it. For example, the figure–ground segregation process involves carving up a set of surfaces into parts, each of which can then be matched against stored templates. This process is unlikely to be distinct from the process of carving up a single object into its parts. But as Hoffman and Richards (1984) argue in this issue, a representation of how an object is decomposed into its parts may be the first representation used in accessing memory during recognition, and the subsequent matching of particular parts, template-style or not, may be less important in determining how to classify a shape.

Feature models

This class of models is based on the early "Pandemonium" model of shape recognition (Selfridge, 1959; Selfridge and Neisser, 1960). In these models, there are no templates for entire shapes; rather, there are mini-templates or 'feature detectors' for simple geometric features such as vertical and horizontal lines, curves, angles, 'T'-junctions, etc. There are detectors for every feature at every location in the input array, and these detectors send out a graded signal encoding the degree of match between the target feature and the part of the input array they are 'looking at'. For every feature (e.g., an open curve), the levels of activation of all its detectors across the input array are summed, or the number of occurrences of the feature are counted (see e.g., Lindsay and Norman, 1977), so the output of this first stage is a set of numbers, one for each feature.

The stored representation of a shape consists of a list of the features composing the shape, in the form of a vector of weights for the different features, a list of how many tokens of each feature are present in the shape, or both. For example, the representation of the shape of the letter 'A' might specify high weights for (1) a horizontal segment, (2) right-leaning diagonal segment, (3) a left-leaning diagonal segment, (4) an upward-pointing acute angle, and so on, and low or negative weights for curved and vertical segments. The intent is to use feature weights or counts to give each shape a characterization that is invariant across transformations of it. For example, since the features are all independent of location, any feature specification will be invariant across translations and scale changes; and if features referring to orientation (e.g. "left-leaning diagonal segment") are eliminated, and only features distinguishing straight segments from curves from angles are retained, then the description will be invariant across frontal plane rotations.

The match between input and memory would consist of some comparison of the levels of activation of feature detectors in the input with the weights of the corresponding features in each of the stored shape representations, for example, the product of those two vectors, or the number of matching features minus the number of mismatching features. The shape that exhibits the highest degree of match to the input is the shape recognized.

The principal problem with feature analysis models of recognition is that no one has ever been able to show how a *natural* shape can be defined in terms of a vector of feature weights. Consider how one would define the shape of a horse. Naturally, one could define it by giving high weights to features like 'mane', 'hooves', 'horse's head', and so on, but then detecting these features would be no less difficult than detecting the horse itself. Or, one could try to define the shape in terms of easily detected features such as vertical lines and curved segments, but horses and other natural shapes are composed of so many vertical lines and curved segments (just think of the nose alone, or the patterns in the horse's hide) that it is hard to believe that there is a feature vector for a horse's shape that would consistently beat out feature vectors for other shapes across different views of the horse. One could propose that there is a hierarchy of features, intermediate ones like 'eye' being built out of lower ones like 'line segment' or 'circle', and higher ones like 'head' being built out of intermediate ones like 'eye' and 'ear' (Selfridge, for example, posited "computational demons" that detect Boolean combinations of features), but no one has shown how this can be done for complex natural shapes.

Another, equally serious problem is that in the original feature models the spatial relationships among features—how they are located and oriented with respect to one another—are generally not specified; only which ones are present in a shape and perhaps how many times. This raises serious problems in distinguishing among shapes consisting of the same features arranged in different ways, such as an asymmetrical letter and its mirror image. For the same reason, simple feature models can turn reading into an anagram problem, and can be shown formally to be incapable of detecting certain pattern distinctions such as that between open and closed curves (see Minsky and Papert, 1972).

One of the reasons that these problems are not often raised against feature models is that the models are almost always illustrated and referred to in connection with recognizing letters of the alphabet or schematic line drawings. This can lead to misleading conclusions because the computational problems posed by the recognition of two-dimensional stimuli composed of a small number of one-dimensional segments may be different in kind from the problems posed by the recognition of three-dimensional stimuli composed of a large number of two-dimensional surfaces (e.g., the latter involves compensating for perspective and occlusion across changes in the viewer's vantage point and describing the complex geometry of curved surfaces). Furthermore, when shapes are chosen from a small finite set, it is possible to choose a feature inventory that exploits the minimal contrasts among the particular members of the set and hence successfully discriminates among those members, but that could be fooled by the addition of new members to the set. Finally, letters or line drawings consisting of dark figures presented against a blank background with no other objects occluding or touching them avoids the many difficult problems concerning the effects on edge detection of occlusion, illumination, shadows, and so on.

Fourier models

Kabrisky (1966), Ginsburg (1971, 1973), and Persoon and Fu (1974; see also Ballard and Brown, 1982) have proposed a class of pattern recognition models that that many researchers in psychophysics and visual physiology adopt implicitly as the most likely candidate for shape recognition in humans. In these models, the two-dimensional input intensity array is subjected to a spatial trigonometric Fourier analysis. In such an analysis, the array is decomposed into a set of components, each component specific to a sinusoidal change in intensity along a single orientation at a specific spatial frequency. That is, one component might specify the degree to which the image gets brighter and darker and brighter and darker, etc., at intervals of 3° of visual angle going from top right to bottom left in the image (averaging over changes in brightness along the orthogonal direction). Each component can be conceived of as a grid consisting of parallel black-and-white stripes of a particular width oriented in a particular direction, with the black and white stripes fading gradually into one another. In a full set of such grating-like components, there is one component for each stripe width or spatial frequency (in cycles per degree) at each orientation (more precisely, there would be a continuum of components across frequencies and orientations).

A Fourier transform of the intensity array would consist of two numbers for each of these components. The first number would specify the degree of contrast in the image corresponding to that frequency at that orientation (that is, the degree of difference in brightness between the bright areas and the dark areas of that image for that frequency in that orientation), or, roughly, the degree to which the image 'contains' that set of stripes. The full set of these numbers is the *amplitude spectrum* corresponding to the image. The second number would specify where in the image the peaks and troughs of the intensity change defined by that component lie. The full set of these numbers of the *phase spectrum* corresponding to the image. The amplitude spectrum and the phase spectrum together define the *Fourier transform* of the image, and the transform contains all the information in the original image. (This is a very crude introduction to the complex subject of Fourier analysis. See Weisstein (1980) and Cornsweet (1970) for excellent nontechnical tutorials).

One can then imagine pattern recognition working as follows. In long-term memory, each shape would be stored in terms of its Fourier transform. The Fourier transform of the image would be matched against the long-term memory transforms, and the memory transform with the best fit to the image transform would specify the shape that is recognized.[1]

How does matching transforms differ from matching templates in the original space domain? When there is an exact match between the image and one of the stored templates, there are neither advantages nor disadvantages to doing the match in the transform domain, because no information is lost in the transformation. But when there is no exact match, it is possible to define metrics of goodness of fit in the transform domain that might capture some of the invariances in the family of retinal images corresponding to a shape. For example, to a first approximation the amplitude spectrum corresponding to a shape is the same regardless of where in the visual field the object is located. Therefore if the matching process could focus on the amplitude spectra of shape and input, ignoring the phase spectrum, then a shape could be recognized across all its possible translations. Furthermore, a shape and its mirror image have the same amplitude spectrum, affording recognition of a shape across reflections of it. Changes in orientation and scale of an object result in corresponding changes in orientation and scale in the transform, but in some models the transform can easily be normalized so that it is invariant with rotation and scaling. Periodic patterns and textures, such as a brick wall, are easily recognized because they give rise to peaks in their transforms corresponding to the period of repetition of the pattern. But most important, the Fourier transform segregates information about sharp edges and small

---

[1] In Persoon and Fu's model (1974), it is not the transform of brightness as a function of visual field position that is computed and matched, but the transform of the tangent angle of the boundary of an object as a function of position along the boundary. This model shares many of the advantages and disadvantages of Fourier analysis of brightness in shape recognition.

details from information about gross overall shape. The latter is specified primarily by the lower spatial-frequency components of the transform (i.e., fat gratings), the former, by the higher spatial-frequency components (i.e. thin gratings). Thus if the pattern matcher could selectively ignore the higher end of the amplitude spectrum when comparing input and memory transforms, a shape could be recognized even if its boundaries are blurred, encrusted with junk, or defined by wiggly lines, dots or dashes, thick bands, and so on. Another advantage of Fourier transforms is that, given certain assumptions about neural hardware, they can be extracted quickly and matched in parallel against all the stored templates (see e.g., Pribram, 1971).

Upon closer examination, however, matching in the transform domain begins to lose some of its appeal. The chief problem is that the invariances listed above hold only for entire scenes or for objects presented in isolation. In a scene with more than one object, minor rearrangements such as moving an object from one end of a desk to another, adding a new object to the desk top, removing a part, or bending the object, can cause drastic changes in the transform. Furthermore the transform cannot be partitioned or selectively processed in such a way that one part of the transform corresponds to one object in the scene, and another part to another object, nor can this be done within the transform of a single object to pick out its parts (see Hoffman and Richards (1984) for arguments that shape representations must explicitly define the decomposition of an object into its parts). The result of these facts is that it is difficult or impossible to recognize familiar objects in novel scenes or backgrounds by matching transforms of the input against transforms of the familiar objects. Furthermore, there is no straightforward way of linking the shape information implicit in the amplitude spectrum with the position information implicit in the phase spectrum so that the perceiver can tell where objects are as well as what they are. Third, changes in the three-dimesional orientation of an object do not result in any simple cancelable change in its transform, even it we assume that the visual system computes three-dimensional transforms (e.g., using components specific to periodic changes in binocular disparity).

The appeal of Fourier analysis in discussions of shape recognition comes in part from the body of elegant psychophysical research (e.g., Campbell and Robson, 1968) suggesting that the visual system partitions the information in the retinal image into a set of channels each specific to a certain range of spatial frequencies (this is equivalent to sending the retinal information through a set of bandpass filters and keeping the outputs of those filters separate). This gives the impression that early visual processing passes on to the shape recognition process not the original array but something like a Fourier transform of the array. However, *filtering* the image according to its spatial frequency components is not the same as *transforming* the image into its spectra. The psychophysical evidence for channels is consistent with the notion that the recognition system operates in the space domain, but rather than processing a single array, it processes a family of arrays, each one containing information about intensity changes over a different scale (or, roughly, each one bandpass-filtered at a different center frequency). By processing several bandpass-filtered images separately, one obtains some of the advantages of Fourier analysis (segregation of gross shape from fine detail) without the disadvantages of processing the Fourier transform itself (i.e. the utter lack of correspondence between the parts of the representation and the parts of the scene).

Structural descriptions

A fourth class of theories about the format in which visual input is matched against memory holds that shapes are represented *symbolically*, as *structural descriptions* (see Minsky, 1975; Palmer, 1975a; Winston, 1975). A structural description is a data structure that can be thought of as a list of propositions whose arguments correspond to parts and whose predicates correspond to properties of the parts and to spatial relationships among them. Often these propositions are depicted as a graph whose nodes correspond to the parts or to properties, and whose edges linking the nodes correspond to the spatial relations (an example of a structural description can be found in the upper left portion of Fig. 6). The explicit representation of spatial relations is one aspect of these models that distinguishes them from feature models and allows them to escape from some of the problems pointed out by Minsky and Papert (1972).

One of the chief advantages of structural descriptions is that they can factor apart the information in a scene without necessarily losing information in it. It is not sufficient for the recognition system simply to supply a list of labels for the objects that are recognized, for we need to know not only what things are but also how they are oriented and where they are with respect to us and each other, for example, when we are reaching for an object or driving. We also need to know about the visibility of objects: whether we should get closer, turn up the lights, or remove intervening objects in order to recognize an object with more confidence. Thus the recognition process in general must not boil away or destroy the information that is not diagnostic of particular objects (location, size, orientation, visibility, and surface properties) until it ends up with a residue of invariant information; it must *factor apart* or *decouple* this information from information about shape, so that different cognitive processes (e.g., shape recognition *versus* reaching) can access the information relevant to their particular tasks without becoming overloaded, distracted, or misled by the irrelevant information that the retina conflates with the relevant information. Thus one of the advantages of a structural description is that the shape of an object can be specified by one set of propositions, and its location in the visual field, orientation, size, and relation to other objects can be specified in different propositions, each bearing labels that processing operations can use for selective access to the information relevant to them.

Among the other advantages of structural descriptions are the following. By representing the different parts of an object as separate elements in the representation, these models break up the recognition process into simpler subprocesses, and more important, are well-suited to model our visual system's reliance on decomposition into parts during recognition and its ability to recognize novel rearrangements of parts such as the various configurations of a hand (see Hoffman and Richards (1984)). Second, by mixing logical and spatial relational terms in a representation, structural descriptions can differentiate among parts that must be present in a shape (e.g., the tail of the letter 'Q'), parts that may be present with various probabilities (e.g., the horizontal cap on the letter 'J'), and parts that must not be present (e.g., a tail on the letter 'O') (see Winston, 1975). Third, structural descriptions represent information in a form that is useful for subsequent visual reasoning, since the units in the representation correspond to objects, parts of objects, and spatial relations among them. Nonvisual information about objects or parts (e.g., categories they belong to, their uses, the situations that they are typically found in) can easily be associated with parts of structural descriptions, especially since many theories hold that nonvisual knowledge is stored in a propositional format that is similar to structural descriptions (e.g., Minsky, 1975; Norman and Rumelhart, 1975). Thus visual recognition can easily invoke knowledge about what is recognized that may be relevant to visual cognition in general, and that knowledge in turn can be used to aid in the recognition process (see the discussion of top-down approaches to recognition below).

The main problem with the structural description theory is that it is not really a full theory of shape recognition. It specifies the format of the representation used in matching the visual input against memory, but by itself it does not specify what types of entities and relations each of the units belonging to a structural description corresponds to (e.g., 'line' *versus* 'eye' *versus* 'sphere'; 'next-to' *versus* 'to-the-right-of' *versus* '37-degrees-with-respect-to'), nor how the units are created in response to the appropriate patterns of retinal stimulation (see the discussion of feature models above). Although most researchers in shape recognition would not disagree with the claim that the matching process deals with something like structural descriptions, a genuine theory of shape recognition based on structural descriptions must specify these components and justify why they are appropiate. In the next section, I discuss a theory proposed by David Marr and H. Keith Nishihara which makes specific proposals about each of these aspects of structural descriptions.

Two fundamental problems with the traditional approaches

There are two things wrong with the textbook approaches to visual representation and recognition. First, none of the theories specifies where perception ends and where cognition begins. This is a problem because there is a natural factoring part of the process that extracts information about the geometry of the visible world and the process that recognizes familiar objects. Take the recognition of a square. We can recognize a square whether its contours are defined by straight black lines printed on a white page, by smooth rows and columns of arbitrary small objects (Kohler, 1947; Koffka, 1935), by differences in lightness or in hue between the square and its background, by differences in binocular disparity (in a random-dot stereogram), by differences in the orientation or size of randomly scattered elements defining visual textures (Julesz, 1971), by differences in the directions of motion of randomly placed dots (Ullman, 1982; Marr, 1982), and so on. The square can be recognized as being a square regardless of how the boundaries are found; for example, we do not have to learn the shape of a square separately for boundaries defined by disparity in random-dot stereograms, by strings of asterisks, etc., nor must we learn the shapes of other figures separately for each type of edge once we have learned how to do so for a square. Conversely, it can be demonstrated that the ultimate recognition of the shape is not necessary for any of these processes to find the boundaries (the boundaries can be seen even if the shape they define is an unfamiliar blob, and expecting to see a square is neither necessary nor sufficient for the perceiver to see the boundaries; see Gibson, 1966; Marr, 1982; Julesz, 1971). Thus the process that recognizes a shape does not care about how its boundaries were found, and the processes that find the boundaries do not care how they will be used. It makes sense to separate the process of finding boundaries, degree of curvature, depth, and so on, from the process of recognizing particular shapes (and from other processes such as reasoning that can take their input from vision).

A failure to separate these processes has tripped up the traditional approaches in the following ways. First, any theory that derives canonical shape representations directly from the retinal arrays (e.g., templates, features) will have to solve all the problems associated with finding edges (see the previous paragraph) at the same time as solving the problem of recognizing particular shapes—an unlikely prospect. On the other hand, any theory that simply assumes that there is some perceptual processing done before the shape match but does not specify what it is is in danger of explaining very little since the putative preprocessing could solve the most important part of the recognition process that the theory is supposed to address (e.g., a claim that a feature like 'head' is supplied to the recognition process). When assumptions about perceptual preprocessing *are* explicit, but are also incorrect or unmotivated, the claims of the recognition theory itself could be seriously undermined: the theory could require that some property of the world is supplied to the recognition process when there is no physical basis for the perceptual system to extract that property (e.g., Marr (1982) has argued that it is impossible for early visual processes to segment a scene into objects).

The second problem with traditional approaches is that they do not pay serious attention to what in general the shape recognition process has to do, or, put another way, what problem it is designed to solve (see Marr, 1982). This requires examining the input and desired output of the recognition process carefully: on the one hand, how the laws of optics, projective geometry, materials science, and so on, relate the retinal image to the external world, and on the other, what the recognition process must supply the rest of cognition with. Ignoring either of these questions results in descriptions of recognition mechanisms that are unrealizable, useless, or both.

The Marr–Nishihara theory

The work of David Marr represents the most concerted effort to examine the nature of the recognition problem, to separate early vision from recognition and visual cognition in general, and to outline an explicit theory of three-dimensional shape recognition built on such foundations. In this section, I will briefly describe Marr's theory. Though Marr's shape recognition model is not without its difficulties, there is a consensus that it addresses the most important problems facing this class of theories, and that its shortcomings define many of the chief issues that researchers in shape recognition must face.

The $2^1/_2$-D sketch

The core of Marr's theory is a claim about the interface between perception and cognition, about what early, bottom-up visual processes supply to the recognition process and to visual cognition in general. Marr, in collaboration with H. Keith Nishihara, proposed that early visual processing culminates in the construction of a representation called the *$2^1/_2$-D sketch*. The 2½-D sketch is an array of cells, each cell dedicated to a particular line of sight from the viewer's vantage point. Each cell in the array is filled with a set of symbols indicating the depth of the local patch of surface lying on that line of sight, the orientation of that patch in terms of the degree and direction in which it dips away from the viewer in depth, and whether an edge (specifically, a discontinuity in depth) or a ridge (specifically, a discontinuity in orientation) is present at that line of sight (see Fig. 1). In other words, it is a representation of the surfaces that are visible when looking in a particular direction from a single vantage point. The 2½-D sketch is intended to gather together in one representation the richest information that early visual processes can deliver, Marr claims that no top-down processing goes into the construction of the 2½-D sketch, and that it does not contain any global information about shape (e.g., angles between lines, types of shapes, object or part boundaries), only depths and orientations of local pieces of surface.

The division between the early visual processes that culminate in the 2½-D sketch and visual recognition has an expository as well as a theoretical advantage: since the early processes are said not to be a part of visual cognition

Figure 1   *Schematic drawing of Marr and Nishihara's 2½-D sketch. Arrows represent surface orientation of patches relative to the viewer (the heavy dots are foreshortened arrows). The dotted line represents locations where orientation changes discontinuously (ridges). The solid line represents locations where depth changes discontinuously (edges). The depths of patches relative to the viewer are also specified in the 2½-D sketch but are not shown in this figure. From Marr (1982).*

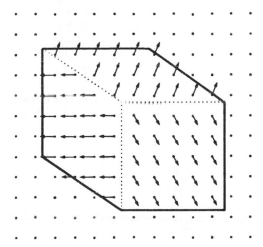

(i.e., not affected by a person's knowledge or intentions), I will discuss them only in bare outline, referring the reader to Marr (1982) and Poggio (1984) for details. The 2½-D sketch arises from a chain of processing that begins with mechanisms that convert the intensity array into a representation in which the locations of edges and other surface details are made explicit. In this 'primal sketch', array cells contain symbols that indicate the presence of edges, corners, bars, and blobs of various sizes and orientations at that location. Many of these elements can remain invariant over changes in overall illumination, contrast, and focus, and will tend to coincide in a relatively stable manner with patches of a single surface in the world. Thus they are useful in subsequent processes that must examine similarities and differences among neighboring parts of a surface, such as gradients of density, size, or shape of texture elements, or (possibly) processes that look for corresponding parts of the world in two images, such as stereopsis and the use of motion to reconstruct shape.

A crucial property of this representation is that the edges and other features are extracted separately at a variety of scales. This is done by looking for points where intensity changes most rapidly across the image using detectors of different sizes that, in effect, look at replicas of the image filtered at different ranges of spatial frequencies. By comparing the locations of intensity changes in each of the (roughly) bandpass-filtered images, one can create families of edge symbols in the primal sketch, some indicating the boundaries of the larger blobs in the image, others indicating the boundaries of finer details. This segregation of edge symbols into classes specific to different scales preserves some of the advantages of the Fourier models discussed above: shapes can be represented in an invariant manner across changes in image clarity and surface detail (e.g., a person wearing tweeds *versus* polyester).

The primal sketch is still two-dimensional, however, and the next stage of processing in the Marr and Nishihara model adds the third dimension to arrive at the 2½-D sketch. The processes involved at this stage compute the depths and orientations of local patches of surfaces using the binocular disparity of corresponding features in the retinal images from the two eyes (e.g., Marr and Poggio, 1977), the relative degrees of movement of features in successive views (e.g., Ullman, 1979), changes in shading (e.g., Horn, 1975), the size and shape of texture elements across the retina (Cutting and Millard, 1984; Stevens, 1981), the shapes of surface contours, and so on. These processes cannot indicate explicitly the overall three-dimensional shape of an object, such as whether it is a sphere or a cylinder; their immediate output is simply a set of values for each patch of a surface indicating its relative distance from the viewer, orientation with respect to the line of sight, and whether either depth or orientation changes discontinuously at that patch (i.e., whether an edge or ridge is present).

The 2½-D sketch itself is ill-suited to matching inputs against stored shape representations for several reasons. First, only the visible surfaces of shapes are represented; for obvious reasons, bottom-up processing of the visual input can provide no information about the back sides of opaque objects. Second, the 2½-D sketch is viewpoint-specific; the distances and orientations of patches of surfaces are specified with respect to the perceiver's viewing position and viewing direction, that is, in part of a spherical coordinate system centered on the viewer's vantage point. That means that as the viewer or the object moves with respect to one another, the internal representation of the object in the 2½-D sketch changes and hence does not allow a successful match against any single stored replica of a past 2½-D representation of the object (see Fig. 2a). Furthermore, objects and their parts are not explicitly demarcated.

Figure 2.   *The orientation of a hand with respect to the retinal vertical* V *(a viewer-centered reference frame), the axis of the body* B *(a global object-centered reference frame), and the axis of the lower arm* A *(a local object-centered reference frame). The retinal angle of the hand changes with rotation of the whole body (middle panel); its angle with respect to the body changes with movement of the elbow and shoulder (right panel). Only its angle with respect to the arm remains constant across these transformations.*

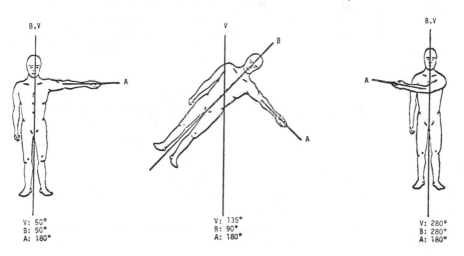

Shape recognition and 3-D models

Marr and Nishihara (1978) have proposed that the shape recognition process (a) defines a coordinate system that is centered on the as-yet unrecognized object, (b) characterizes the arrangement of the object's parts with respect to that coordinate system, and (c) matches such characterizations against canonical characterizations of objects' shapes stored in a similar format in memory. The object os described with respect to a coordinate system that is centered on the object (e.g., its origin lies on some standard point on the object and one or more of its axes are aligned with standard parts of the object), rather than with respect to the viewer-centered coordinate system of the 2½-D sketch, because even though the locations of the object's parts with respect to the viewer change as the object as a whole is moved, the locations of its parts with respect to the object itself do not change (see Fig. 2b). A structural description representing an object's shape in terms of the arrangement of its parts, using parameters whose meaning is determined by a coordinate system centered upon that object, is called the *3-D model description* in Marr and Nishihara's theory.

Centering a coordinate system on the object to be represented solves only some of the problems inherent in shape recognition. A single object-centered description of a shape would still fail to match an input object when the object bends at its joints (see Fig. 2c), when it bears extra small parts (e.g., a horse with a bump on its back), or when there is a range of variation among objects within a class. Marr and Nishihara address this *stability* problem by proposing that information about the shape of an object is stored not in a single model with a global coordinate system but in a hierarchy of models each representing parts of different sizes and each with its own coordinate system. Each of these local coordinate systems is centered on a part of the shape represented in the model, aligned with its axis of elongation, symmetry, or (for movable parts) rotation.

For example, to represent the shape of a horse, there would be a top-level model with a coordinate system centered on the horse's torso. That coordinate system would be used to specify the locations, lengths, and angles of the main parts of the horse: the head, limbs, and tail. Then subordinate models are defined for each of those parts: one for the head, one for the front right leg, etc. Each of those models would contain a coordinate system centered on the part that the model as a whole represents, or on a part subordinate to that part (e.g., the thigh for the leg subsystem). The coordinate system for that model would be used to specify the positions, orientations, and lengths of the subordinate parts that comprise the part in question. Thus, within the head model, there would be a specification of the locations and angles of the neck axis and of the head axis, probably with respect to a coordinate system centered on the neck axis. Each of these parts would in turn get its own model, also consisting of a coordinate axis centered on a part, plus a characterization of the parts subordinate to it. An example of a 3-D model for a human shape is shown in Fig. 3.

Employing a hierarchy of corrdinate systems solves the stability problems alluded to above, because even though the position and orientation of the hand relative to the torso can change wildly and unsystematically as a person bends the arm, the position of the hand relative to the arm does not change (except possibly by rotating within the range of angles permitted by bending of the wrist). Therefore the description of the shape of the arm remains constant only when the arrangement of its parts is specified in terms of angles and positions relative to the arm axis, not relative to the object as a whole (see Fig. 2). For this to work, of course, positions, lengths, and angles must be specified in terms of ranges (see Fig. 3d) rather than by precise values, so as to accommodate the changes resulting from movement or individual variation among exemplars of a shape. Note also that the hierarchical arrangement of 3-D models compensates for individual variation in a second way: a horse with a swollen or broken knee, for example, will match the 3-D model defining the positions of a horse's head, torso, limbs, and tail relative to the torso axis, even if the subordinate limb model itself does not match the input limb.

Organization and accessing of shape information in memory

Marr and Nishihara point out that using the 3-D model format, it is possible to define a set of values at each level of the hierarchy of coordinate systems that correspond to a central tendency among the members of well-defined classes of shapes organized around a single 'plan'. For example, at the top level of the hierarchy defining limbs with respect to the torso, one can define one set of values that most quadruped shapes cluster around, and a different set of values that most bird shapes cluster around. At the next level down one can define values for subclasses of shapes such as songbirds *versus* long-legged waders.

This modular organization of shape descriptions, factoring apart the arrangement of parts of a given size from the internal structure of those parts, and factoring apart shape of an individual type from the shape of the class of objects it belongs to, allows input descriptions to be matched against memory in a number of ways. Coarse information about a shape specified in a top-level coordinate system can be matched against models for general classes (e.g., quadupeds) first, constraining the class of shapes that are checked the next level down, and so on. Thus when recognizing the shape of a person, there is no need to match it against shape descriptions of particular types of

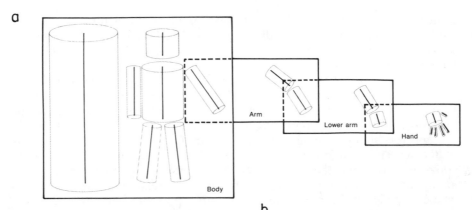

a

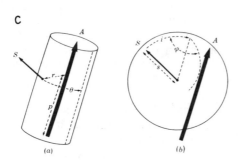

c

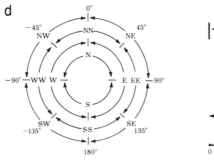

d

b

		Origin location			Part orientation		
Shape	Part	ρ	r	θ	i	ϕ	s
Human	head	DE	AB	NN	NN	NN	AB
	arm	DE	CC	EE	SE	EE	BC
	arm	DE	CC	WW	SE	WW	BC
	torso	CC	AB	NN	NN	NN	CC
	leg	CC	CC	EE	SS	NN	CC
	leg	CC	CC	WW	SS	NN	CC
Arm	upper arm	AA	AA	NN	NN	NN	CC
	lower arm	CC	AA	AA	NE	NN	CC
Lower Arm	forearm	AA	AA	NN	NN	NN	DD
	hand	DD	AA	NN	NN	NN	BB
Hand	palm	AA	AA	NN	NN	NN	CC
	thumb	AA	BB	NN	NE	NN	BC
	finger	CC	BB	NN	NN	NN	CC
	finger	CC	AB	NN	NN	NN	CC
	finger	CC	AB	SS	NN	NN	CC
	finger	CC	BB	SS	NN	NN	CC

guppies, parakeets, or beetles once it has been concluded that the gross shape is that of a primate. (Another advantage of using this scheme is that if a shape is successfully matched at a higher level but not at any of the lower levels, it can still be classified as failing into a general class or pattern, such as being a bird, even if one has never encountered that type of bird before). An alternative way of searching shape memory is to allow the successful recognition of a shape in a high-level model to trigger the matching of its subordinate part-models against as-yet unrecognized parts in the input, or to allow the successful recognition of individual parts to trigger the matching of their superordinate models against the as-yet unrecognized whole object in the input containing that part. (For empirical studies on the order in which shape representations are matched against inputs, see Jolicoeur *et al.* 1984a; Rosch *et al.* 1976; Smith *et al.* 1978. These studies suggest that the first index into shape memory may be at a 'basic object' level, rather than the most abstract level, at least for prototypical exemplars of a shape.)

Representing shapes of parts
Once the decomposition of a shape into its component axes is accomplished, the shapes of the components that are centered on each axis must be specified as well. Marr and Nishihara conjecture that shapes of parts may be described in terms of *generalized cones* (Binford, 1971). Just as a cone can be defined as the surface traced out when a circle is moved along a straight line perpendicular to the circle while its diameter steadily shrinks, a generalized cone can be defined as the surface traced out when *any* planar closed shape is moved along *any* smooth line with its size smoothly changing in *any* way. Thus to specify a particular generalized cone, one must specify

---

Figure 3.   *Marr and Nishishara's 3-D model description for a human shape. A shows how the whole shape is decomposed into a hierarchy of models, each enclosed by a rectangle. B shows the information contained in the model description: the subordinate models contained in each superordinate, and the location and orientation of the defining axis of each subordinate with respect to a coordinate system centered on a part of the superordinate. The meanings of the symbols used in the model are illustrated in C and D: the endpoint of a subordinate axis is defined by three parameters in a cylindrical coordinate system centered on a superordinate part (left panel of C); the orientation and length of the subordinate axis are defined by three parameters in a spherical coordinate system centered on the endpoint and aligned with the superordinate part (right panel of C). Angles and lengths are specified by ranges rather than by exact values (D). From Marr and Nishihara (1978).*

the shape of the axis (i.e., how it bends, if at all), the two-dimensional shape of the generalized cone's cross-section, and the gradient defining how its area changes as a function of position along the axis. (Marr and Nishihara point out that shapes formed by biological growth tend to be well-modeled by generalized cones, making them good candidates for internal representations of the shapes of such parts.) In addition, surface primitives such as rectangular, circular, or bloblike markings can also be specified in terms of their positions with respect to the axis model.

Deriving 3-D descriptions from the 2½-D sketch
Unfortunately, this is an aspect of the Marr and Nishihara model that has not been developed in much detail. Marr and Nishihara did outline a limited process for deriving 3-D descriptions from the two-dimensional silhouette of the object. The process first carves the silhouette into parts at extrema of curvature, using a scheme related to the one proposed by Hoffman and Richards (1984). Each part is given an axis coinciding with its direction of elongation, and lines are created joining endpoints to neighboring axes. The angles between axes and lines are measured and recorded, the resulting description is matched against top-level models in memory, and the best-matched model is chosen. At that point, constraints on how a part is situated and oriented with respect to the superordinate axis in that model can be used to identify the viewer-relative orientation of the part axis in the 2½-D sketch. That would be necessary if the orientation of that part cannot be determined by an examination of the sketch itself, such as when its axis is pointing toward the viewer and hence is foreshortened. Once the angle of an axis is specified more precisely, it can be used in selecting subordinate 3-D models for subsequent matching.

The Marr and Nishihara model is the most influential contemporary model of three-dimensional shape recognition, and it is not afflicted by many of the problems that afflict the textbook models of shape representation summarized earlier. Nonetheless, the model does have a number of problems, which largely define the central issues to be addressed in current research on shape recognition. In the next section, I summarize some of these problems briefly.

Current problems in shape recognition research

Choice of shape primitives to represent parts
The shape primitives posited by Marr and Nishihara—generalized cones centered on axes of elongation or symmetry—have two advantages: they can

easily characterize certain important classes of objects, such as living things, and they can easily be derived from their silhouettes. But Hoffman and Richards (1984) point out that many classes of shapes cannot be easily described in this scheme, such as faces, shoes, clouds, and trees. Hoffman and Richards take a slightly different approach to the representation of parts in a shape description. They suggest that the problem of *describing* parts (i.e., assigning them to categories) be separated from the problem of *finding* parts (i.e., determining how to carve an object into parts). If parts are only found by looking for instances of certain part categories (e.g., generalized cones) then parts that do not belong to any of those categories would never be found. Hoffman and Richards argue that, on the contrary, there is a psychologically plausible scheme for finding part boundaries that is ignorant of the nature of the parts it defines. The parts delineated by these boundaries at each scale can be categorized in terms of a taxonomy of lobes and blobs based on the patterns of inflections and extrema of curvature of the lobe's surface. (Hoffman (1983) has worked out a taxonomy for primitive shape descriptors, called 'codons', for two-dimensional plane curves). They argue not only that the decomposition of objects into parts is more basic for the purposes of recognition than the description of each part, but that the derivation of part boundaries and the classification of parts into sequences of codon-like descriptors might present fewer problems than the derivation of axis-based descriptions, because the projective geometry of extrema and inflections of curvature allows certain reliable indicators of these extrema in the image to be used as a basis for identifying them (see Hoffman, 1983).

Another alphabet of shape primitives that has proven useful in computer vision consists of a set of canonical volumetric shapes such as spheres, parallelopipeds, pyramids, cones, and cylinders, with parameterized sizes and (possibly) aspect ratios, joined together in various ways to define the shape of an object (see e.g., Hollerbach, 1975; Badler and Bajcsy, 1978). It is unlikely that a single class of primitives will be sufficient to characterize all shapes, from clothes lying in a pile to faces to animals to furniture. That means that the derivation process must be capable of determining prior to describing and recognizing a shape which type of primitives are appropriate to it. There are several general schemes for doing this. A shape could be described in parallel in terms of all the admissible representational schemes, and descriptions in inappropriate schemes could be rejected because they are unstable over small changes in viewing position or movement, or because no single description within a scheme can be chosen over a large set of others within that scheme. Or there could be a process that uses several coarse properties of an object, such as its movement, surface texture and color, dimensionality, or sound to give it an initial classification into broad categories such as animal *versus* plant *versus* artifact each with its own scheme of primitives and their organization (e.g., see Richards (1979, 1982) on "playing 20 questions" with the perceptual input).

Assigning frames of reference to a shape

In a shape representation, size, location, and orientation cannot be specified in absolute terms but only with respect to some frame of reference. It is convenient to think of a frame of reference as a coordinate system centered on or aligned with the reference object, and transformations within or between reference frames as being effected by an analogue of matrix multiplication taking the source coordinates as input and deriving the destination coordinates as output. However, a reference frame need not literally be a coordinate system. For example, it could be an array of arbitrarily labelled cells, where each cell represents a fixed position relative to a reference object. In that case, transformations within or between such reference frames could be effected by fixed connections among corresponding source and destination cells (e.g., a network of connections linking each cell with its neighbor to the immediate right could effect translation when activated iteratively; see e.g., Trehub, 1977).

If a shape is represented for the purpose of recognition in terms of a coordinate system or frame of reference centered on the object itself, the shape recognition system must have a way of determining what the object-centered frame of reference is prior to recognizing the object. Marr and Nishihara conjecture that a coordinate system used in recognition may be aligned with an object's axes of elongation, bilateral symmetry, radial symmetry (for objects that are radially symmetrical in one plane and extended in an orthogonal direction), rotation (for jointed objects), and possibly linear movement. Each of these is suitable for aligning a coordinate system with an object because each is derivable prior to object recognition and each is fairly invariant for a type of object across changes in viewing position.

This still leaves many problems unsolved. For starters, these methods only fix the orientation of one axis of the cylindrical coordinate system. The direction of the cylindrical coordinate system for that axis (i.e., which end is zero), the orientation of the zero point of its radial scale, and the handedness of the radial scale (i.e., whether increasing angle corresponds to going clockwise or counterclockwise around the scale) are left unspecified, as is the direction of one of the scales used in the spherical coordinate system specified within the cylindrical one (assuming its axes are aligned with the axis of the cylindrical system and the line joining it to the cylindrical system) (see Fig. 3c). Furthermore, even the choice of the orientation of the principal axis will be difficult when an object is not elongated or symmetrical, or when the principal axis is occluded, foreshortened, or physically compressed. For example, if the top-level description of a cow shape describes the dispositions of its parts with respect to the cow's torso, then when the cow faces the viewer the torso is not visible, so there is no way for the visual system to describe, say, the orientations of the leg and head axes relative to its axis.

There is evidence that our assignment of certain aspects of frames of reference to an object is done independently of its intrinsic geometry. The positive–negative direction of an intrinsic axis, or the assignment of an axis to an object when there is no elongation or symmetry, may be done by computing a global up–down direction. Rock (1973, 1983) presents extensive evidence showing that objects' shapes are represented relative to an up–down direction. For example, a square is ordinarily 'described' internally as having a horizontal edge at the top and bottom; when the square is tilted 45°, it is described as having vertices at the top and bottom and hence is perceived as a different shape, namely, a diamond. The top of an object is not, however, necessarily the topmost part of the object's projection on the retina: Rock has shown that when subjects tilt their heads and view a pattern that, unknown to them, is tilted by the same amount (so that it projects the same retinal image), they often fail to recognize it. In general, the up–down direction seems to be assigned by various compromises among the gravitational upright, the retinal upright, and the prevailing directions of parallelism, pointing, and bilateral symmetry among the various features in the environment of the object (Attneave, 1968; Palmer and Bucher, 1981; Rock, 1973). In certain circumstances, the front–back direction relative to the viewer may also be used as a frame of reference relative to which the shape is described; Rock *et al.* (1981) found that subjects would fail to recognize a previously-learned asymmetrical wire form when it was rotated 90° about the vertical axis.

What about the handedness of the angular scale in a cylindrical coordinate system (e.g., the θ parameter in Fig. 3)? One might propose that the visual system employs a single arbitrary direction of handedness for a radial scale that is uniquely determined by the positive–negative direction of the long axis orthogonal to the scale. For example, we could use something analogous to the 'right hand rule' taught to physics students in connection with the orientation of a magnetic field around a wire (align the extended thumb of your right hand with the direction of the flow of current, and look which way your fingers curl). There is evidence, however, that the visual system does *not* use any such rule. Shepard and Hurwitz (1984, in this issue; see also Hinton and Parsons, 1981; Metzler and Shepard, 1975) point out that we do not in general determine how parts are situated or oriented with respect to the left–right direction on the basis of the intrinsic geometry of the object (e.g., when we are viewing left and right hands). Rather, we assign the object a left–right direction in terms of our own egocentric left and right sides. When an object's top and bottom do not correspond to an egocentric or gravitational top–bottom direction, we mentally rotate it into such an orientation, and when two unfamiliar objects might differ in handedness, we rotate one into the orientation of the other (taking greater amounts of time for greater angles of rotation. Mental rotation is discussed further later in this paper). Presumably this failure to assign objects intrinsic left and right directions is an evolutionary consequence of the fact that aside from human artifacts and body parts, virtually no class of ecologically significant shapes need be distinguished from their enantiomorphs (Corballis and Beale, 1976; Gardner, 1967).

To the extent that a shape is described with respect to a reference frame that depends on how the object is oriented with respect to the viewer or the environment, shape recognition will fail when the object moves with respect to the viewer or environment. In cases where we do succeed at recognizing objects across its different dispositions and where object-centered frames cannot be assigned, there are several possible reasons for such success. One is that multiple shape descriptions, corresponding to views of the object with different major axes occluded, are stored under a single label and corresponding parts in the different descriptions are linked. Another is that the representation of the object is rotated into a canonical orientation or until the description of the object relative to the frame matches a memorized shape description; alternatively, the reference frame or canonical orientation could be rotated into the orientation of the object. Interestingly, there is evidence from Cooper and Shepard (1973) and Shepard and Hurwitz (1984) that the latter option (rotating an empty reference frame) is difficult or impossible for humans to do: advance information about the orientation of an upcoming visual stimulus does not spare the perceiver from having to rotate the stimulus mentally when it does appear in order to judge its handedness.[2] A third possibility stems from Hoffman and Richards's (1984) suggestion that part segmentation may be independent of orientation, and that only the representations of spatial relations among parts are orientation-sensitive. If so, recognition of an isolated part can be used as an index to find the objects in memory that contain that part. Finally, in some cases recognition might fail outright with changes in orientation but the consequences might be innocu-

---

[2]Hinton and Parsons (1981) have shown that when the various stimuli to be judged all conform to a single shape schema (e.g., alphanumeric characters with a vertical spine and strokes attached to the right side of the spine, such as 'R', 'L', and 'F'), advance information about orientation saves the subject from having to rotate the stimulus. However, it is possible that in their experiment subjects rotated a concrete image of a vertical spine plus a few strokes, rather than an empty reference frame.

ous. Because of the pervasiveness of gravity, many shapes will rarely be seen in any position but the upright (e.g., faces, trees), and many of the differences in precise shape among objects lacking axes of symmetry, movement, rotation, or elongation are not ecologically significant enough for us to distinguish among them in memory (e.g., differences among bits of gravel or crumpled newspaper). Naturally, to the extent that any of the suggestions made in this paragraph are true, the importance of Marr and Nishihara's argument for canonical object-centered descriptions lessens.[3]

Frames of reference for the visual field

We not only represent the shapes of objects internally; we also represent the locations and orientations of objects and surfaces in the visual field. The frames of reference that we use to represent this information will determine the ease with which we can make various spatial judgments. The relevant issues are the *alignment* of the frames of reference, and the *form* of the frames of reference.

Early visual representations are in a viewer-centered and approximately spherical frame of reference; that is, our eyes give us information about the world in terms of the azimuth and elevation of the line of sight at which the features are found relative to the retina, and their distance from the viewing position (this is the coordinate system used for the 2½-D sketch). Naturally, this is a clumsy representation to use in perceiving invariant spatial relations, since the information will change with eye movements. The system can compensate for eye movements by superimposing a head-centered coordinate system on top of the retinal system and moving the origin of that coordinate system in conjunction with eye movement commands. Thus every cell in the 2½-D sketch would be represented by the fixed 'address' defined with respect to the retina, and also by its coordinates with respect to the head, which would be dynamically adjusted during eye movements so that fixed locations in the world retain a constant coordinate address within the head-centered system. A third coordinate system, defined over the same information, could represent position with respect to the straight ahead direction of the body

---

[3]Specifying the origin of the object-centered coordinate system presents a slightly different set of issues than specifying the orientation of its axes. An origin for an object-centered frame can be determined by finding its visual center of mass or by assigning it to one end of a principal axis. It is noteworthy that there are no obvious cases where we fail to recognize an object when it is displaced, where we see a shape as ambiguous by virtue of assigning different 'centers' or 'reference locations' to it (analogous to the diamond/tilted square ambiguity), or where we have to mentally translate an object in order to recognize it or match it against a comparison object. This indicates either that the procedure that assigns an origin to an object on the basis of its intrinsic geometry always yields a unique solution for an object, or that, as Hinton (1979a) suggests, we do not compute an origin at all in shape descriptions, only a set of significant directions.

and it could be updated during head movements to represent the invariant position of surfaces across those movements. Other coordinate systems could be defined over these visible surface representations as well, such as coordinate systems aligned with the gravitational upright and horizontal ground (see Shepard and Hurwitz, 1984), with fixed salient landmarks in the world, or with the prevailing directions of large surfaces (e.g., the walls in a tilted room). These coordinate systems for objects' positions with respect to one's body or with respect to the environment could be similar to those used to represent the parts of an object with respect to the object as a whole. Presumably they are also like coordinate systems for objects' shapes in being organized hierarchically, so that a paper clip might be represented by its position with respect to the desk tray it is in, whose position is specified with respect to the desk, whose position is specified with respect to the room. Beyond the visual world, the origin and orientation of large frames of reference such as that for a room could be specified in a hierarchy of more schematic frames of reference for entities that cannot be seen in their entirety, such as those for floor plans, buildings, streets, neighborhoods and so on (see e.g., Kuipers, 1978; Lynch, 1960; McDermott, 1980).

The possible influence of various frames of reference on shape perception can be illustrated by an unpublished experiment by Laurence Parsons and Geoff Hinton. They presented subjects with two Shepard–Metzler cube figures, one situated 45° to the left of the subject, another at 45° to the right. The task was to turn one of the objects (physically) to whatever orientation best allowed the subject to judge whether the two were identical or whether one was a mirror-reversed version of the other (subjects were allowed to move their heads around the neck axis). If objects were represented in coordinate systems centered upon the objects themselves, subjects would not have to turn the object at all (we known from the Shepard and Metzler studies that this is quite unlikely to be true for these stimuli). If objects are represented in a coordinate system aligned with the retina, subjects should turn one object until the corresponding parts of the two objects are perpendicular to the other, so that they will have the same orientations with respect to their respective lines of sight. And if shapes are represented in a coordinate system aligned with salient environmental directions (e.g., the walls), one object would be turned until its parts are parallel to those of the other, so that they will have the same orientations with respect to the room. Parsons and Hinton found that subjects aligned one object so that it was nearly parallel with another, with a partial compromise toward keeping the object's retinal projections similar (possibly so that corresponding cube faces on the two objects would be simultaneously visible). This suggests that part orientations are represented primarily with respect to environmentally-influenced frames.

The choice of a reference object, surface, or body part is closely tied to the format of the coordinate system aligned with the frame of reference, since rotatable objects (such as the eyes) and fixed landmarks easily support coordinate systems containing polar scales, whereas reference frames with orthogonal directions (e.g., gravity and the ground, the walls of a room) easily support Cartesian-like coordinate systems. The type of coordinate system employed has effects on the ease of making certain spatial judgments. As mentioned, the 2½-D sketch represents information in a roughly spherical coordinate system, with the result that the easiest information to extract concerning the position of an edge or feature is its distance and direction with respect to the vantage point. As Marr (1982) points out, this representation conceals many of the geometric properties of surfaces that it would be desirable to have easy access to; something closer to a Cartesian coordinate system centered on the viewer would be much handier for such purposes. For example, if two surfaces in different parts of the visual field are parallel, their orientations as measured in a spherical coordinate system will be different, but their orientations as measured in a coordinate system with a parallel component (e.g., Cartesian) will be the same (see Fig. 4). If a surface is flat, the represented orientations of all the patches composing its surface will be identical in Cartesian, but not in spherical coordinates. Presumably, size constancy could also be a consequence of such a coordinate system, if a given range of coordinates in the left–right or up–down directions always stood for

Figure 4.   *Effects of rectangular versus polar coordinate systems on making spatial judgments. Whether two surfaces are parallel can be assessed by comparing their angles with respect to the straight ahead direction in a rectangular coordinate system (b), but not by comparing their angles with respect to the lines of sight in a polar system (a). From Marr (1982).*

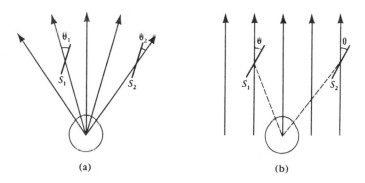

(a)   (b)

a constant real world distance regardless of the depth of the represented surface.

One potentially relevant bit of evidence comes from a phenomenon studied by Corcoran (1977), Natsoulas (1966), and Kubovy *et al.* (1984, Reference note 1). When an asymmetric letter such as 'd' is traced with a finger on the back of a person's head, the person will correctly report what the letter is. But when the same letter is traced on the person's forehead, the mirror image of that letter is reported instead (in this case, 'b'). This would follow if space (and not just visible space) is represented in a parallel coordinate system aligned with a straight ahead direction, such as that shown in Fig. 4b. The handedness of a letter would be determined by whether its spine was situated to the left or right of the rest of its parts, such that 'left' and 'right' would be determined by a direction orthogonal to the straight ahead direction, regardless of where on the head the letter is drawn. The phenomenon would not be expected in an alternative account, where space is represented using spherical coordinates centered on a point at or behind the eyes (e.g., Fig. 4a), because then the letter would be reported as if 'seen' from the inside of a transparent skull, with letters traced on the back of the head reported as mirror-reversed, contrary to fact.

In many experiments allowing subjects to choose between environmental, Cartesian-like reference frames and egocentric, spherical reference frames, subjects appear to opt for a compromise (e.g., the Parsons and Hinton and Kubovy *et al.* studies; see also Attneave, 1972; Gilinsky, 1955; Uhlarik *et al.* 1980). It is also possible that we have access to both systems, giving rise to ambiguities when a single object is alternatively represented in the two systems, for example, when railroad tracks are seen either as parallel or as converging (Boring, 1952; Gibson, 1950; Pinker, 1980a), or when the corner formed by two edges of the ceiling of a room can be seen both as a right angle and as an obtuse angle.

Deriving shape descriptions

One salient problem with the Marr and Nishihara model of shape recognition in its current version is that there is no general procedure for deriving an object-centered 3-D shape description from the 2½-D sketch. The algorithm proposed by Marr and Nishihara using the two-dimensional silhouette of a shape to find its intrinsic axes has trouble deriving shape descriptions when axes are foreshortened or occluded by other parts of the object (as Marr and Nishihara pointed out). In addition, the procedures it uses for joining up part boundaries to delineate parts, to find axes of parts once they are delineated, and to pair axes with one another in adjunct relations rely on some limited heuristics that have not been demonstrated to work other than for objects composed of generalized cones—but the perceiver cannot in general know prior to recognition whether he or she is viewing such an object. Furthermore, there is no explicit procedure for grouping together the parts that belong together in a single hierarchical level in the 3-D model description. Marr and Nishihara suggest that all parts lying within a 'coarse spatial context' surrounding an axis can be placed within the scope of the model specific to that axis, but numerous problems could arise when unrelated parts are spatially contiguous, such as when a hand is resting on a knee. Some of these problems perhaps could be resolved using an essentially similar scheme when information that is richer than an object's silhouette is used. For example, the depth, orientation, and discontinuity information in the $2\frac{1}{2}$-D sketch could assist in the perception of foreshortened axes (though not when the blunt end of a tapering object faces the viewer squarely), and information about which spatial frequency bandpass channels an edge came from could help in the segregation of parts into hierarchical levels in a shape description.

A general problem in deriving shape representations from the input is that, as mentioned, the choice of the appropriate reference frame and shape primitives depends on what type of shape it is, and shapes are recognized via their description in terms of primitives relative to a reference frame. In the remainder of this section I describe three types of solutions to this chicken-and-egg problem.

Top–down processing

One response to the inherent difficulties of assigning descriptions to objects on the basis of their retinal images is to propose that some form of ancillary information based on a person's knowledge about regularities in the world is used to choose the most likely description or at least to narrow down the options (e.g., Gregory, 1970; Lindsay and Norman, 1977; Minsky, 1975; Neisser, 1967). For example, a cat-owner could recognize her cat upon seeing only a curved, long, grey stripe extending out from underneath her couch, based on her knowledge that she has a long-tailed grey cat that enjoys lying there. In support of top–down, or, more precisely, knowledge-guided perceptual analysis, Neisser (1967), Lindsay and Norman (1977), and Gregory (1970) have presented many interesting demonstrations of possible retinal ambiguities that may be resolved by knowledge of physical or object-specific regularities, and Biederman (1972), Weisstein and Harris (1974) and Palmer (1975b) and others have shown that the recognition of an object, a part of an object, or a feature can depend on the identity that we attribute to the context object or scene as a whole.

Despite the popularity of the concept of top–down processing within cognitive science and artificial intelligence during much of the 1960s and 1970s, there are three reasons to question the extent to which general knowledge plays a role in describing and recognizing shapes. First, many of the supposed demonstrations of top–down processing leave it completely unclear what kind of knowledge is brought to bear on recognition (e.g., regularities about the geometry of physical objects in general, about particular objects, or about particular scenes or social situations), and how that knowledge is brought to bear (e.g., altering the order in which memory representations are matched against the input, searching for particular features or parts in expected places, lowering the goodness-of-fit threshold for expected objects, generating and fitting templates, filling in expected parts). Fodor (1983) points out that these different versions of the top-down hypothesis paint very different pictures of how the mind is organized in general: if only a restricted type of knowledge can influence perception in a top–down manner, and then only in restricted ways, the mind may be constructed out of independent modules with restricted channels of communication among them. But if all knowledge can influence perception, the mind could consist of an undifferentiated knowledge base and a set of universal inference procedures which can be combined indiscriminately in the performance of any task. Exactly which kind of top–down processing is actually supported by the data can make a big difference in one's conception of how the mind works; Fodor argues that so far most putative demonstrations of top–down phenomena are not designed to distinguish among possible kinds of top-down processing and so are uninformative on this important issue.

A second problem with extensive top–down processing is that there is a great deal of information about the world that is contained in the light array, even if that information cannot be characterized in simple familiar schemes such as templates or features (see Gibson, 1966, 1979; Marr, 1982). Given the enormous selection advantage that would be conferred on an organism that could respond to what was really in the world as opposed to what it expected to be in the world whenever these two descriptions were in conflict, we should seriously consider the possibility that human pattern recognition has the most sophisticated bottom-up pattern analyses that the light array and the properties of our receptors allow. And as Ullman (1984, this issue) points out, we do appear to be extremely accurate perceivers even when we have no basis for expecting one object or scene to occur rather than another, such as when watching a slide show composed of arbitrary objects and scenes.

Two-stage analysis of objects
Ullman (1984) suggests that our visual systems may execute a universal set of 'routines' composed of simple processes operating on the 2½-D sketch, such as tracing along a boundary, filling in a region, marking a part, and

sequentially processing different locations. Once universal routines are executed, their outputs could characterize some basic properties of the prominent entities in the scene such as their rough shape and spatial relationships. This characterization could then trigger the execution of routines specific to the recognition of particular objects or classes of objects. Because routines can be composed of arbitrary sequences of very simple but powerful processes, it might be possible to compile both a core of generally useful routines, plus a large set of highly specific routines suitable for the recognition of very different classes of objects, rather than a canonical description scheme that would have to serve for every object type. (In Ullman's theory visual routines would be used not only for the recognition of objects but also for geometric reasoning about the surrounding visual environment such as determining whether one object is inside another or counting objects.) Richards (1979, 1982) makes a related proposal concerning descriptions for recognition, specifically, that one might first identify various broad classes of objects such as animal, vegetable, or mineral by looking for easily sensed hallmarks of these classes such as patterns of movement, color, surface texture, dimensionality, even coarse spectral properties of their sounds. Likely reference frames and shape primitives could then be hypothesized based on this first-stage categorization.

Massively parallel models
There is an alternative approach that envisions a very different type of solution from that suggested by Richards, and that advocates very different types of mechanisms from those described in this issue by Ullman. Attneave (1982), Hinton (1981) and Hrechanyk and Ballard (1982) have outlined related proposals for a model of shape recognition using massively parallel networks of simple interconnected units, rather than sequences of operations performed by a single powerful processor (see Ballard *et al.* 1983; Feldman and Ballard, 1982; Hinton and Anderson, 1981), for introductions to this general class of computational architectures).
A favorite analogy for this type of computation (e.g., Attneave, 1982) is the problem of determining the shape of a film formed when an irregularly shaped loop of wire is dipped in soapy water (the shape can be characterized by quantizing the film surface into patches and specifying the height of each patch). The answer to the problem is constrained by the 'least action' principle ensuring that the height of any patch of the film must be close to the heights of all its neighboring patches. But how can this information be used if one does not know beforehand the heights of all the neighbors of any patch? One can solve the problem iteratively, by assigning every patch an arbitrary initial height except for those patches touching the wire loop, which

are assigned the same heights as the piece of wire they are attached to. Then the heights of each of the other patches is replaced by the average height of its neighbors. This is repeated through several iterations; eventually the array of heights converges on a single set of values corresponding to the shape of the film, thanks to constraints on height spreading inward from the wire. The solution is attained without knowing the height of any single interior patch *a priori*, and without any central processor.

Similarly, it may be possible to solve some perceptual problems using networks of simple units whose excitatory and inhibitory interconnections lead the entire network to converge to states corresponding to certain geometric constraints that must be satisfied when recognition succeeds. Marr and Poggio (1976) proposed such a 'cooperative' model for stereo vision that simultaneously finds the relative distance from the viewer of each feature in pair of stereoscopic images *and* which feature in one image corresponds with a given feature in the other. It does so by exploiting the constraints that each feature must have a single disparity and that neighboring features mostly have similar disparities.

In the case of three-dimensional shape recognition, Attneave, Hinton, and Hrechanyk and Ballard point out that there are constraints on how shape elements and reference frames may be paired that might be exploitable in parallel networks to arrive at both simultaneously. First, every part of an object must be described with respect to the same object-centered reference frame (or at least, every part of an object in a circumscribed region at a given scale of decomposition; see the discussion of the Marr and Nishihara model). For example, if one part is described as the front left limb of a animal standing broadside to the viewer and facing to the left, another part of the same object cannot simultaneously be described as the rear left limb of that animal facing to the right. Second, a description of parts relative to an object-centered frame is to be favored if that description corresponds to an existing object description in memory. For example, a horizontal part will be described as the downward-pointing leg of a chair lying on its back rather than as the forward-facing leg of an unfamiliar upright object.

These constraints, it is argued, can be used to converge on a unique correct object-centered description in a network of the following sort. There is a *retina-based unit* for every possible part at every retinal size, location, and orientation. There is also an *object-based unit* for every orientation, location, and size of a part with respect to an object axis. Of course, these units cannot be tied to *individual* retina-based units, but each object-based unit can be connected to the entire set of retina-based units that are geometrically consistent with it. Every shape description in memory consists of a *shape unit* that is connected to its constituent object-based units. Finally, all the pairs of

Figure 5. *A portion of a massively parallel network model for shape recognition. Triangular symbols indicate special multiplicative connections: the product of activation levels of a retina-based and a mapping unit is transmitted to an object-based unit, and the product of the activation levels in those retina-based and object-based units is transmitted to the mapping unit. From Hinton (1981).*

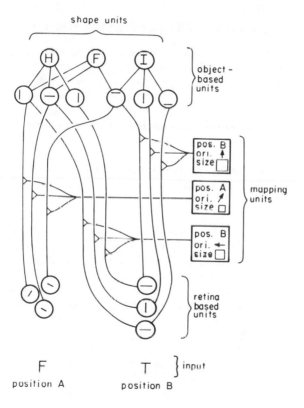

object- and retina-based units that correspond to a single orientation of the object axis relative to the viewer are themselves tied together by a *mapping unit,* such that the system contains one such unit for each possible spatial relation between object and viewer. An example of such a network, taken from Hinton (1981), is shown in Fig. 5.

The system's behavior is characterized as follows. The visual input activates retina-based units. Retina-based units activate all the object-based units they are connected to (this will include all object-based units that are geometrically compatible with the retinal features, including units that are inappropriate for the current object). Object-based units activate their corresponding shape units (again, both appropriate and inappropriate ones). Joint activity in particular retina- and object-based units activate the mapping units linking the two, that is, the mapping units that represent vantage points (relative to an object axis) for which those object-based features project as those retina-based features. Similarly, joint activity in retina-based and mapping units activate the corresponding object-based units. Shape units activate their corresponding object-based units; and (presumably) shape units inhibit other shape units and mapping units inhibit other mapping units. Hinton (1981) and Hrechanyk and Ballard (1982) argue that such networks should enter into a positive feedback loop converging on a single active shape unit, representing the recognized shape, and a single active mapping unit, representing the orientation and position of its axis with respect to the viewer, when a familiar object is viewed.

In general, massively parallel models are effective at avoiding the search problems that accompany serial computational architectures. In effect, the models are intended to assess the goodness-of-fit between all the transformations of an input pattern and all the stored shape descriptions in parallel, finding the pair with the highest fit at the same time. Since these models are in their infancy, it is too early to evaluate the claims associated with them. Among other things, it will be necessary to determine: (a) whether the model can be interfaced to preprocessing systems that segregate an object from its background and isolate sets of parts belonging to a single object-centered frame at a single scale; (b) whether the initial activation of object-based units by retina-based units is selective enough to head the network down a path leading toward convergence to unique, correct solutions; (c) whether the number of units and interconnections among units needed to represent the necessary combinations of shapes, parts, and their dispositions is neurologically feasible; and (d) whether these networks can overcome their current difficulty at representing and recognizing *relations* among parts in complex objects and scenes, in addition to the parts themselves.

Visual imagery

Visual imagery has always been a central topic in the study of cognition. Not only is it important to understand our ability to reason about objects and scenes that are remembered rather than seen, but the study of imagery is tied to the question of the number and format of mental representations, and of the interface between perception and cognition. Imagery may also be a particularly fruitful topic for study among the higher thought processes because of its intimate connection with shape recognition, benefitting from the progress made in that area. Finally, the subject of imagery is tied to scientific and literary creativity, mathematical insight, and the relation between cognition and emotion (see the papers in Sheikh, 1983); though the scientific study of imagery is mostly concerned with more pedestrian spatial abilities such as memory for literal appearance, spatial transformations, and matching images against visual stimuli, it has been argued that an understanding of these abilities may give us the tochold we need to approach the less tractable topics in the future (Shepard, 1978; Shepard and Cooper, 1982).

Imagery is in some ways a more difficult topic to study than recognition, and progress in the area is slower and consensus rarer. Unlike recognition, the direct inputs and outputs of the imagery system are not known beforehand; they must be discovered at the same time as the operation of the system itself. This has two implications. First, it is difficult to characterize antecedently the 'function' that the imagery system computes (cf. Marr, 1982). Second, there is the practical problem that the imagery system cannot be engaged automatically in experimental settings by presenting a person with particular physical inputs; imagery must be engaged through more indirect pathways involving a person's conceptual system (e.g., presenting him or her with certain types of spatial problems, giving instructions to use imagery). Thus it can be difficult to determine when the imagery is used or even whether there is a distinct imagery system.

Philosophical objections to imagery

During much of this century the coherence of the concept of an image itself has been called into question, and there have been claims that there is no such thing as an image—that talk of imagery is just a figure of speech (e.g., Ryle, 1949). However, most of the arguments within this debate really concerned the use of representations and processes in explanations of intelligence and mental life. Now that there is something close to a working consensus among cognitive scientists that intelligence can be characterized as computations over data structures or representations (see Block, 1980; Fodor, 1975; Haugeland, 1981; Pylyshyn, 1980), many of the criticisms of the concept of imagery are now moot, or at least can be absorbed into the debate over the representational and computational theories of mind in general (see Block (1981, 1983) for further arguments). In particular, I think it would be wise to avoid worrying about the following three non-issues:

(1) *The homunculus problem.* How can the mind contain 'images' unless there was some little man in the head to look at the images? This is simply not a problem under the computational theory of mind: images may be construed as data structures, and there is no more of a conceptual problem with positing mechanistic operations that can access those data structures than there is in positing mechanistic operations that access other mental representations such as linguistic or logical structures, or positing operations that access data in a computer. In particular, the study of shape recognition has led people to posit many types of operations that take as input array-like data structures created by sensory receptors, such as the 2½-D sketch, and it would be a short step to claim that the same processes could access such data structures generated from memory rather than from the eyes (whether or not this is *true* is, of course, a different matter).

(2) *The epiphenomenon problem.* Maybe images exist, but they are epiphenomenal to the actual computations that constitute thinking about visual objects. That is, they play no causal role, and are just like the lights that flash on and off on the front panel of a computer. The problem here is an ambiguity in the word 'image'. It could be taken to refer either to the subjective experience that people have when they report thinking in images, or to a mental representation that a theory might posit to help explain visual thinking. If 'image' is used in the former sense, then it is noncontroversially epiphenomenal if one subscribes to the computational theory of mind in general. In no computational theory of a mental process does subjective experience *per se* play a causal role; only representations and processes do, and the subjective experience, if it is considered at all, is assumed to be a correlate of the processing. If, on the other hand, 'image' is meant to refer to a representation posited in a theory of spatial memory and reasoning, then no one could hold that it is epiphenomenal: any theory positing a representation that never played a causal role would be rejected as unlikely to be true using ordinary parsimony criteria.

(3) *The subjectivity issue.* It is dangerous to take people's introspective reports about the contents or properties of their images as evidence in characterizing imagery, because such reports can be unreliable and subject to bias, because the referents of people's descriptions of imagery are unclear, and because interesting cognitive processes are likely to take place beneath the level of conscious accessibility. Again, a non-issue: all parties agree that much of image processing, whatever it is, is inaccessible to consciousness, that experimental data and computational and neurological feasibility are the proper source of constraints on imagery theories, and that introspective reports are psychological phenomena to be accounted for, not accurate descriptions of underlying mechanisms.

Imagery theories

I believe we have reached the point where it is particular *theories* of imagery, not analyses of the concept of imagery, that are in question, and that the 'imagery debate' is now a scientific controversy rather than a philosophical conundrum. This controversy largely concerns two questions. First, does the architecture of the mind contain any structures and processes that are specific to imagery, or does imagery simply consist of the application of general cognitive processes to data structures whose content happens to be about the visual world? Second, if it does make sense to talk of imagery as a dedicated module, does it consist of the processing of pixels in an array with properties similar to the 2½-D sketch, or does it consist of the processing of structural descriptions?

The most forceful proponent of the view that imagery is not a distinct cognitive module is Zenon Pylyshyn (1981). Pylyshyn argues that imagery simply consists of the use of general thought processes to simulate physical or perceptual events, based on tacit knowledge of how physical events unfold. For example, mental rotation effects (e.g., Shepard and Hurwitz (1984); also discussed below) occur because subjects are thinking in real time about the course of a physical rotation. They know implicitly that physical objects cannot change orientation instantaneously and that the time taken by a rotation is equal to the angle of rotation divided by the rotation rate. They perform the relevant computation, then wait the corresponding amount of time before indicating their response. Pylyshyn argues that virtually all known demonstrations of imagery phenomena, experimental or informal, can be interpreted as the use of tacit knowledge to simulate events rather than as the operation of a dedicated processor. In particular, he argues, the representation of space or of movement in images does not tell us anything about the format of imagery representation, least of all that there is anything 'spatial' or 'moving' in the image itself; the demonstrations just tell us about the content of information that can be represented in imagery.

Though Pylyshyn has not proposed an explicit model of the general purpose cognitive mechanisms that subserve imagery, the type of mechanism that would be congenial to his view would be a structural description. As mentioned, structural descriptions use a symbolic format similar to that used in the semantic networks proposed as representations of general knowledge.

A second class of theories has been proposed by Allan Paivio (1971) Roger Shepard (1981) and Stephen Kosslyn (1980, 1983) (see also Kosslyn *et al.* (1984, this issue) and Farah (1984, this issue)). They have proposed that imagery uses representations and processes that are ordinarily dedicated to visual perception, rather than abstract conceptual structures subserving thought in general. Furthermore, it is proposed that at least one of these representations used in perception and imagery has a spatial or array-like structure. By an array-like structure, I mean the following: images are patterns of activation in a structure consisting of units (or cells) that represent, by being on or off (or filled or unfilled) the presence or absence of a part or patch of the surface of an object at a particular disposition in space (orientation or location). The medium is structured so that each cell is adjacent to a fixed set of other cells, in such a way that the metric axioms are satisfied.[4] This makes it meaningful to speak of properties like 'position', 'proximity', and 'direction' of cells or pairs of cells; these properties are defined by the adjacencies among cells within the medium and need not correspond to physical position, distance, or direction within the neural instantiation of the array (though presumably they are related to proximity measured in number of neural connections). The processes that occur within that medium are sensitive to the location of a cell within the medium; that is, there are primitive operations that access a particular cell by absolute or relative location, that move the contents of one cell to a neighboring one within the medium, and so on. Furthermore, location within the medium is systematically related to the disposition in space of the represented object or feature, so that adjacent cells represent dispositions of the represented object or feature that differ by some minimal amount. An array of values in a computer memory functioning as a graphics bit map is an example of the type of array-like medium characterized in this paragraph, but such media can also be quite different from bit maps.[5]

Shepard (1981) has proposed an elegant though only partially worked-out set of conjectures, according to which a shape is represented by a two-dimensional manifold curved in three-dimensional space to form a closed surface, such as a sphere. Each position within the manifold corresponds to one orien-

---

[4]The metric axioms are (a) the distance between a point and itself is less than the distance between a point and any other point; (b) the distance between point a and point b is the same as the distance between point b and point a; (c) the distance between point a and point b plus the distance between point b and point c must be greater than or equal to the distance between point a and point c.

[5]Pylyshyn (1980, 1981) rightly emphasizes that it is crucial to distinguish among the *representation* of geometric properties like distance, position, and direction, the corresponding physical properties in the world themselves, and these properties defined over the surface of the brain. Pylyshyn accuses certain theorists of confusing these notions, but in my opinion Pylyshyn's argument loses its force by failing to acknowledge another sense of notions like distance, namely that defined by the intercell adjacencies in an array representation and respected by the processes that operate within such an array. According to the theories outlined in the text, position and distance in the array represent position and distance in the world, and possibly (depending on details of the neural instantiation of these mechanisms) rough position and distance within certain regions of the brain. Thus rather than confusing distance in the world, the internal representation of distance in the world, distance among cells in the internal structure representing the world, and distance in the brain, these theorists are making assertions about how these different senses of distance are related.

tation of the shape, with nearby positions corresponding to nearby orientations. The shape of the manifold captures the various symmetries in the
represented object, so that the point representing the letter 'H' rotated 175°
will be closer to the point representing its upright orientation than either of
them is to the point representing its 90° orientation. When points are activated in the medium (i.e., when one perceives or imagines a shape at a
particular orientation), activation spreads through the manifold, and when
fronts of activation originating from different sources meet (i.e., when two
views of a shape are seen or imagined), a straight-line path between the
sources is activated, corresponding to the shortest angular trajectory that the
shape would have to pass through to rotate one orientation into the other.
Shepard uses this proto-model to make sense of a wide set of findings on
mental rotation and apparent movement; see Shepard (1981) for details, and
Pinker and Kosslyn (1983) for explication and commentary.

Kosslyn has proposed a different theory, instantiated in an explicit and
detailed computational model (Kosslyn, 1980, 1983; Kosslyn and Shwartz,
1977; also briefly summarized in this issue by Kosslyn *et al.* (1984) and by
Farah (1984)). Here the medium, which Kosslyn calls the "visual buffer", is
two-dimensional and Euclidean, and the position of cells within the array
corresponds to position within the visual field (i.e., a line of sight from the
vantage point of the viewer; in this regard it is similar to a 2½-D sketch—see
Pinker (1980b)). Cells, when activated, represent patches of the surface of a
represented shape, so that the pattern of activation within the buffer is
isomorphic to the shape of the visible surfaces of the object. As in Shepard's
proposal, this medium can be filled from information arriving from the visual
system (subsequent to preprocessing such as the detection of edges and surface properties); or from information in long-term memory—this is what
generating a mental image consists of. In Kosslyn's theory the long term
memory representations of objects' shapes and surface properties used in
imagery are assumed to be shared with those used in recognition (see Farah
(1984) for neuropsychological evidence that these representations are the
same), and are assumed to have the format of a structural description augmented with whatever information is necessary to reconstruct the appearance of the surfaces of the object. The image generation processes (which
are the focus of the article by Farah (1984)) can fill the buffer with patterns
representing several objects from different long-term memory files, and can
place the objects in different positions, orientations, and sizes with respect
to one another. Once in the buffer, the pattern of activated cells can be
rotated, scaled in size, or translated, and the resulting patterns can be
examined by operations that detect shapes and spatial configurations (presumably, mechanisms similar to the visual routines proposed by Ullman

(1984) in this issue). The upper panel in Fig. 6 is an illustration of the general architecture of Kosslyn's model. (A slightly different hybrid model in this class has been proposed by Attneave (1974), who suggests that a two- or three-dimensional array can specify the locations of objects by containing labels or pointers to symbolic descriptions, rather than edge or surface primitives depicting the object's shape.)

Hinton (1979a, b) has proposed a model for imagery belonging to a third class. It shares the following assumptions with Kosslyn's model: there are processes dedicated to the manipulation of spatial information in imagery;

Figure 6.   *Two ways of representing viewer-specific information in imagery. The top panel schematically illustrates an array model; the lower panel schematically illustrates a structural description model. The parameters within parentheses symbolize the disposition of a part in local coordinate systems centered on superordinate parts (see Fig. 2 and 3); parameters within hexagons in the lower panel symbolize the horizontal and vertical directions and depth with respect to a single vantage point.*

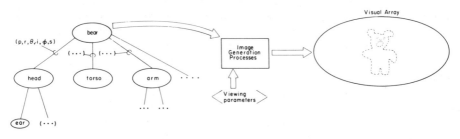

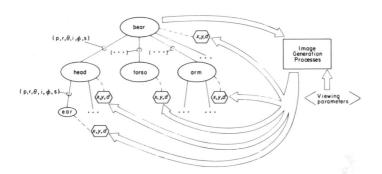

there is a special format for information represented in imagery, involving a global, viewer-centered reference frame; and there is an array-like scale within which the spatial disposition of the represented shape is specified. However, in Hinton's model there is no array whose cells correspond to local portions of the visual field and represent local patches of the shape. Rather, imagery consists of information appended to a structural description of the object's shape. In this long-term memory representation, units correspond to entire parts defined by a hierarchical decomposition of the shape of the object, and the spatial relations between adjacent parts are defined with respect to a frame of reference centered on one of the parts (thus it is similar to Marr and Nishihara's 3-D model description). Image generation consists of activating a certain set of part nodes, and appending to them a *second* representation of their spatial dispositions. This second set of coordinates is *not* specified with respect to a local, object-centered frame of reference, but with respect to a global reference frame centered on the viewer. A set of processes can then operate on these temporary viewer-centered coordinates appended to the activated nodes in order to ascertain spatial relations holding among parts of an object at different levels of its hierarchical decomposition or among parts of different objects. The lower panel in Fig. 6 is a sketch of the general properties of Hinton's model. An additional feature of Hinton's model is that the various quantitative parameters used in specifying spatial dispositions are encoded as pointers to one-dimensional arrays within which an activated cell represents a particular position, orientation, or size. (See Anderson (1983) who also presents a model that is centered around structural descriptions but which contains special processes for the manipulation of spatial information in images).

Current issues in the study of visual imagery

Distinguishing among the three classes of models just described is not the only focus of current research on imagery (for example, Kosslyn *et al.* (1984) and Farah (1984) examine the decomposition of imagery into modules, and do not directly address the format of the short-term memory structure underlying images). The following is a summary of some important current topics in imagery research; I will highlight how data bear on the models described above but will also describe classes of research that are independent of that controversy. For more general literature reviews on imagery research, see Kosslyn (1980), Kosslyn and Shwartz (1981), Shepard and Cooper (1982), and Finke and Shepard (In press).

Cognitive penetration

These phenomena are relevant to the distinction between theories appealing to tacit knowledge alone *versus* theories appealing to dedicated imagery processes. Pylyshyn (1979, 1981) cites cases where people's knowledge and belief may influence the time and ease with which they use imagery in certain tasks. Pylyshyn argues that if the operation of a putative processing module is sensitive to the contents of a person's beliefs, then it cannot be a primitive component of the cognitive architecture inasmuch as the mode of operation of the primitative architecture is by definition sensitive only to the syntactic form of representations, not their content. Thus sensitivity to the contents of beliefs is evidence that the process in question is a manifestation of whatever mechanisms manipulate the representation underlying knowledge in general.

Although the form of Pylyshyn's argument is generally accepted (all things being equal), its application to particular sets of data, especially in the case of imagery, is controversial. The problem is that the penetrability criterion pertains to individual information processing *components*, but we can only gather direct evidence that beliefs are penetrating individual *tasks* involving many components (Fodor, 1983; Kosslyn *et al.* 1979). If a person's beliefs influence the rate of mental rotation, the time to generate an image, and so on, it could simply be that the executive has access to certain parameters that can be set prior to the execution of an operation, such as transformation rate, decision criteria, or the choice of shapes to imagine or transformations to execute (for example, the rotation operator might have a rate parameter that can be set externally, but all other aspects of its operation might be fixed). Which processing stage is the one influenced by a person's beliefs makes all the difference in the world, but identifying such stages is as difficult as making any other claim about representations and processes based on experimental data. (There is also controversy over the facts of which imagery tasks actually are penetrable by beliefs; see e.g., Finke, 1980; Kosslyn, 1981; Pinker, Choate and Finke, 1984a; Reed *et al.*, 1983).

Constraints on imagery

If imagery is nothing but the use of tacit knowledge to simulate physical events, then the only constraints on what we can do in our images should stem from what we know can or cannot occur in the world. However, there have been many reports, some introspective, some experimental, that people cannot form images of arbitrary specifications of spatial properties and relations. For example, we cannot imagine a shape whose orientation, location, subjective size, or direction with respect to the vantage point are simply indeterminate, undefined, or unspecified; each image must make commitments to particular values of these parameters. Similarly, we cannot imagine two objects that are next to one another without one being to the left of the other; nor can we imagine the front and back of an opaque intact object simultaneously, nor the visual space in front of and behind the head (see e.g., Fiske *et al.* 1979; Hinton, 1979b; Pinker and Finke, 1980; Poincaré, 1913; Johnson-Laird, 1983; Keenan and Moore, 1979).

Note that these possible constraints stand in contrast to long-term memory for visual information in general. As Pylyshyn (1973) has pointed out, we often remember that an object was in a room or near another object without being able to recall where in the room or on what side of the object it was; similarly, Nickerson and Adams (1979) have shown that people are quite inaccurate at remembering spatial relations among the parts of familiar objects such as a Lincoln penny. The constraints also contrast with the optionality of other properties in imagery, such as color, surface texture, local parts, and details of edges, which are often reported as being totally unspecified in images. This means that the constraints are not just constraints on which properties are defined in the world, because just as an object must have an orientation when viewed, it must have a certain color and texture.

When there are constraints on which geometric properties are optional in images and which are obligatory, when these constraints hold of imagery in particular and not of long term memory about visual information in general, and when they are not predictable from physical and geometric constraints on objects in the world, we have evidence that imagery is represented by special mechanisms. In particular, in a structural description, any geometric attribute that can be factored out of a shape description (e.g., orientation, size, relative location) can be lost and hence undefined, and abstract spatial relations (e.g., 'next to') can be specified easily. In contrast, in an array model it is impossible to form an image representation lacking a size, absolute or relative location, or orientation, because shapes are represented only by being placed somewhere in the array medium, thereby receiving some specification of location, size, and so on automatically. Thus the constraints, if they are robust, would speak against a totally factored structural description.

Mental transformations and couplings among between geometric properties
The most famous body of research on imagery in the past decade has been concerned with image transformations (Cooper and Shepard, 1973; Shepard and Metzler, 1971; Shepard and Hurvitz, 1984); see also the section on "Assigning reference frames" above). Shepard and his collaborators have shown that when people have to decide whether two 3-D objects have the same shape, the time they take is a linear function of the difference in their depicted orientations. When they have to judge the handedness of alphanumeric characters or random polygons (i.e., whether one is normal or mirror-re-

versed), time increases monotonically with degree of deviation in orientation from the upright. Shepard's interpretation of these findings is that subjects engage in a smooth, continuous process of mental rotation, transforming the orientation of an imagined shape until it coincides in a template-like manner with a second, perceived shape or with a shape stored in a canonical upright orientation in memory. By itself, the increase in reaction time with orientation would not necessarily support the claim that a continuous rotation is imagined, but Shepard and Cooper have independent evidence that the rotation process computes intermediate representations in the angular trajectory (see Shepard and Cooper (1982) for a review). There have also been demonstrations of phenomena interpretable as mental translation or scanning (Finke and Pinker, 1982, 1983; Kosslyn *et al.*, 1978; Pinker *et al.*, 1984a), and size scaling (Bundesen and Larsen, 1975; Kosslyn, 1980).

In interpreting these data, it is important to separate two aspects of the phenomenon: why transformations are necessary at all, and why the transformations are gradual (e.g., why people take increasing time for greater orientation disparities, rather than simply taking a constant additional amount of time when there is any difference in orientation at all). I think that the *necessity* of performing image transformations tells us about which pairs of geometric attributes are obligatorily coupled in images, rather than being factored apart, leading to similar conclusions to those suggested in the previous section on imagery constraints. Consider the following structural description of a viewed object:

Object X:
　　Shape:
$$\left[\text{(Object-centered 3-D model)} \right]$$

　　Viewer-relative
　　location: (x, y, d)

　　Viewer-relative
　　orientation: (s, t)

　　Size: (z)

Now consider what would happen if one had to verify that two stimuli had the same shape, or whether one stimulus did or did not correspond in shape to a standard in memory. If the judgment could be made on the basis of structural descriptions such as this one, exploiting the explicit decoupling of geometric attributes in it, then depicted orientation should make no difference. All one has to do is examine the part of the structural description that specifies shape, and ignore the parts specifying orientation, location, and size. In fact, the factoring apart of orientation, location, and size in structural descriptions, allowing processes to ignore selectively the geometric attributes that are irrelevant to their tasks, is considered one of the chief selling points of this format. However, the facts of mental transformations indicate that this account cannot be completely correct: when judging shape, people are systematically affected by the irrelevant attributes of orientation and size. Similarly, when verifying whether an imagined object has a part, people are affected by the size of the object or of the part (Kosslyn, 1980); and when verifying whether one point lies in a certain direction with respect to another, they are affected by the distance between them (Finke and Pinker, 1983). There is also evidence that the imagined size of an object affects the rate of rotation (Shwartz, 1979; Pinker, unpublished data; though see also Bundesen *et al.*, 1981). Finally, when matching an imagined shape against a physically presented one, differences in orientation, size, location, and combinations of these differences all affect the speed of the match (Bundesen and Larsen, 1975; Cooper and Shepard, 1973; Farah, In press; Kosslyn, 1980; Shepard and Cooper, 1982).

The phenomena of mental image transformations, then, suggest that the completely factored structural description as shown above cannot be the one used in imagery. Exactly what about it is wrong is not completely clear. The phenomena are consistent with the spatial models of Shepard and Kosslyn in that in those models, shape and orientation (and, in Kosslyn's model, size and location) are *not* factored apart; they are 'in' one and the same set of activated cells. Thus the value of one attribute may affect the accessing of another when two representations differing in the first attribute are compared; the comparison process might be similar in some ways to template matching. Hinton and Parsons (1981) argue otherwise; they suggest that shape and orientation are factored apart in image representations except for the handedness of the object-centered reference frame, which is determined in the viewer-centered reference frame (see the earlier section on "Assigning reference frames"). Hence normalization of orientation is necessary whenever shapes must be discriminated from their mirror-reversed versions, the situation in most of the mental rotation experiments. Mental rotation also occurs, however, when the foils are not mirror-images (e.g., Cooper and Podgorny, 1976; Shwartz, 1981, Reference note 4); whether or not Hinton and Parson's account is correct in these cases will depend on whether the relevant shape representations depend on the handedness of their reference frame (e.g., whether random polygons are represented in terms of a list of their angles going clockwise from the topmost angle). Another, related possibility for the necessity of computing geometric transformations is that the shape description does not have a global specification of viewer-relative orientation, only specifications appended to each part. The description of the dispositions of the object's parts would change with orientation, requiring a normalization of orientation before shape can be extracted. In any case, the fact that mental transformations must occur when processing information in images indicates that images cannot consist of a viewpoint-invariant object-centered description plus a global specification of orientation.

Why the transformations must be executed incrementally is another issue. Logically there is no reason why the processes that update the represented orientation of a shape could not arrive at new orientations in one fell swoop. If orientation is simply a parameter appended to a shape description, one value could simply be replaced by another. Even in an array theory like Kosslyn's, the process that moves surface primitives from cell to cell (based on the coordinates of the first cell and the nature of the transformation) could calculate the coordinates of the target destination in one step rather than calculating a series of destinations separated by small increments.

Explanations for the gradualness of image transformations divide into three classes. In theories with an array component, neighboring cells are used to represent adjacent orientations and the orientation changes are accomplished by hardwired connections between cells within some bounded neighborhood (e.g., Hinton, 1979a; Shepard, 1981; Trehub, 1977). Since there are hardwired connections only between neighboring cells, larger transformations require the network of connections to be activated iteratively, transferring activation from initial to final state through intermediate states in bucket brigade fashion.[6]

The second class of account appeals not to constraints on the transformation mechanisms but on the executive processes that control it. For example, Kosslyn (1980) proposes that incremental transformations are selected because they minimize noise introduced into the depicted shape by the transformation operation, and because they allow a simple control strategy when the target orientation is not known in advance: the executive can monitor the successive representations and stop the transformation when the represented shape is familiar or matches some target (Marr (1982) makes a similar conjecture). In these accounts, the necessity of choosing gradual transformations

---

[6]The local nature of the wiring in these networks could either be an accidental consequence of principles of neural organization, or could have been selected during evolution to mirror the continuity of the motion of physical objects, as Shepard (1981) and Hayes-Roth (1979) have conjectured.

ultimately derives from the coupling of shape and orientation (size, location, etc.) in imagery, because only if they are coupled would the size of the transformation affect the process of recognizing a target shape.

The third class of account comes from Pylyshyn (1981) and Mitchell and Richman (1980), who also argue that it is executive processes that cause the transformation to be incremental, but attribute the source of this choice to a different factor, namely one's tacit knowledge that movement in the world is continuous and one's desire or tendency to simulate the time course of physical events. In particular, experiments in which subjects are told explicitly to transform a pattern (e.g., Kosslyn *et al.*, 1978); or in which subjects know that the experiment is about 'rotation', 'movement', and so on, are open to this explanation, it is argued, because subjects could literally construe their task as the mental simulation of motion. The account becomes less plausible in cases where subjects are left to their own devices and are asked to solve the task as quickly as possible, with no mention of imagery or of transformations (e.g., Cooper and Shepard, 1973; Finke and Pinker, 1982, 1983; Pinker *et al.*, 1984a). Instead, tacit knowledge, accounts would have to claim that subjects carry with them the habit of simulating physical events whenever they make spatial judgments. However, such an account would then need to explain what it is about the mind that would cause it to adopt such unnecessary habits (Kosslyn, 1981) and why mental transformations are not carried out when various sorts of advance information are provided to the subject (e.g., Cooper and Shepard, 1973; Finke and Pinker, 1983; Pinker *et al.*, 1984a).

Goodness and cohesiveness of parts

The definition of the primitive units represented in structural description and array theories is one of the key features that differentiate them. In structural descriptions, the primitives correspond to cohesive parts of objects and their dispositions with respect to reference frames centered on superordinate parts. In an array representation, the primitives correspond to local patches of surface or to edges, located with respect to a single reference frame centered on the viewer (see Fig. 6). Hence, in structural descriptions, it should be easy to make judgments about spatial relations among cohesive parts specified within the same reference frame, whereas in arrays, the parts do not have a special status and the difficulty of a judgment should be determined by factors such as distance and size rather than part cohesiveness or membership in a family of parts in the same reference frame. Thus it has been taken as evidence against array representations that it is extremely difficult to see parts in complex objects that are low in *Gestalt* 'goodness' or that do not correspond to one of the units in one's internal description or

Figure 7.   *Effects of descriptions on the visualization of parts. Different parts are more or less easy to detect in an imagined pattern depending on whether the whole is conceptualized as two overlapping triangles, two overlapping parallelograms, two adjacent hourglasses, or a diamond contained in a large hourglass. From Reed (1974).*

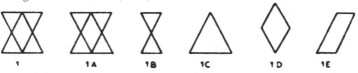

conceptualization of the objects (Hinton, 1979a; Palmer, 1977; Reed, 1974; see also Fig. 7).

Unfortunately, these demonstrations become less than decisive in settling the array–*versus*–description issue because most explicit imagery theories have multiple mechanisms. For example, in Kosslyn's array theory, objects' shapes are stored in long-term memory as structural descriptions involving the objects' parts, and image generation consists of the successive activation in the array of patterns for those parts (Kosslyn *et al.*, 1983). Since imagined parts begin to fade as soon as they are generated, (Kosslyn, 1980), at any given time an image of a complex shape will contain only subsets of parts that were originally generated in close temporal proximity. These will usually be parts that have a distinct identity and that belong to the same reference frame in memory. Hence relations that cut across parts or reference frames will be difficult to make, just as in the structural description account. Conversely, in a structural description theory that allows a global set of viewer-centered coordinates to be appended to each part description (e.g., as shown in the lower panel of Fig. 6), relations among parts in different reference frames should *not* be difficult to perceive. In both theories, limitations on the number of parts kept active at one time, and the use of structural descriptions at one level of shape representation, are the source of the explanation for these phenomena. Discriminating among the theories will be easier when each makes more precise commitments as to how the limitations in capacity are measured, and what determines the choice of reference frames.

Imagery and perception

There is a large body of research exploring similarities between imagining a pattern and perceiving one (see Finke, 1980;Finke and Shepard, In press; Shepard and Podgorny, 1978; Shepard and Cooper, 1982). These include chronometric patterns in discriminating magnitudes of perceived and imagined objects; perceptual aftereffects following the formation of images, and parallels in the scaling of magnitudes or similarities among perceived and remembered stimuli. Finke (1980) and Finke and Shepard (In press) discuss the relevance of this large body of findings to theories of imagery. Finke distinguishes among similarities between imagery and perception according to the locus of the relevant perceptual effect in the nervous system. For example, one can conceive of perceptual effects that are due to properties of the sensory receptors and lower-level feature analyzers and grouping processes (i.e., those processes leading to what Marr calls the Primal Sketch), those that are due to properties of the higher level analysis of objects' shapes, sizes, surface features, orientations, and so on; and those that are due to general knowledge and cognitive skills, such as a person's tacit knowledge of the workings of his or her perceptual system. Finke argues that among the phenomena that are similar in imagery and perception, there are some that can be attributed to the second of these three levels, that is, phenomena that reflect the operation of middle-level perceptual processes that are independent of a person's knowledge and beliefs. If so, it would argue that imagery is more than the application of one's general purpose knowledge about physical or perceptual processes.

In search of the imagery medium
The research most directly addressed to distinguishing between the array and structural description theories has attempted to discover evidence for the putative medium underlying images. According to the array theory there is a fixed medium underlying all visual images, regardless of their content; according to the alternative, the representation underlying the image of an object is simply the activated representation of that object's shape in memory (see Farah, 1984 for discussion). If an imagery medium exists, its parts should correspond to fixed points in the visual field, it should display the same eccentricity, isotropy, and contrast constraints as one would find in the corresponding perceptual medium, regardless of which objects are being represented, and it should have an identifiable locus or loci in the nervous system. There are inherent methodological difficulties in determining whether such a medium exists because people's tacit knowledge of their own perceptual experience could make it easy for them simply to remember how something originally appeared to them when forming an image, rather than forming a pure image and allowing the inherent structure of imagery representations to affect its "appearance" (Pylyshyn, 1981). Nonetheless, there have been several interesting lines of investigation, and attempts to overcome the methodological problems.

For example, Finke and Kosslyn (1980), Finke and Kurtzman (1981), and Pennington and Kosslyn (1981, Reference note 2; see the paper by Kosslyn *et al.* in this issue) have attempted to show that images have decreased resolution at peripheral eccentricities and oblique orientations, just like physical patterns, but that these effects were not known to the subjects, at least not consciously. Kosslyn (1983) has also shown that imagining a pattern at a particular location over a prolonged period makes it harder to imagine a new pattern at that location, as if a single neural substrate was being fatigued or habituated. Bisiach and Luzzati (1978) have shown that brain-injured patients suffering from attentional neglect of one visual hemifield also show signs of neglect in images of objects in that hemifield. For example, when imagining a piazza and describing the buildings facing them they fail to describe the buildings on one side—but fail to describe a different set of buildings, those that would be seen in the same part of the visual field, when imagining themselves facing in a different direction. And Farah (1984) argues that the process that converts long-term memory representations into the format corresponding to imagery can be selectively impaired and that this impairment is caused by damage only to certain parts of the brain.[7]

Computing and updating viewer-centered representations
The instrospective and experimental evidence on imagery suggests images represent the surfaces visible from a fixed vantage point, rather than just the intrinsic geometry of an object (see Hinton, 1979b; Pinker, 1980b; Pinker and Finke, 1980). The major models of imagery, both of the array and structural description variety, are designed to capture this fact. However, computing the dispositions and visible surfaces of parts from a description of their shape plus a specification of a vantage point, and updating that representation during image transformations, can be a nontrivial computational problem, especially as images are subject to transformations that alter the sets of surfaces that are visible (e.g., rotation in depth, translation or panning that brings new objects into view, zooming to reveal formerly blurred detail).

Furthermore, simply computing the rotation and translation transformations themselves can be problematic, especially in array theories. If the viewer-centered coordinates are specified in polar coordinates, then rotations in the frontal plane around the fovea are easy to compute, but not rotations in depth, about noncentral axes, or translations. If rectangular coordinates are used, sideways or up-and-down translations are easy to compute, but not diagonal translations or rotations. One possibility is that aside from the vie-

---

[7]Evidence on position-specific neglect following brain injury supports theories that have specific neural loci representing specific locations in the visual field. Hinton's (1979a) hybrid structural description model has this property, since location parameters are claimed to be given a 'place' representation in unidimensional neural arrays. There is, however, a prediction that differentiates Hinton's model from array theories: according to Hinton, entire objects or parts should be neglected when they are represented at particular locations, whereas according to Kosslyn, arbitrary chunks of a part (whatever material overlaps the missing region) can be inaccessible.

wer-centered coordinate system that defines the fixed 'address' of each array cell, rectangular and cylindrical coordinate systems can be dynamically centered on or linked to patterns for objects in the array, giving the cells a second, transient set of coordinates. Imagined transformations and the positioning of objects and parts with respect to one another could then be accomplished by processes that manipulate these transient, more appropriate coordinates (see the section on "Frames of reference for the visual field"; also Pinker, 1980c, Reference note 3; 1981; Trehub, 1977).

Thus the complexity of mechanisms needed in an imagery theory hinges crucially on which geometric transformations we actually can compute in generating and updating our images. It may turn out, for example, that the image generation processes (i.e., those discussed at length by Farah (1984) are not as powerful as one might think. I have found that subjects can accurately remember the projected positions of objects in scenes when they are told to visualize the way the scene looked from a vantage point that the subjects had actually experienced. However, when the subjects had to visualize the scene as it would appear from a different, hypothetical viewing distance, the subjects were unable to predict the projected positions of the objects accurately (unless a rich context framework was visible at the time of making the judgments). Instead, the subjects simply reconstructed the perspective they had actually witnessed and then uniformly scaled its size to approximate the novel perspective view (Pinker, 1983). In a different set of experiments, (Pinker *et al.*, 1984b), I found that subjects could not visualize in a single step the appearance of a three-dimensional object from an arbitrary viewing angle, even when they had advance information about the viewing angle. Instead they first visualized it in some canonical orientation, and then mentally rotated it into the target orientation.

These findings argue against an image generation process that takes as input an object-centered shape representation plus a specification of an arbitrary viewpoint, and computes as output the corresponding viewer-centered representation. Instead it suggests that the memory representation from which images are generated uses a viewer-centered format and that the generation process simply activates this representation intact (at which point image transformation processes could begin to operate). This could have interesting implications for the representation of shape in general. My experimental evidence suggests that long-term image representations are primarily viewer-centered. Both parsimony considerations and neurological evidence summarized by Farah (1984) suggest that the long term representations of shape used in recognition are the same as those used in imagery. And Marr and Nishihara argue that shape representations used in recognition are primarily object-centered. One of these three claims has to give.

What is imagery good for?

The question of whether we have cognitive representations and processes dedicated to imagery is closely related to the question of what advantages such representations bring to reasoning and thinking. If general knowledge systems could do everything that a putative imagery system could do and could do it as well or better, one would have to question why the imagery system is there. No one questions the need for memories and reasoning processes that deal with visual information or hypothetical scenes or physical interactions; the question is whether any of the special properties that have been attributed to the imagery system—such as sharing one of the representational media used in perception, representing information in a single viewer-centered coordinate system, conflating shape, orientation, and position, or executing transformations continuously—are computationally desirable.

There have been several conjectures about the possible usefulness of these and other properties of the imagery system. None of these conjectures is strongly grounded as yet in computational complexity theory or in experimental investigations, but all have a certain intuitive appeal and all are amenable to such investigations. Here is a sample of prominent suggestions:

(1) *Global coordinate system.* In the section on shape recognition, I reviewed compelling arguments for representing objects' shapes in distributed coordinate systems rather than a global one (see e.g., Fig. 2). Efficient though this scheme is for recognition, it can be problematical when one must reason about spatial relations among non-adjacent parts. Consider how one could answer a question such as "is the midpoint of a horse's tail higher or lower than its lips?" The position of the midpoint of the tail is specified with respect to the tail as a whole; the position, angle, and size of the tail are specified with respect to the torso; the position, angle, and size of the lips are specified with respect to the face, whose position, size, and angle are specified with respect to the head, whose position, size, and angle are specified with respect to the torso. One cannot simply look up any pair of coordinates to answer the question, because the coordinates of the midpoint of the tail and those of the lips have completely different meanings. Comparing the positions of the two objects could be done by transforming the geometric parameters of one of them into the coordinate system of the other, but that would require several successive coordinate transforms. Not only might such a series of transformations be time-consuming and error-prone, but noise in the representation of one of the parameters or noise introduced by the transformation processes could accumulate from transformation to transformation and the final comparison could be severely inaccurate. For example, errors of a few degrees in the representation of the angle of a giraffe's neck could lead to

large errors in the judgment of how far ahead of its feet its snout extends.

If the position, orientation, and size of each of a set of parts could be specified in terms of a single coordinate system, relations between parts within the same 3-D model would be a bit more difficult to compute, but relations among parts separated by many intervening models would be easier and more accurate. Hinton (1979b) has suggested that visual imagery consists of the use of a global viewer-centered reference frame to represent the dispositions of arbitrary collections of parts for the purpose of judging spatial relations among them (see Finke and Pinker (1983) for some relevant experimental evidence). Shepard and Hurvitz (1984) also point out that mental rotation can serve to bring one object into alignment with the reference frame of another, or into alignment with a viewer-centered reference frame, to facilitate the computation of reference-frame-specific predicates such as 'right' and 'left' (see also the section above on "Assigning reference frames").

This advantage is not tied to a single theory of imagery; it could be obtained whether the global coordinates are listed as tags on nodes in structural descriptions, of whether they are the addresses of the cells in an array medium occupied by the represented surfaces of the object (see Fig. 6). There are, however, diferences in the extent to which the advantages could be exploited in the two models; in an array model, the boundaries of various parts or details of their surfaces can be compared in the same global reference frame whenever an object or part is activated, whereas in the structural description account, only relations among entire parts are possible. Thus it has been argued that array representations are especially efficient when properties that cut across part boundaries, such as the empty space defined by a pile of objects on a table, must be computed (Funt, 1976; Hayes-Roth, 1979; see also Waltz, 1979).

(2) *Incidental properties.* When we learn about a new object, we record a number of facts about its structure, but not every potentially useful fact. For example, we do not record explicitly the shape of the ear of a sheep, or whether any of the parts of a car are triangular, or how many windows there are in one's house. Such information is often implicit in the information we do record, but it is simply not listed as an explicit proposition in memory. If there are routines analogous to the ones proposed in this issue by Ullman (1984) that can recognize these properties from visual input, then perhaps they can also recognize them from information stored in memory that is similar in form to the visual input. That is, we might store a relatively uncommitted, literal record of the appearance of objects from which we can compute properties that we could not anticipate the need for knowing when we initially saw the object. Kosslyn (1980) reports an extensive series of experiments and intuitive demonstrations showing that imagery is used when people are re-

quired to answer questions about parts of objects that are 'poorly associated' with the objects (that is, parts that we are not likely to have thought of in connection with that object before) and not deducible from the properties of the superordinate class to which the object belongs. Thus "does a bee have a dark head" requires the use of imagery (as assessed by effects of size and scanning, as well as by introspective reports), but "does a bee have a stinger" or "does a bee have wheels" do not.

(3) *Incremental representation in perception.* Ullman (1984) argues that certain types of visual recognition are solved by routines that can add information to the visual input, yielding "incremental representations" that subsequently are used by that routine or by other routines (e.g. 'coloring' regions, marking objects). Though Ullman suggests that visual routines are fast, unconscious, low-level recognition operations, it is also possible that some of these operations are identical to what are often called imagery operations (sequences of which, presumably, can become automatized with practice and hence could become fast and unconscious). Thus it is noteworthy that Ullman's operation of 'boundary tracing', which is similar to the operations of mental scanning and extrapolation proposed in connection with imagery, appears to occur at the same rate (in degrees of visual angle per second) as image scanning (Finke and Pinker, 1983; Jolicoeur *et al.*, 1984b). It is also possible that the generation and template-like matching of images against perceptual input (see Shepard and Cooper (1982) for a review) is a visual routine that can be used to recognize objects when one number of a small set of candidate objects is expected and when it is difficult to compute a 3-D model for the input. This could happen if the input pattern lacks stable axes or a stable decomposition into parts, when it must be discriminated from mirror-reversed versions, or when the input is severely degraded.

(4) *Reasoning in isomorphic domains.* If images are representations in a medium with certain fixed properties, and can be subjected to transformations such as rotation and scaling, then imagery could be used as an analogue computer, to solve problems whose entities and relations are isomorphic to objects and spatial relations. That is, certain abstract problems could best be solved by translating their entities into imagined objects, transforming them using available image transformations, detecting the resulting spatial relations and properties, and translating those relations and properties back to the problem domain.

For example, if every imagined object is constrained to have a single set of coordinates within a global coordinate system (e.g., the array proposed by Kosslyn), then it is impossible to represent the fact that one object is next to another without also committing oneself to which is to the left. (This is not true for abstract propositional representations, where the two-place predicate "next to" can be asserted of a pair of objects with no such commitment.) Furthermore, if there is a routine that can compute which of two objects is to the left of another on the basis of its global coordinates or the position of the cells it occupies in the array, then transitivity of left-to-right position falls out of the transitivity of the coordinates or of cell position within the array. The result of these properties is that problems such as three-term syllogisms (e.g., John is nobler than Bill, Sam is less noble than Bill, who is the noblest?) can be solved straightforwardly by imagining an object for each entity in the problem and placing them to the left and right of one another in an order corresponding to the dimension of comparison (Huttenlocher, 1968; Shaver *et al.*, 1975; see also Johnson-Laird, 1983).

Shepard (1978) and Shepard and Cooper (1982) also note that the use of imagery in mathematical and scientific problem solving may be effective because the medium used to represent images and the operations transforming them might embody physical and geometric constraints on terrestrial objects and space. When there are isomorphisms between physical objects in space and other domains (e.g., electromagnetic fields and elastic lines or surfaces), imagining a concrete analogue of an entity, transforming it, and then translating it back to the original domain could make explicit certain properties and equivalences in that domain that were only implicit beforehand.

A concluding remark

In this tutorial review, I have made no effort to conceal the disagreement and lack of resolution that surrounds many of the issues discussed. This should be taken not as a sign of disarray, but as a sign of the vigor of a newly revitalized branch of cognitive psychology. After a period of relative stagnation, researchers in visuospatial cognition are striving to synthesize a large number of new empirical findings, theoretical constructs, and external constraints. The past decade has seen Marr's important statements of the problems that visual recognition must solve and of the criteria of adequacy for theories of shape representation, his introduction into discussions in visual cognition of physical, optical, and geometric constraints that the visual system can exploit, and his concrete proposals on several classes of visual representations and algorithms. It has also witnessed a burgeoning of experimental data on imagery and recognition made possible by the chronometric methodology of Shepard and Kosslyn; tentative resolutions of the principal conceptual objections to theories of visual representations; the development of explicit computations and neural models of processes and structures that were previously characterized only in vague metaphors; and the application to visual imagery of concepts used in shape recognition such as distributed coordinate systems, object- and viewer-centered reference frames, and the 2½-D sketch. Most recently, we have seen an exposition of properties of alternative computational architectures, including the massively parallel systems that visual processing surely requires at some levels. Theories and data in visual cognition are being applied for the first time to neighboring disciplines that previously had been largely insulated from theoretical considerations, such as computer vision systems, individual difference psychology, and neuropsychology, and these disciplines are now in a position, in turn, to inform basic research on visual cognition. There are disagreements and confusion over specifics, to be sure, and syntheses between independent bodies of research that have yet to be made, but it seems clear what the problems to be solved are, what sorts of data and arguments are relevant, and what degrees of precision and explicitness it is reasonable to hope for in our theories.

References

Anderson, J.A. and Hinton, G.E. (1981) Models of information processing in the brain. In Hinton, G.E. and Anderson, J.A. (eds.), *Parallel Models of Associative Memory*. Hillsdale, NJ, Erlbaum.

Anderson, J.R. (1978) Arguments for representations for mental imagery. *Psychol. Rev., 85*, 249–277.

Anderson, J.R. (1983) *The Architecture of Cognition*. Cambridge, MA, Harvard University Press.

Attneave, F. (1968) Triangles as ambiguous figures. *Am. J. Psychol., 81*, 447–453.

Attneave, F. (1972) Representation of physical space. In A.W. Melton and E.J. Martin (eds.), *Coding Processes in Human Memory*. Washington, DC, V.H. Winston.

Attneave, F. (1974) How do you know? *Am. Psychol., 29*, 493–499.

Attneave, F. (1982) Pragnanz and soap bubble systems: A theoretical exploration. In J. Beck (ed.), *Organization and Representation in Perception*. Hillsdale, NJ, Erlbaum.

Badler, N. and Bajcsy, R. (1978) Three-dimensional representations for computer graphics and computer vision. *Comp. Graph. 12*, 153–160.

Ballard, D. and Brown, C. (1982) *Computer Vision*. Englewood Cliffs, NJ, Prentice Hall.

Ballard, D., Hinton, G.E. and Sejnowski, T.J. (1983) Parallel visual computation. *Nature, 306*, 21–26.

Biederman, I. (1972) Perceiving real-world scenes. *Science, 177*, 77–80.

Binford, T.O. (1971) Visual perception by computer. Presented to the IEEE conference on Systems and Control, December, Miami.

Bisiach, E. and Luzzatti, G.R. (1978) Unilateral neglect of representational space. *Cortex, 14*, 129–133.

Block, N. (ed.) (1980) *Readings in Philosophy of Psychology, Vol. I* Cambridge, MA, Harvard University Press.

Block, N. (ed.) (1981) *Imagery*. Cambridge, MA, MIT Press.

Block, N. (1983) Mental pictures and cognitive science. *Phil. Rev., 92*, 499–542.

Boring, E.G. (1952) Visual perception as invariance. *Psychol. Rev., 59*, 142–150.

Bundesen, C.C. and Larsen, A. (1975) Visual transformation of size. *J. exp. Psychol.: Hum. Percep. Perf., 1*, 214–220.

Bundesen, C.C., Larsen, A. and Farrell, J.E. (1981) Mental transformations of size and orientation. In A.D. Baddeley and J.B. Long (eds.), *Attention and Performance, Vol. 9*. Hillsdale, NJ, Erlbaum.

Campbell, F.W. and Robson, J.G. (1968) Application of Fourier analysis to the visbility of gratings. *J. Physiol., 197*, 551–566.

Cooper, L.A. and Shepard, R.N. (1973) Chronometric studies of the rotation of mental images. In W.G. Chase (ed.), *Visual Information Processing*. New York, Academic Press.

Cooper, L.A. and Podgorny, P. (1976) Mental transformations and visual comparison processes: Effects of complexity and similarity. *J. exp. Psychol.: Hum. Percep. Perf., 2*, 503–514.

Corballis, M.C. and Beale, I.L. (1976) *The Psychology of Left and Right*. Hillsdale, NJ, Erlbaum.

Corcoran, D.W.J. (1977) The phenomena of the disembodied eye or is it a matter of personal geography? *Perception, 6*, 247–253.

Cornsweet, T.N. (1970) *Visual Perception*. New York, Academic Press.

Cutting, J.E. and Millard, R.T. (1984) Three gradients and the perception of flat and curved surfaces. *J. exp. Psychol.: Gen., 113*, 221–224.

Farah, M.J. (1984) The neurological basis of mental imagery: A componential analysis. *Cog., 18*, 245–272.

Farah, M.J. (In press) Psychophysical evidence for a shared representational medium for visual images and percepts. *J. exp. Psychol.: Gen.*

Feldman, J.A. and Ballard, D.H. (1982) Connectionist models and their properties. *Cog. Sci., 6*, 205–254.

Finke, R.A. (1980) Levels of equivalence in imagery and perception. *Psychol. Rev., 87*, 113–132.

Finke, R.A. and Kosslyn, S.M. (1980) Mental imagery acuity in the peripheral visual field. *J. exp. Psychol.: Hum. Percep. Perf., 6*, 244–264.

Finke, R.A. and Kurtzman, H.S. (1981) Area and contrast effects upon perceptual and imagery acuity. *J. exp. Psychol.: Hum. Percep. Perf., 7*, 825–832.

Finke, R.A. and Pinker, S. (1982) Spontaneous mental image scanning in mental extrapolation. *J. exp. Psychol.: Learn. Mem. Cog., 8*, 142–147.

Finke, R.A. and Pinker, S. (1983) Directional scanning of remembered visual patterns. *J. exp. Psychol.: Learn. Mem. Cog., 9*, 398–410.

Finke, R.A. and Shepard, R.N. (In press) Visual functions of mental imagery. In L. Kaufman and J. Thomas (eds.), *Handbook of Perception and Human Performance*. New York, Wiley.

Fiske, S.T., Taylor, S.E., Etcoff, N.L. and Laufer, J.K. (1979) Imaging, empathy, and causal attribution. *J. exp. soc. Psychol., 15*, 356–377.

Fodor, J.A. (1975) *The Language of Thought*, New York, Crowell.

Fodor, J.A. (1983) *Modularity of Mind*. Cambridge, MA, MIT Press/Bradford Books.

Funt, B.V. (1976) WHISPER: a computer implementation using analogues in reasoning. Ph.D. Thesis, University of British Columbia.

Gardner, M. (1967) *The Ambidextrous Universe*. London, Allen Lane/Penguin Books.

Gibson, J.J. (1950) *The Perception of the Visual World*. Boston, Houghton-Mifflin.

Gibson, J.J. (1966) *The Senses Considered as Perceptual Systems*. Boston, Houghton-Mifflin.

Gibson, J.J. (1979) *The Ecological Approach to Visual Perception*. Boston, Houghton-Mifflin.

Gilinsky, A. (1955) The effect of attitude on the perception of size. *Am. J. Psychol., 68*, 173–192.

Ginsburg, A.P. (1971) Psychological correlates of a model of the human visual system. *Proceedings of the IEEE National Aerospace and Electronics Conference, 283*–290.

Ginsburg, A.P. (1973) Pattern recognition techniques suggested from psychological correlates of a model of the human visual system. *Proceedings of the IEEE National Aerospace and Electronics Conference*, 309–316.

Gregory, R.L. (1970) *The Intelligent Eye*. London, Weidenfeld and Nicholson.

Haugeland, J. (ed.) (1981) *Mind Design: Philosophy, Psychology, Artificial Intelligence*. Montgomery, VT, Bradford Books.

Hayes-Roth, F. (1979) Understanding mental imagery: Interpretive metaphors versus explanatory models. *Behav. Br. Sci., 2*, 553–554.

Hinton, G.E. (1979a) Some demonstrations of the effects of structural descriptions in mental imagery. *Cog. Sci., 3*, 231–250.

Hinton, G.E. (1979b) Imagery without arrays. *Behav. Br. Sci., 2*, 555–556.

Hinton, G.E. (1981) A parallel computation that assigns canonical object-based frames of reference. Proceedings of the International Joint Conference on Artificial Intelligence, Vancouver, Canada.

Hinton, G.E. and Anderson, J.A. (eds.) (1981) *Parallel Models of Associative Memory*. Hillsdale, NJ, Erlbaum.

Hinton, G.E. and Parsons, L.M. (1981) Frames of reference and mental imagery. In A. Baddeley and J. Long (eds.), *Attention and Performance IX*. Hillsdale, NJ, Erlbaum.

Hoffman, D.D. (1983) Representing shapes for visual recognition. Doctoral dissertation, MIT.

Hoffman, D.D. and Richards, M. (1984) Parts of recognition, *Cog., 18*, 65–96.

Hollerbach, J.M. (1975) Hierarchical shape description of objects by selection and modification of prototypes. MIT Artificial Intelligence Laboratory Technical Report #346.

Horn, B.K.P. (1975) Obtaining shape from shading information. In P.H. Winston (ed.), *The Psychology of Computer Vision*. New York, McGraw-Hill.

Hrechanyk, L.M. and Ballard, D.H. (1982) A connectionist model of form perception. Proceedings of the IEEE Special Workshop on Computer Vision, Rindge, NH.

Huttenlocher, J. (1968) Constructing spatial images: A strategy in reasoning. *Psychol. Rev., 75*, 550–560.

Jackendoff, R. (1983) *Semantics and Cognition*. Cambridge, MA, MIT Press.

James, W. (1890; reprinted 1980) *Principles of Psychology*. New York, Holt, Rinehart and Winston.

Johnson-Laird, P.N. (1983) *Mental Models*. Cambridge, MA, Harvard University Press.

Jolicoeur, P., Gluck, M.A. and Kosslyn, S.M. (1984a) Pictures and names: Making the connection. *Cog. Psychol., 16*, 243–275.

Jolicoeur, P., Ullman, S. and Mackay, M.E. (1984b) Boundary tracing: A possible basic operation in the perception of spatial relations. Research Bulletin, Department of Psychology, University of Saskatchewan.

Julesz, B. (1971) Experiments in the visual perception of texture. *Scient. Am., 232*, 34–43.

Kabrisky, M. (1966) *A Proposed Model for Visual Information Processing in the Human Brain*. Urbana, IL, University of Illinois Press.

Keenan, J.M. and Moore, R.E. (1979) Memory for images of concealed objects: A re-examination of Neisser and Kerr. *J. exp. Psychol. Hum. Learn. Mem., 5*, 374–385.

Koffka, K. (1935) *Principles of Gestalt Psychology*. New York, Harcourt Brace Jovanovich.

Kohler, W. (1947) *Gestalt Psychology*. New York, Mentor/Liveright.

Kosslyn, S.M. (1980) *Image and Mind*. Cambridge, MA, Harvard University Press.

Kosslyn, S.M. (1981) The medium and the message in mental imagery: a theory. *Psychol. Rev., 88*, 46–66.

Kosslyn, S.M. (1983) *Ghosts in the Mind's Machine*. New York, Norton.

Kosslyn, S.M., Ball, T.M. and Reiser, B.J. (1978) Visual images preserve metric spatial information: evidence from studies of imagery scanning. *J. exp. Psychol.: Hum. Percep. Perf., 4*, 47–60.

Kosslyn, S.M., Brunn, J., Cave, K. and Wallach, R. (1984) Individual differences in mental imagery ability: A computational analysis. *Cog., 18*, 195–243.

Kosslyn, S.M., Pinker, S., Smith, G.E., and Shwartz, S.P. (1979) On the demystification of mental imagery. *Behav. Br. Sci., 2*, 535–548.

Kosslyn, S.M., Reiser, B.J., Farah, M.J. and Fliegel, S.L. (1983) Generating visual images: units and relations. *J. exp. Psychol. Gen., 112*, 278–303.

Kosslyn, S.M. and Shwartz, S.P. (1977) A simulation of visual imagery. *Cog. Sci., 1*, 265–295.

Kosslyn, S.M. and Shwartz, S.P. (1981) Empirical constraints on theories of mental imagery. In A.D. Baddeley and J.B. Long (eds.), *Attention and Performance, Vol. 9*. Hillsdale, NJ, Erlbaum.

Kuipers, B. (1978) Modeling spatial knowledge. *Cog. Sci., 2*, 129–141.

Lindsay, P.H. and Norman, D.A. (1977) *Human Information Processing: An Introduction to Psychology*, 2nd ed. New York, Academic Press.

Lynch, K. (1960) *The Image of the City*. Cambridge, MA, MIT Press.

Marr, D. (1982) *Vision*. San Francisco, Freeman.

Marr, D., and Nishihara, H.K. (1978) Representation and recognition of the spatial organization of three-dimensional shapes. *Proc. R. Soc. Lond., 200*, 269–294.

Marr, D. and Poggio, T. (1977) Cooperative computation of stereo disparity. *Science, 194*, 283–287.

McDermott, D. (1980) Spatial inferences with ground, metric formulas on simple objects. Research report #173, Yale University Department of Computer Science.

Metzler, J. and Shepard, R.N. (1975) Transformational studies of the internal representation of three-dimensional objects. In R. Solso (ed.), *Theories in Cognitive Psychology· The Loyola Symposium*. Hillsdale, NJ, Erlbaum.

Minsky, M. (1975) A framework for representing knowledge. In P.H. Winston (ed.), *The Psychology of Computer Vision*. New York, McGraw-Hill.

Minsky, M. and Papert, S. (1972) *Perceptrons*, 2nd ed. Cambridge, MA, MIT Press.

Mitchell, D.B. and Richman, C.L. (1980). Confirmed reservations: mental travel. *J. exp. Psychol. Hum. Percep. Perf., 6*, 58–66.

Natsoulas, T. (1966) Locus and orientation of the perceiver (ego) under variable, constant, and no perspective instructions. *J. Person. Soc. Psychol., 3*, 190–196.

Neisser, U. (1967) *Cognitive Psychology*. New York, Appleton-Century-Crofts.

Nickerson, R.S. and Adams, M.J. (1979) Long-term memory for a common object. *Cog. Psychol., 3*, 287–307.

Norman, D.A. and Rumelhart, D.E. (1975) *Explorations in Cognition*. San Francisco, Freeman.

Palmer, S.E. (1975a) Visual perception and world knowledge: Notes on a model of sensory–cognitive interaction. In D.A. Norman and D.E. Rumelhart (eds.), *Explorations in Cognition*. San Francisco, Freeman.

Palmer, S.E. (1975b) The effects of contextual scenes on the identification of objects. *Mem. Cog., 3*, 519–526.

Palmer, S.E. (1977) Hierarchical structure in perceptual representation. *Cog. Psychol., 9*, 441–474.

Palmer, S.E. and Bucher, N. (1981) Configural effects in perceived pointing of ambiguous triangles. *J. exp. Psychol. Hum. Percep. Perf., 7*, 88–114.

Paivio, A. (1971) *Imagery and Verbal Processes*. New York, Holt, Rinehart and Winston.

Persoon, E. and Fu, K. (1974) Shape description using Fourier descriptives. *Proceedings of the Second International Joint Congress on Pattern Recognition*, 126–130.

Pinker, S. (1980a) Mental imagery and the visual world. Occasional Paper #4, MIT Center for Cognitive Science.

Pinker, S. (1980b) Mental imagery and the third dimension. *J. exp. Psychol. Gen., 109*, 354–371.

Pinker, S. (1981) What spatial representation and syntax acquisition don't have in common. *Cog., 10*, 243–248.

Pinker, S. (1983) Perspective information in visualized scenes. Paper presented at the Annual Meeting of the Psychonomic Society, San Diego, November 17–19, 1983.

Pinker, S., Choate, P. and Finke, R.A. (1984a) Mental extrapolation in patterns constructed from memory. *Mem. Cog.*.

Pinker, S. and Finke, R.A. (1980) Emergent two-dimensional patterns in images rotated in depth. *J. exp. Psychol. Hum. Percep. Perf., 6*, 69–84.

Pinker, S. and Kosslyn, S.M. (1983) Theories of mental imagery. In A.A. Sheikh (ed.), *Imagery: Current Theory, Research and Application*. New York, Wiley, 1983.

Pinker, S., Stromswold, K., and Beck, L. (1984b) Visualizing objects at prespecified orientations. Paper presented at the annual meeting of the Psychonomic Society, San Antonio, November.

Poggio, T. (1984) Vision by man and machine. *Scient. Am., 250*, 106–116.

Poincaré, H. (1913) *The Foundations of Science*. Lancaster, PA, Science Press.

Pribram, K.H. (1971). *Languages of the Brain*. Englewood Cliffs, NJ, Prentice-Hall.

Pylyshyn, Z.W. (1973) What the mind's eye tells the mind's brain: a critique of mental imagery. *Psychol. Bull., 80*, 1–24.

Pylyshyn, Z.W. (1979) The rate of "mental rotation" of images: a test of a holistic analogue hypothesis. *Mem. Cog., 7*, 19–28.

Pylyshyn, Z.W. (1980) Computation and cognition: issues in the foundations of cognitive science. *Behav. Br. Sci., 3*, 382–389.
Pylyshyn, Z.W. (1981) The imagery debate: Analogue media versus tacit knowledge. *Psychol. Rev., 88*, 16–45.
Reed, S.K. (1974) Structural descriptions and the limitations of visual images. *Mem. Cog., 2*, 329–336.
Reed, S.K., Hock, H.S. and Lockhead, G. (1983) Tacit knowledge and the effect of pattern configuration on mental scanning. *Mem. Cog., 11*, 137–143.
Richards, W. (1979) Natural computation: Filling a perceptual void. Presented at the 10th Annual Pittsburgh Conference on Modeling and Simulation, April, University of Pittsburgh.
Richards, W. (1982) How to play twenty questions with nature and win. MIT Artificial Intelligence Laboratory Memo # 660.
Rock, I. (1973) *Orientation and Form*. New York, Academic Press.
Rock, I. (1983) *The Logic of Perception*. Cambridge, MA, MIT Press/Bradford Books.
Rock, I., di Vita, J. and Barbeito, R. (1981) The effect on form perception of change of orientation in the third dimension. *J. exp. Psychol. Hum. Percep. Perf., 7*, 719–732.
Rosch, E., Mervis, C.B., Gray, W., Johnson, D. and Boyes-Braem, P. (1976) Basic objects in natural categories. *Cog. Psychol., 8*, 382–439.
Ryle, G. (1949) *The Concept of Mind*. London, Hutchinson.
Selfridge, O.G. (1959) Pandemonium: A paradigm for learning. In *Symposium on the Mechanization of Thought Processes*. London: HMSO.
Selfridge, O.G. and Neisser, U. (1960) Pattern recognition by machine. *Scient. Am., 203*, 60–68.
Shaver, P., Pierson, L. and Lang, S. (1975) Converging evidence for the functional significance of imagery in problem-solving. *Cog., 3*, 359–376.
Sheikh, A.A. (ed.) (1983) *Imagery: Theory, Research, and Application*. New York, Wiley.
Shepard, R.N. (1978) The mental image. *Am. Psychol., 33*, 125–137.
Shepard, R.N. (1981) Psychophysical complementarity. In M. Kubovy and J. Pomerantz (eds.), *Perceptual Organization*. Hillsdale, NJ, Erlbaum.
Shepard, R.N. and Cooper, L.A. (1982) *Mental Images and their Transformations*. Cambridge, MA, MIT Press/Bradford Books.
Shepard, R.N. and Hurwitz, S. (1984) Upward direction, mental rotation, and discrimination of left and right turns in maps, *Cog., 18*, 161–193.
Shepard, R.N. and Metzler, J. (1971) Mental rotation of three-dimensional objects. *Science, 171*, 701–703.
Shepard, R.N. and Podgorny, P. (1978) Cognitive processes that resemble perceptual processes. In W.K. Estes (ed.), *Handbook of Learning and Cognitive Processes, Vol. 5*. Hillsdale, NJ, Erlbaum.
Shwartz, S.P. (1979) Studies of mental image rotation: Implications for a computer simulation of visual imagery. Doctoral dissertation, The Johns Hopkins University.
Smith, E.E., Balzano, G.J. and Walker J. (1978) Nominal, perceptual, and semantic codes in picture categorization. In J.W. Cotton and R.L. Klatzky (eds.), *Semantic Factors in Cognition*. Hillsdale, NJ, Erlbaum.
Stevens, K.A. (1981). The information content of texture gradients. *Biol. Cybernet., 42*, 95–105.
Trehub, A. (1977) Neuronal models for cognitive processes: Networks for learning, perception and imagination. *J. theor. Biol., 65*, 141–169.
Uhlarik, J., Pringle, R., Jordan, K. and Misceo, G. (1980) Size scaling in two-dimensional pictorial arrays. *Percep. Psychophys., 27*, 60–70.
Ullman, S. (1979) *The Interpretation of Visual Motion*. Cambridge, MA, MIT Press.
Ullman, S. (1984) Visual routines. *Cog., 18*, 97–159.
Waltz, D. (1979) On the function of mental imagery. *Behav. Br. Sci., 2*, 569–570.
Weisstein, N. (1980) The joy of Fourier analysis. In C.S. Harris (ed.), *Visual Coding and Adaptability*. Hillsdale, NJ, Erlbaum.
Weisstein, N. and Harris, C.S. (1974) Visual detection of line segments: An object superiority effect. *Science, 186*, 752–755.

Winston, P.H. (1975) Learning structural descriptions from examples. In P.H. Winston (ed.), *The Psychology of Computer Vision*. New York, McGraw-Hill.

Reference Notes

1. Kubovy, M., Turock, D., Best, T.L. and Marcus, J. (1984) The virtual vantage point for the identification of cutaneous patterns. Unpublished paper. Rutgers University.
2. Pennington, N. and Kosslyn, S.M. (1981) The oblique effect in mental imagery. Unpublished manuscript, Harvard University.
3. Pinker, S. (1980c) The mental representation of 3-D space. Unpublished manuscript, MIT.
4. Shwartz, S.P. (1981) The perception of disorientated complex objects. Unpublished manuscript. Yale University.

Resumé

Cet article est une revue didactique sur les questions essentielles de la cognition visuelle. Il est centré sur la reconnaissance des formes et sur la représentation des objets et des relations spatiales en perception et en imagerie. L'auteur donne d'abord un bref rapport sur l'état de la question puis fait une présentation plus approfondie des théories contemporaines, des données et des prospectives. Il discute différentes théories de la reconnaissance des formes telles que les descriptions structurales en termes de patrons, traits, Fourier, Marr–Nishihara, et les modèles parallèles. Il discute aussi les propositions du type cadres de référence, primitifs, traitements de haut en bas et architectures de calcul utilisées dans la reconnaissance spatiale. Suit une discussion sur l'imagerie mentale ou sont abordés les concepts utilisés dans les recherches sur l'imagerie, les théories de l'imagerie, les rapports entre imagerie et perception, les transformations d'image, les complexités de calcul dans le traitement des images, les questions neurologiques et le rôle fonctionnel possible de l'imagerie. On insiste sur les relations entre les théories de la reconnaissance et l'imagerie ainsi que sur la pertinence des articles de ce volume sur ces sujets.

2

Parts of recognition*

D.D. HOFFMAN

University of California, Irvine

W.A. RICHARDS

Massachusetts Institute of Technology

Abstract

We propose that, for the task of object recognition, the visual system decomposes shapes into parts, that it does so using a rule defining part boundaries rather than part shapes, that the rule exploits a uniformity of nature—transversality, and that parts with their descriptions and spatial relations provide a first index into a memory of shapes. This rule allows an explanation of several visual illusions. We stress the role inductive inference in our theory and conclude with a précis of unsolved problems.

1. Introduction

Any time you view a statue, or a simple line drawing, you effortlessly perform a visual feat far beyond the capability of the most sophisticated computers today, through well within the capacity of a kindergartener. That feat is shape recognition, the visual identification of an object using only its shape. Figure 1 offers an opportunity to exercise this ability and to make several observations. Note first that, indeed, shape alone is sufficient to recognize the objects; visual cues such as shading, motion, color, and texture are not present in the figure. Note also that you could not reasonably predict the contents of the figure before looking at it, yet you recognized the objects.

*We are grateful to Thomas Banchoff, Aaron Bobick, Mike Brady, Carmen Egido, Jerry Fodor, Jim Hodgson, Jan Koenderink, Jay Lebed, Alex Pentland, John Rubin, Joseph Scheuhammer, and Andrew Witkin for their helpful discussions and, in some cases, for reading earlier drafts. We are also grateful to Alan Yuille for comments and corrections on the mathematics in the appendices. Preparation of this paper was supported in part by NSF and AFOSR under a combined grant for studies in Natural Computation, grant 79-23110-MCS, and by the AFOSR under an Image Understanding contract F49620-83-C-0135. Technical support was kindly provided by William Gilson; artwork was the creation of Julie Sandell and K. van Buskirk. Reprints may be obtained from D. Hoffman, School of Social Sciences, University of California, Irvine, CA 92717, U.S.A.

Figure 1.   *Some objects identifiable entirely from their profiles.*

Clearly your visual system is equipped to describe the shape of an object and to guess what the object is from its description. This guess may just be a first guess, perhaps best thought of as a first index into a memory of shapes, and might not be exactly correct; it may simply narrow the potential matches and trigger visual computations designed to narrow them further.

This first guess is more precisely described as an inference, one the truth of whose premises—the descriptions of shape—does not logically guarantee the truth of its conclusion—the identity of the object. Because the truth of the conclusion does not follow logically from the truth of the premises, the strength of the inference must derive from some other source. That source, we claim, is the regularity of nature, its uniformities and general laws. The design of the visual system exploits regularities of nature in two ways: they underlie the mental categories used to represent the world and they permit inferences from impoverished visual data to descriptions of the world.

Regularities of nature play both roles in the visual task of shape recognition, and both roles will be examined. We will argue that, just as syntactic analysis decomposes a sentence into its constituent structure, so the visual system decomposes a shape into a hierarchy of parts. Parts are not chosen arbitrarily; the mental category 'part' of shapes is based upon a regularity of nature discovered by differential topologists—transversality. This is an example of a regularity in the first role. The need arises for a regularity in the second role because although parts are three-dimensional, the eye delivers only a two-dimensional projection. In consequence the three-dimensional parts must be inferred from their two-dimensional projections. We propose that this inference is licensed by another regularity, this time from the field of singularity theory.

2. Why parts?

Before examining a part definition and its underlying regularity, we should ask: Given that one wants to recognize an object from its shape, why partition the shape at all? Could template matching or Fourier descriptors rise to the occasion? Possibly. What follows is not so much intended to deny this as to indicate the usefulness of parts.

To begin, then, an articulation of shapes into parts is useful because one never sees an entire shape in one glance. Clearly the back side is never visible (barring transparent objects), but even the front side is often partially occluded by objects interposed between the shape and the observer. A Fourier approach suffers because all components of a Fourier description can change radically as different aspects of a shape come into view. A part theory, on the other hand, can plausibly assume that the parts delivered by early vision correspond to the parts stored in the shape memory (after all, the contents of the shape memory were once just the products of early visual processing), and that the shape memory is organized such that a shape can be addressed by an inexhaustive list of its parts. Then recognition can proceed using the visible parts.

Parts are also advantageous for representing objects which are not entirely rigid, such as the human hand. A template of an outstretched hand would correlate poorly with a clenched fist, or a hand giving a victory sign, etc. The proliferation of templates to handle the many possible configurations of the hand, or of any articulated object, is unparsimonious and a waste of memory. If part theorists, on the other hand, pick their parts prudently (criteria for prudence will soon be forthcoming), and if they introduce the notion of spatial relations among parts, they can decouple configural properties from the shape of an object, thereby avoiding the proliferation of redundant men tal models.

The final argument for parts to be considered here is phenomenological: we see them when we look at shapes. Figure 2, for instance, presents a cosine surface, which observers almost uniformly see organized into ring-like parts. One part stops and another begins roughly where the dotted circular contours are drawn. But if the figure is turned upside down the organization changes such that each dotted circular contour, which before lay between parts, now lies in the middle of a part. Why the parts change will be explained by the partitioning rule to be proposed shortly; the point of interest here is simply that our visual systems do in fact cut surfaces into parts.

Figure 2.   *The cosine surface at first appears to be organized into concentric rings, one ring terminating and the next beginning approximately where the dashed circular contours are drawn. But this organization changes when the figure is turned upside down.*

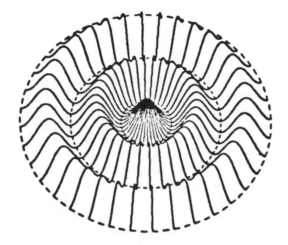

3. Parts and uniformities of nature

Certainly any proper subset of a surface is a part of that surface. This definition of part, however, is of little use for the task of shape recognition. And although the task of shape recognition constrains the class of suitable part definitions (see Section 5), it by no means forces a unique choice. To avoid an *ad hoc* choice, and to allow a useful correspondence between the world and mental representations of shape, the definition of part should be motivated by a uniformity of nature.[1]

One place not to look for a defining regularity is in the shapes of a part. One could say that all parts are cylinders, or cones, or spheres, or polyhedra, or some combination of these; but this is legislating a definition, not discovering a relevant regularity. And such a definition would have but limited applicability, for certainly not all shapes can be decomposed into just cylinders, cones, spheres, and polyhedra.

If a defining regularity is not to be found in part shapes, then another place

---

[1]Unearthing an appropriate uniformity is the most creative, and often most difficult, step in devising an explanatory theory for a visual task. Other things being equal, one wants the most general uniformity of nature possible, as this grants the theory and the visual task the broadest possible scope.

Figure 3.   *An illustration of the transversality regularity. When any two surfaces inter-*
penetrate at random they always meet in concave discontinuities, as indicated
by the dashed contours.

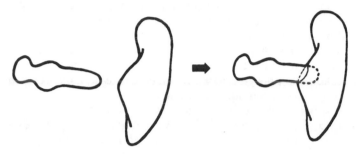

to look is part intersections. Consider the two three-dimensional blobs depicted in the left of Fig. 3. Certainly these two spatially separated shapes are
different parts of this figure. Indeed, each spatially distinct object in a visual
scene is a part of that scene. Now if two such separate objects are interpenetrated to form one new composite object, as shown in the right of Fig. 3, then
the two objects, which were before separate parts of the visual scene, are
surely now prime candidates to be parts of the new composite shape. But can
we tell, simply by examining the new composite shape, what the original
parts are? That is, is there a way to tell where one part stops and the next
part begins on the new composite shape? Fortunately there is a way, one
which depends on a regularity in the way two shapes generically intersect.
This regularity is called transversality (for a detailed discussion of transversality see Guillemin and Pollack (1974)).

● *Transversality regularity.* When two arbitrarily shaped surfaces are made
  to interpenetrate they always[2] meet in a contour of concave discontinuity
  of their tangent planes.

To see this more clearly, observe the silhouette of the composite shape
shown in the right of Fig. 3. Notice that this composite silhouette is not
smooth at the two points where the silhouette of one of its parts intersects
the silhouette of the other part. At these two points the direction of the
silhouette's outline (i.e., its tangent direction) changes abruptly, creating a
concave cusp (i.e., a cusp which points into the object, not into the

―――――――――
[2]The word *always* is best interpreted "with probability one assuming the surfaces interpenetrate at random".

background) at each of the two points. In fact, such concave discontinuities arise at every point on the surface of the composite shape where the two parts meet. These contours of concave discontinuity of the tangent plane of the composite shape will be the basis for a partitioning rule in the next section. But three observations are in order.

First, though it may sound esoteric, transversality is a familiar part of our everyday experience. A straw in a soft drink forms a circular concave discontinuity where it meets the surface of the drink. So too does a candle in a birthday cake. The tines of a fork in a piece of steak, a cigarette in a mouth, all are examples of this ubiquitous regularity.

Second, transversality does not double as a theory of part growth or part formation (D'Arcy Thompson, 1968). We are not claiming, for example, that a nose was once physically separated from the face and then got attached by interpenetration. We simply note that when two spatially separated shapes are interpenetrated, their intersection is transversal. Later we will see how this regularity underlies the visual definition of separate parts of any composite shape, such as the nose of a face or a limb of a tree, regardless of how the composite shape was created.

Finally, transversality does encompass movable parts. As mentioned earlier, one attraction of parts is that, properly chosen, they make possible a decoupling of configuration and shape in descriptions of articulated objects. But to do this the parts must cut an object at its articulations; a thumb–wrist part on the hand, for instance, would be powerless to capture the various spatial relations that can exist between the thumb and the wrist. Now the parts motivated by transversality will be the movable units, fundamentally because a transversal intersection of two surfaces remains transversal for small pertubations of their positions. This can be appreciated by reviewing Fig. 3. Clearly the intersection of the two surfaces remains a contour of concave discontinuity even as the two surfaces undergo small independent rotations and translations.

4. Partitioning: The minima rule

On the basis of the transversality regularity we can propose a first rule for dividing a surface into parts: divide a surface into parts along all contours of concave discontinuity of the tangent plane. Now this rule cannot help us with the cosine surface because this surface is entirely smooth. The rule must be generalized somewhat, as will be done shortly. But in its present form the rule can provide insight into several well-known perceptual demonstrations.

4.1. Blocks world

We begin by considering shapes constructed from polygons. Examine the staircase of Fig. 4. The rule predicts that the natural parts are the steps, and not the faces on the steps. Each step becomes a 'part' because it is bounded by two lines of concave discontinuity in the staircase. (A face is bounded by a concave and a convex discontinuity.) But the rule also makes a less obvious prediction. If the staircase undergoes a perceptual reversal, such that the 'figure' side of the staircase becomes 'ground' and *vice versa*, then the step boundaries must change. This follows because only *concave* discontinuities define step boundaries. And what looks like a concavity from one side of a surface must look like a convexity from the other. Thus, when the staircase reverses, convex and concave discontinuities must reverse roles, leading to new step boundaries. You can test this prediction yourself by looking at the step having a dot on each of its two faces. When the staircase appears to reverse note that the two dots no longer lie on a single step, but lie on two adjacent steps (that is, on two different 'parts').

Similar predictions from the rule can also be confirmed with more complicated demonstrations such as the stacked cubes demonstration shown in Fig. 5. The three dots which at first appear to lie on one cube, lie on three different cubes when the figure reverses.

Still another quite different prediction follows from our simple partitioning rule. If the rule does not define a unique partition of some surface, then the division of that surface into parts should be perceptually ambiguous (unless,

Figure 4.   *The Schroder staircase, published by H. Schroder in 1858, shows that part boundaries change when figure and ground reverse. The two dots which at first appear to lie on one step suddenly seem to lie on two adjacent steps when the staircase reverses.*

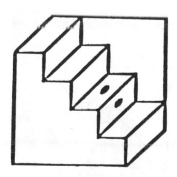

of course, there are additional rules which can eliminate the ambiguity). An elbow-shaped block provides clear confirmation of this prediction (see Fig. 6). The only concave discontinuity is the vertical line in the crook of the elbow; in consequence, the rule does not define a unique partition of the block. Perceptually, there are three plausible ways to cut the block into parts (also shown in Fig. 6). All three use the contour defined by the partitioning rule, but complete it along different paths.

Figure 5.   *Stacked cubes also show that parts change when figure and ground reverse. Three dots which sometimes lie on one cube will lie on three different cubes when the figure reverses.*

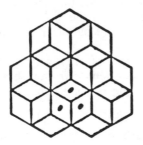

Figure 6.   *Elbow-shaped blocks show that a rule partitioning shapes at concave discontinuities is appropriately conservative. The rule does not give a closed contour on the top block, and for good reason. Perceptually, three different partitions seem reasonable, as illustrated by the bottom three blocks.*

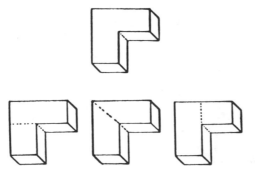

4.2. Generalization to smooth surfaces

The simple partitioning rule directly motivated by transversality leads to interesting insights into our perception of the parts of polygonal objects. But how can the rule be generalized to handle smooth surfaces, such as the cosine surface? To grasp the generalization, we must briefly digress into the differential geometry of surfaces in order to understand three important concepts: surface normal, principal curvature, and line of curvature. Fortunately, although these concepts are quite technical, they can be understood intuitively.

The surface normal at a point on a surface can be thought of as a unit length needle sticking straight out of (orthogonal to) the surface at that point, much like the spines on a sea urchin. All the surface normals at all points on a surface are together called a field of surface normals. Usually there are two possible fields of surface normals on a surface—either outward pointing or inward pointing. A sphere, for instance, can either have the surface normals all pointing out like spines, or all pointing to its center. Let us adopt the convention that the field of surface normals is always chosen to point into the figure (i.e., into the object). Thus a baseball has inward normals whereas a bubble under water, if the water is considered figure, has outward normals. Reversing the choice of figure and ground on a surface implies a concomitant change in the choice of the field of surface normals. And, as will be discussed shortly, a reversal of the field of surface normals induces a change in sign of each principal curvature at every point on the surface.

It is often important to know not just the surface normal at a point but also how the surface is curving at the point. The Swiss mathematician Leonhard Euler discovered around 1760 that at any point on any surface there is always a direction in which the surface curves least and a second direction, always orthogonal to the first, in which the surface curves most. (Spheres and planes are trivial cases since the surface curvature is identical in all directions at every point.) These two directions at a point are called the principal directions at that point and the corresponding surface curvatures are called the principal curvatures. Now by starting at some point and always moving in the direction of the greatest principal curvature one traces out a line of greatest curvature. By moving instead in the direction of the least principal curvature one traces out a line of least curvature. On a drinking glass the family of lines of greatest curvature is a set of circles around the glass. The lines of least curvature are straight lines running the length of the glass (see Fig. 7).

With these concepts in hand we can extend the partitioning rule to smooth surfaces. Suppose that wherever a surface has a concave discontinuity we smooth the discontinuity somewhat, perhaps by stretching a taut skin over it.

Figure 7.   *Lines of curvature are easily depicted on a drinking glass. Lines of greatest curvature are circles. Lines of least curvature are straight lines.*

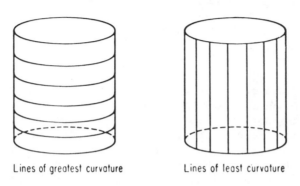

Lines of greatest curvature   Lines of least curvature

Then a concave discontinuity becomes a contour where, locally, the surface has greatest negative curvature. In consequence we obtain the following generalized partitioning rule for surfaces.

• *Minima rule.* Divide a surface into parts at loci of negative minima of each principal curvature along its associated family of lines of curvature.

The minima rule is applied to two surfaces in Fig. 8. The solid contours indicate members of one family of lines of curvature, and the dotted contours are the part boundaries defined by the minima rule. The bent sheet of paper on the right of Fig. 8 is particularly informative. The lines of curvature shown for this surface are sinusoidal, whereas the family of lines not shown are perfectly straight and thus have zero principal curvature (and no associated minima). In consequence, the product of the two principal curvatures at each point, called the *Gaussian curvature*, is always zero for this surface. Now if the Gaussian curvature is always zero on this surface, then the Gaussian curvature cannot be used to divide the surface into parts. But we see parts on this surface. Therefore whatever rule our visual systems use to partition surfaces cannot be stated entirely in terms of Gaussian curvature. In particular, the visual system cannot be dividing surfaces into parts at loci of zero Gaussian curvature (parabolic points) as has been proposed by Koenderink and van Doorn (1982b).

The minima rule partitions the cosine surface along the circular dotted contours shown in Fig. 2. It also explains why the parts differ when figure and ground are reserved. For when the page is turned upside down the visual system reverses its assignment of figure and ground on the surface (perhaps

Figure 8. *Part boundaries, as defined by the smooth surface partitioning rule, are indicated by dashed lines on several different surfaces. The families of solid lines are the lines of curvature whose minima give rise to the dashed partitioning contour.*

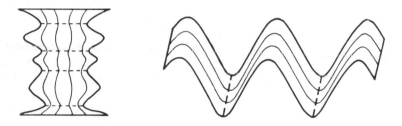

due to a preference for an interpretation which places the object below rather than overhead). When figure and ground reverse so does the field of surface normals, in accordance with the convention mentioned earlier. But simple calculations show that when the normals reverse so too does the sign of the principal curvatures. Consequently minima of the principal curvatures must become maxima and *vice versa*. Since minima of the principal curvatures are used for part boundaries, it follows that these part boundaries must also move. In sum, parts appear to change because the partitioning rule, motivated by the transversality regularity, uses minima of the principal curvatures, and because these minima relocate on the surface when figure and ground reverse. A more rigorous treatment of the partitioning rule is provided in Appendix 1.

5. Parts: Constraints from recognition

The task of visual recognition constrains one's choice of parts and part descriptions. We evaluate the part scheme proposed here against three such constraints—*reliability, versatility*, and *computability*—and then note a non-constraint, *information preservation*.

Reliability. Recognition is fundamentally a process of matching descriptions of what one sees with descriptions already in memory. Imagine the demands on memory and on the matching process if every time one looked at an object one saw different parts. A face, for example, which at one instant appeared to be composed of eyes, ears, a nose, and a mouth, might at a later instant metamorphose into a potpourri of eye–cheek, nose–chin, and mouth–

ear parts—a gruesome and unprofitable transmutation. Since no advantage accrues for allowing such repartitions, in fact since they are uniformly deleterious to the task of recognition, it is reasonable to disallow them and to require that the articulation of a shape into parts be invariant over time and over change in viewing geometry. This is the constraint of reliability (see Marr, 1982; Marr and Nishihara, 1978; Nishihara, 1981; Sutherland, 1968); the parts of a shape should be related reliably to the shape. A similar constraint governs the identification of linguistic units in a speech stream (Liberman *et al*, 1967; Fodor, 1983). Apparently the shortest identifiable unit is the syllable; shorter units like phones are not related reliably to acoustic parameters.

The minima rule satisfies this reliability constraint because it uses only surface properties, such as extrema of the principal curvatures, which are independent (up to a change in sign) of the coordinate system chosen to parametrize the surface (Do Carmo, 1976). Therefore the part boundaries do not change when the viewing geometry changes. (The part boundaries do change when figure and ground reverse, however.)

Versatility. Not all possible schemes for defining parts of surfaces are sufficiently versatile to handle the infinite variety in shape that objects can exhibit. Other things being equal, if one of two partitioning schemes is more versatile than another, in the sense that the class of objects in its scope properly contains the class of objects in the scope of the other scheme, the more versatile scheme is to be preferred. A partitioning scheme which can be applied to any shape whatsoever is most preferable, again other things being equal. This versatility constraint can help choose between two major classes of partitioning schemes: boundary-based and primitive-based. A *boundary-based* approach defines parts by their contours of intersection, not by their shapes. A *primitive-based* approach defines parts by their shapes, not by their contours of intersection (or other geometric invariants, such as singular points).

Shape primitives currently being discussed in the shape representation literature include spheres (Badler and Bajcsy, 1978; O'Rourke and Badler, 1979), generalized cylinders (Binford, 1971; Brooks *et al.*, 1979; Marr and Nishihara, 1978; Soroka, 1979), and polyhedra (Baumgart, 1972; Clowes, 1971; Guzman, 1969; Huffman, 1971; Mackworth, 1973; Waltz, 1975), to name a few (see Ballard and Brown, 1982). The point of interest here is that, for all the interesting work and conceptual advances it has fostered, the primitive-based approach has quite limited versatility. Generalized cylinders, for instance, do justice to animal limbs, but are clearly inappropriate for faces, cars, shoes, ... the list continues. A similar criticism can be levelled against each proposed shape primitive, or any conjunction of shape primitives. Perhaps a large enough conjunction of primitives could handle most shapes we do in fact encounter, but the resulting proposal would more resemble a restaurant menu than a theory of shape representation.

A boundary-based scheme on the other hand, if its rules use only the geometry (differential or global) of surfaces, can apply to any object whose bounding surface is amenable to the tools of differential geometry—a not too severe restriction.[3] Boundary rules simply tell one where to draw contours on a surface, as if with a felt marker. A boundary-based scheme, then, is to be preferred over a primitive-based scheme because of its greater versatility.

The advantage of a boundary-based scheme over a primitive-based scheme can also be put this way: using a boundary-based scheme one can locate the parts of an object without having any idea of what the parts look like. This is not possible with the primitive-based scheme. Of course one will want descriptions of the parts one finds using a boundary-based scheme, and one may (or may not) be forced to a menu of shapes at this point. Regardless, a menu of part shapes is not necessary for the task of locating parts. In fact a menu-driven approach restricts the class of shapes for which parts can be located. The minima rule, because it is boundary-based and uses only the differential geometry of surfaces, satisfies the versatility constraint—all geometric surfaces are within its scope.[4]

Computability. The partitioning scheme should in principle be computable using only information available in retinal images. Otherwise it is surely worthless. This is the constraint of *computability*. Computability is not to be confused with efficiency. Efficiency measures how quickly and inexpensively something can be computed, and is a dubious criterion because it depends not only on the task, but also on the available hardware and algorithms. Computability, on the other hand, states simply that the scheme must in principle be realizable, that it use only information available from images.

We have not yet discussed whether our parts are computable from retinal

---

[3]Shapes outside the purview of traditional geometric tools might well be represented by fractal-based schemes (Mandelbrot, 1982; Pentland 1983). Candidate shapes are trees, shrubs, clouds—in short, objects with highly crenulate or ill-defined surfaces.

[4]One must, however, discover the appropriate scales for a natural surface (Hoffman, 1983a, b; Witkin, 1983). The locations of the part boundaries depend, in general, on the scale of resolution at which the surface is examined. In consequence an object will not receive a single partitioning based on the minima rule, but will instead receive a nested hierarchy of partitions, with parts lower in the hierarchy being much smaller than parts higher in the hierarchy. For instance, at one level in the hierarchy for a face one part might be a nose. At the next lower level one might find a wart on the nose. The issue of scale is quite difficult and beyond the scope of this paper.

images (but see Appendix 2). And indeed, since minima of curvature are third derivative entities, and since taking derivatives exaggerates noise, one might legitimately question whether our part boundaries are computable. This concern for computability brings up an important distinction noted by Marr and Poggio (1977), the distinction between theory and algorithm. A theory in vision states what is being computed and why; an algorithm tells how. Our partitioning rule is a theoretical statement of what the part boundaries should be, and the preliminary discussion is intended to say why. The rule is not intended to double as an algorithm so the question of computability is still open. Some recent results by Yuille (1983) are encouraging though. He has found that directional zero-crossings in the shading of a surface are often located on or very near extrema of one of the principal curvatures along its associated lines of curvature. So it might be possible to read the part boundaries directly from the pattern of shading in an image, avoiding the noise problems associated with taking derivatives (see also Koenderink and van Doorn, 1980, 1982a). It is also possible to determine the presence of part boundaries directly from occluding contours in an image (see Appendix 2).

Information preservation: A non-constraint. Not just any constraints will do. The constraints must follow from the visual task; otherwise the constraints may be irrelevant and the resulting part definitions and part descriptions inappropriate. Because the task of recognition involves classification, namely the assignment of an individual to a class or a token to a type, not all the information available about the object is required. Indeed, in contrast to some possible needs for machine vision (Brady, 1982b, 1982c), we stress that a description of a shape for recognition need not be information preserving, for the goal is not to reconstruct the image. Rather it is to make explicit just what is key to the recognition process. Thus, what is critical is the form of the representation, what it makes explicit, how well it is tailored to the needs of recognition. Raw depth maps preserve all shape information of the visible surfaces, but no one proposes them as representations for recognition because they are simply not tailored for the task.

6. Projection and parts

We have now discussed how 'parts' of shapes may be defined in the three-dimensional world. However the eye sees only a two-dimensional projection. How then can parts be inferred from images? Again, we proceed by seeking a regularity of nature. As was noted earlier, the design of the visual system exploits regularities of nature in two ways: they underlie the mental categories used to represent the world and they license inferences from impoverished visual data to descriptions of the world. The role of transversality in the design of the mental category 'part' of shape is an example of the first case. In this section we study an example of the second case. We find that lawful properties of the singularities of the retinal projection permit an inference from retinal images to three-dimensional part boundaries. For simplicity we restrict attention to the problem of inferring part boundaries from silhouettes.

Consider first a discontinuous part boundary (i.e., having infinite negative curvature) on a surface embedded in three dimensions (Fig. 3). Such a contour, when imaged on the retina, induces a concave discontinuity in the resulting silhouette (notice the concave cusps in the silhouette of Fig. 3). Smooth part boundaries defined by the minima partitioning rule can also provide image cusps, as shown in the profiles of Fig. 1. It would be convenient to infer the presence of smooth and discontinuous part boundaries in three dimensions from concave discontinuities in the two-dimensional silhouette, but unfortunately other surface events can give rise to these discontinuities as well. A torus (doughnut), for instance, can have two concave discontinuities in its silhouette which do not fall at part boundaries defined by the minima rule (see Fig. 9).

Fortunately, it is rare that a concave discontinuity in the silhouette of an object does not indicate a part boundary, and when it does not this can be detected from the image data. So one can, in general, correctly infer the presence or absence of part boundaries from these concave discontinuities. The proof of this useful result (which is banished to Appendix 2) exploits regularities of the singularities of smooth maps between two-dimensional manifolds. We have seen how a regularity of nature underlies a mental category, *viz.*, 'part' of shape; here we see that another regularity (e.g., a singularity regularity) licenses an inference from the retinal image to an instance of this category.

Figure 9.   *A torus can have concave discontinuities (indicated by the arrows) which do not correspond to part boundaries.*

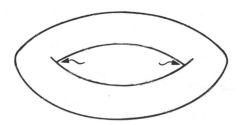

Figure 10. *A reversing figure, similar to Attneave (1974), appears either as an alternating chain of tall and short mountains or as a chain of tall mountains with twin peaks.*

The singularity regularity, together with transversality, motivates a first partitioning rule for plane curves: *Divide a plane curve into parts at concave cusps.* Here the word *concave* means concave with respect to the silhouette (figure) side of the plane curve. A concavity in the figure is, of course, a convexity in the ground.

This simple partitioning rule can explain some interesting perceptual effects. In Fig. 10, for instance, the same wiggly contour can look either like valleys in a mountain range or, for the reversed figure–ground assignment, like large, twin-peaked mountains. The contour is carved into parts differently when figure and ground reverse because the partitioning rule uses only concave cusps for part boundaries. And what is a concave cusp if one side of the contour is figure must become a convex cusp when the other side is figure, and *vice versa.* There is an obvious parallel between this example and the reversible staircase discussed earlier.

6.1. Geometry of plane curves

Before generalizing the rule to smooth contours we must briefly review two concepts from the differential geometry of place curves: principal normal and curvature. The principal normal at a point on a curve can be thought of as a unit length needle sticking straight out of (orthogonal to) the curve at that point, much like a tooth on a comb. All the principal normals at all points on a curve together form a field of principal normals. Usually there are two possible fields of principal normals—either leftward pointing or rightward pointing. Let us adopt the convention that the field of principal normals is always chosen to point into the figure side of the curve. Reversing the choice of figure and ground on a curve implies a concomitant change in the choice of the field of principal normals.

Curvature is a well-known concept. Straight lines have no curvature, circles have constant curvature, and smaller circles have higher curvature than larger circles. What is important to note is that, because of the convention forcing the principal normals to point into the figure, concave portions of a smooth curve have negative curvature and convex portions have positive curvature.

6.2. Parts of smooth curves

It is an easy matter now to generalize the partitioning rule. Suppose that wherever a curve has a concave cusp we smooth the curve a bit. Then a concave cusp becomes a point of negative curvature having, locally, the greatest absolute value of curvature. This leads to the following generalized partitioning rule: *Divide a plane curve into parts at negative minima of curvature.*[5]

Several more perceptual effects can be explained using this generalized partitioning rule. A good example is the reversing figure devised by Attneave (see Fig. 11). He found that by simply scribbling a line through a circle and separating the two halves one can create two very different looking contours. As Attneave (1971) points out, the appearance of the contour depends upon

Figure 11. *Attneave's reversing figure, constructed by scribbling a line down a circle. The apparent shape of a contour depends on which side is perceived as figure.*

---

[5]Transversality directly motivates using concave cusps as part boundaries. Only by smoothing do we include minima as well (both in the case of silhouette curves and in the case of part boundaries in three dimensions). Since the magnitude of the curvature at minima decreases with increased smoothing, it is useful to introduce the notion of the strength or goodness of a part boundary. The strength of a part boundary is higher the more negative the curvature of the minimum. Positive minima have the least strength, and deserve to be considered separately from the negative minima, a possibility suggested to us by Shimon Ullman.

which side is taken to be part of the figure, and does not depend upon any prior familiarity with the contour.

Now we can explain why the two halves of Attneave's circle look so different. For when figure and ground reverse, the field of principal normals also reverses in accordance with the convention. And when the principal normals reverse, the curvature at every point on the curve must change sign. In particular, minima of curvature must become maxima and *vice versa*. This repositioning of the minima of curvature leads to a new partitioning of the curve by the partitioning rule. In short, the curve looks different because it is organized into fundamentally different units or chunks. Note that if we chose to define part boundaries by inflections (see Hollerbach, 1975; Marr, 1977), or by both maxima and minima of curvature (see Duda and Hart, 1973), or by all tangent and curvature discontinuities (Binford, 1981), then the chunks would not change when figure and ground reverse.

A clear example of two very different chunkings for one curve can be seen in the famous face–goblet illusion published by Turton in 1819. If a face is taken to be figure, then the minima of curvature divide the curve into chunks corresponding to a forehead, nose, upper lip, lower lip, and chin. If instead the goblet is taken to be figure then the minima reposition, dividing the curve into new chunks corresponding to a base, a couple of parts of the stem, a bowl, and a lip on the bowl. It is probably no accident that the parts defined by minima are often easily assigned verbal labels.

Demonstrations have been devised which, like the face–goblet illusion, allow more than one interpretation of a single contour but which, unlike the face–goblet illusion, do not involve a figure–ground reversal. Two popular examples are the rabbit–duck and hawk–goose illusions (see Fig. 13). Because these illusions do not involve a figure–ground reversal, and because in consequence the minima of curvature never change position, the partitioning rule

Figure 12. *The reversing goblet can be seen as a goblet or a pair of facial profiles (adapted from Turton, 1819). Defining part boundaries by minima of curvature divides the face into a forehead, nose, upper lip, lower lip, and chin. Minima divide the goblet into a base, a couple parts of the stem, a bowl, and a lip on the bowl.*

Figure 13. *Some ambiguous shapes do not involve a reversal of figure and ground. Consequently, the part boundaries defined by minima of curvature do not move when these figures change interpretations. In this illustration, for instance, a rabbit's ear turns into a duck's bill without moving, and a hawk's head turns into a goose's tail, again without moving.*

must predict that the part boundaries are identical for both interpretations of each of these contours. This prediction is easily confirmed. What is an ear on the rabbit, for instance, becomes an upper bill on the duck.

If the minima rule for partitioning is really used by our visual systems, one should expect it to predict some judgments of shape similarity. One case in which its prediction is counterintuitive can be seen in Fig. 14. Look briefly at the single half-moon on the right of the figure. Then look quickly at the two half-moons on the left and decide which seems more similar to the first (go ahead). In an experiment performed on several similar figures, we found that nearly all subjects chose the bottom half-moon as more similar. Yet if you look again you will find that the bounding contour for the top half-moon is identical to that of the right half-moon, only figure–ground reversed. The bounding contour of the bottom half-moon, however, has been mirror reversed, and two parts defined by minima of curvature have been swapped. Why does the bottom one still look more similar? The minima rule gives a simple answer. The bottom contour, which is not figure–ground reversed from the original contour, has the same part boundaries. The top contour, which is figure–ground reversed from the original, has entirely different part boundaries.

7. Holes: A second type of part

The minima rule for partitioning surfaces is motivated by a fact about generic intersections of surfaces: surfaces intersect transversally. As Fig. 3 illustrates, this implies that if two surfaces are interpenetrated and left together to form a composite object then the contour of their intersection is a contour of

Figure 14. *A demonstration that some judgments of shape similarity can be predicted by the minima partitioning rule. In a quick look, the bottom left half-moon appears more similar to the right half-moon than does the top left one. However the bounding contour of the top left half-moon is identical to that of the right half-moon, whereas the bounding contour of the bottom left half-moon has been mirror reversed and has had two parts interchanged.*

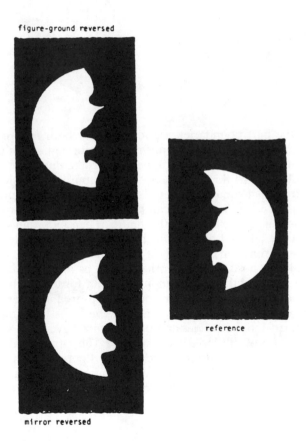

concave discontinuity on the composite surface. Now suppose instead that after the two surfaces are interpenetrated one surface is pulled out of the other, leaving behind a depression, and then discarded. The depression created in this manner has just as much motivation for being a 'part' on the basis of transversality as the parts we have discussed up to this point.

As can be seen by examining the right side of Fig. 3, the contour that divides one part from the other on the composite object is precisely the same contour that will delimit the depression created by pulling out the penetrating part. But whereas in the case of the composite object this contour is a contour of *concave* discontinuity, in the case of the depression this contour is a contour of *convex* discontinuity. And smoothing this contour leads to positive extrema of a principal curvature for the case of a depression. We are led to conclude that a shape can have at least two kinds of parts—'positive parts' which are bounded by negative extrema of a principal curvature, and 'negative parts' (holes) bounded by positive extrema of a principal curvature.

This result presents us with the task of finding a set of rules that determine when to use positive extrema or negative extrema as part boundaries. We do not have these rules yet, but here is an example of what such rules might look like. If a contour of negative extrema of a principal curvature is not a closed contour, and if it is immediately surrounded (i.e., no intervening extrema) by a closed contour of positive extrema of a principal curvature, then take the contour of positive extrema as the boundary of a (negative) part.

Note in any case that what we will not have are single parts bounded by both negative and positive extrema of a principal curvature.

8. Perception and induction

Inferences and regularities of nature have cropped up many times in the theory and discussions presented here. It is useful to explore their significance more fully.

Perceptual systems inform the perceiver about properties of the world she needs to know. The need might be to avoid being eaten, to find what is edible, to avoid unceremonious collisions, or whatever. The relevant knowledge might be the three-dimensional layout of the immediate surrounds, or that ahead lies a tree loaded with fruit, or that crouched in the tree is an unfriendly feline whose perceptual systems are also at work reporting the edible properties of the world. Regardless of the details, what makes the perceptual task tricky is that the data available to a sensorium invariably underdetermine the properties of the world that need to be known. That is, in general there are infinitely many states of the world which are consistent with the available sense data. Perhaps the best known example is that although the world is three-dimensional, and we perceive it as such, each retina is only two-dimensional. Since the mapping from the world to the retina is many-to-one, the possible states of the world consistent with a retinal image, or any series of retinal images, are many. The upshot of all this is that knowledge of the world is inferred. Inference lies at the heart of perception (Fodor and Pylyshyn, 1981; Gregory, 1970; Helmholtz, 1962; Hoffman, 1983b; Marr, 1982).

An inference, reduced to essentials, is simply a list of premises and a conclusion. An inference is said to be *deductively valid* if and only if the conclusion is logically guaranteed to be true given that the premises are true. So, for example, the following inference, which has three premises and one conclusion, is deductively valid: "A mapping from 3-D to 2-D is many-to-one. The world is 3-D. A retinal image is 2-D. Therefore a mapping from the world to a retinal image is many-to-one." An inference is said to be *inductively strong* if and only if it is unlikely that the conclusion is false while its premises are true, and it is not deductively valid (see Skyrms, 1975).[6] So the following inference is inductively strong: "The retinal disparities across my visual field are highly irregular. Therefore whatever I am looking at is not flat." Though this inference is inductively strong, it can prove false, as is in fact the case whenever one views a random dot stereogram.

In perceptual inferences the sensory data play the role of the premises, and the assertions about the state of the world are the conclusions. Since the state of the world is not logically entailed by the sensory data, perceptual inferences are not of the deductive variety—therefore they are inductive.

This is not good news. Whereas deductive inference is well understood, inductive inference is almost not understood at all. Induction involves a morass of unresolved issues, such as projectibility (Goodman, 1955), abduction (Levi, 1980; Peirce, 1931), and simplicity metrics (Fodor, 1975). These problems, though beyond the scope of this paper, apply with unmitigated force to perceptual inferences and are thus of interest to students of perception (Nicod, 1968).

But, despite these difficulties, consider the following question: If the premises of perceptual inferences are the sensory data and the conclusion is an assertion about the state of the world, what is the evidential relation between perceptual premises and conclusions? Or to put it differently, how is it possible that perceptual interpretations of sensory data bear a nonarbitrary (and

---

[6]The distinction between deductively valid and inductively strong inferences is not mere pedantry; the distinction has important consequences for perception, but is often misunderstood. Gregory (1970, p. 160), for instance, realizes the distinction is important for theories of perception, but then claims that "Inductions are generalizations of instances." This is but partly true. Inductive inferences may proceed from general premises to general conclusions, from general premises to particular conclusions, as well as from particular premises to general conclusions (Skyrms, 1975). The distinction between inductive and deductive inferences lies in the evidential relation between premises and conclusions.

even useful) relation to the state of the world? Or to put it still differently, why are perceptual inferences inductively strong?

Surely the answer must be, at least in part, that since the conclusion of a perceptual inference is a statement about the world, such an inference can be inductively strong only if it is motivated by laws, regularities, or uniformities of nature. To see this in a more familiar context, consider the following inductively strong inference about the world: "If I release this egg, it will fall". The inference here is inductively strong because it is motivated by a law of nature—gravity. Skeptics, if there are any, will end up with egg on their feet.

Laws, regularities, and uniformities in the world, then, are crucial for the construction of perceptual inferences which have respectable inductive strength. Only by exploiting the uniformities of nature can a perceptual system overcome the paucity of its sensory data and come to useful conclusions about the state of the world.

If this is the case, it has an obvious implication for perceptual research: identifying the regularities in nature which motivate a particular perceptual inference is not only a good thing to do, but a *sine qua non* for explanatory theories of perception.[7] An explanatory theory must state not only the premises and conclusion of a particular perceptual inference, but also the lawful properties of the world which license the move from the former to the latter. Without all three of these ingredients a proposed theory is incomplete.

---

[7]At least two conditions need to be true of a regularity, such as rigidity, for it to be useful: (1) It should in fact be a regularity. If there were not rigid objects in the world, rigidity would be useless. (2) It should allow inductively strong inferences from images to the world, by making the 'deception probability', to be defined shortly, very close to zero. For instance, let w (world) stand for the following assertion about four points in the world: "are in rigid motion in 3-D". Let i (image) stand for the following assertion about the retinal images of the same four points: "have 2-D positions and motions consistent with being the projections of rigid motion in 3-D". Then what is the probability of w given i? The existence of rigid objects does not in itself make this conditional probability high. Using Bayes' theorem we find that $P(w|i) = P(w) \cdot P(i|w)/[P(w) \cdot P(i|w) + P(-w) \cdot P(i|-w)]$. Since the numerator and the first term of the denominator are identical, this conditional probability is near one only if $P(w) \cdot P(i|w) \gg P(-w) \cdot P(i|-w)$. And since $P(-w)$, though unknown is certainly much greater than zero, $P(w|i)$ is near one only if $P(i|-w)$—let's call this the 'deception probability'—is near zero. Only if the deception probability is near zero can the inference from the image to the world be inductively strong. A major goal of 'structure from motion' proofs (Bobick, 1983; Hoffman and Flinchbaugh, 1982; Longuet-Higgins and Prazony, 1981; Richards *et al.*, 1983; Ullman, 1979) is to determine under what conditions this deception probability is near zero. Using an assumption of rigidity, for instance, Ullman has found that with three views of three points the deception probability is one, but with three views of four points it is near zero.

9. Conclusion

The design of the visual system exploits regularities of nature in two ways: they underlie the mental categories used to represent the world and they license inferences from incomplete visual data to useful descriptions of the world. Both uses of regularities underlie the solution to a problem in shape recognition. Transversality underlies the mental category 'part' of shape; singularities of projection underlie the inference from images to parts in the world.

The partitioning rules presented in this paper are attractive because (1) they satisfy several constraints imposed by the task of shape recognition, (2) they are motivated by a regularity of nature, (3) the resulting partitions look plausible, and (4) the rules explain and unify several well-known visual illusions.

Remaining, however, is a long list of questions to be answered before a comprehensive, explanatory theory of shape recognition is forthcoming. A partial list includes the following. How are the partitioning contours on surfaces to be recovered from two-dimensional images? How should the surface parts be described? All we have so far is a rule for cutting out parts. But what qualitative and metrical descriptions should be applied to the resulting parts? Can the answer to this question be motivated by appeal to uniformities and regularities in the world? What spatial relations need to be computed between parts? Although the part definitions don't depend upon the viewing geometry, is it possible or even necessary that the predicates of spatial relations do (Rock, 1974; Yin, 1970)? How is the shape memory organized? What is the first index into this memory?

The task of vision is to infer useful descriptions of the world from changing patterns of light falling on the eye. The descriptions can be reliable only to the extent that the inferential processes which build them exploit regularities in the visual world, regularities such as rigidity and transversality. The discovery of such regularities, and the mathematical investigation of their power in guiding particular visual inferences, are promising directions for the researcher seeking to understand human vision.

Appendix 1

Surface partitioning in detail

This appendix applies the surface partitioning rule to a particular class of surfaces: surfaces of revolution. The intent is to convey a more rigorous understanding of the rule and the partitions it yields. Since this section is quite mathematical, some readers might prefer to look at the results in Fig. 16 and skip the rest.

Notation. Tensor notation is adopted in this section because it allows concise expression of surface concepts, (see Dodson and Poston, 1979; Hoffman, 1983a; Lipschutz, 1969). A vector in $\Re^3$ is $\mathbf{x} = (x^1, x^2, x^3)$. A point in the parameter plane is (u^1, u^2). A surface patch is $\mathbf{x} = \mathbf{x}(u^1, u^2) = (x^1(u^1, u^2), x^2(u^1, u^2), x^3(u^1, u^2))$. Partial derivatives are denoted by subscripts:

$$\mathbf{x}_1 = \frac{\partial \mathbf{x}}{\partial u^1}, \mathbf{x}_2 = \frac{\partial \mathbf{x}}{\partial u^2}, \mathbf{x}_{12} = \frac{\partial^2 \mathbf{x}}{\partial u^1 \partial u_2}, \text{etc.}$$

A tangent vector is $d\mathbf{x} = \mathbf{x}_1 du^1 + \mathbf{x}_2 du^2 = \mathbf{x}_i du^i$ where the Einstein summation convention is used. The first fundamental form is

$$| = d\mathbf{x} \cdot d\mathbf{x} = \mathbf{x}_i \cdot \mathbf{x}_j du^i du^j = g_{ij} du^i du^j$$

where the g_{ij} are the first fundamental coefficients and $i, j = 1, 2$.

The differential of the normal vector is the vector $d\mathbf{N} = \mathbf{N}_i du^i$ and the second fundamental form is

$$\| = d^2\mathbf{x} \cdot \mathbf{N} = \mathbf{x}_{ij} \cdot \mathbf{N} du^i du^j = b_{ij} du^i du^j$$

where the b_{ij} are the second fundamental coefficients and $i, j = 1, 2$.

A plane passing through a surface S orthogonal to the tangent plane of S at some point P and in a direction $du^i:du^j$ with respect to the tangent plane intersects the surface in a curve whose curvature at P is the *normal curvature* of S at P in the direction $du^i:du^j$. The normal curvature in a direction $du^i:du^j$ is $k_n = \|/|$. The two perpendicular directions for which the values of k_n take on maximum and minimum values are called the *principal directions*, and the corresponding curvatures, k_1 and k_2, are called the *principal curvatures*. The *Gaussian curvature* at P is $K = k_1 k_2$. A *line of curvature* is a curve on a surface whose tangent at each point is along a principal direction.

Partitions of a surface of revolution. A surface of revolution is a set $S \subset \Re^3$ obtained by rotating a regular plane curve α about an axis in the plane which does not meet the curve. Let the $x^1 x^3$ plane be the plane of α and the x^3 axis the rotation axis. Let

$$\alpha(u^1) = (x(u^1), z(u^1)), a < u^1 < b, z(u^1) > 0.$$

Let u^2 be the rotation angle about the x^3 axis. Then we obtain a map

$$\mathbf{x}(u^1, u^2) = (x(u^1)\cos(u^2), x(u^1)\sin(u^2), z(u^1))$$

Figure 15. *Surface of revolution.*

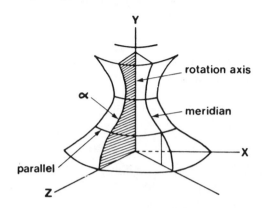

from the open set $U = \{(u^1, u^2) \in \Re^2; 0 < u^2 < 2\pi, a < u^1 < b\}$ into S (Fig. 15). The curve α is called the *generating curve* of S, and the x^3 axis is the *rotation axis* of S. The circles swept out by the points of α are called the *parallels* of S, and the various placements of α on S are called the *meridians* of S.

Let $\cos(u^2)$ be abbreviated as c and $\sin(u^2)$ as s. Then $\mathbf{x}_1 = (x_1 c, x_1 s, z_1)$ and $\mathbf{x}_2 = (-xs, xc, 0)$. The first fundamental coefficients are then

$$g_{ij} = \mathbf{x}_i \cdot \mathbf{x}_j = \begin{pmatrix} x_1^2 + z_1^2 & 0 \\ 0 & x^2 \end{pmatrix}.$$

The surface normal is

$$\mathbf{N} = \frac{\mathbf{x}_1 \times \mathbf{x}_2}{|\mathbf{x}_1 \times \mathbf{x}_2|} = \frac{(z_1 c, z_1 s, -x_1)}{\sqrt{z_1^2 + x_1^2}}.$$

If we let u be arc length along α then $\sqrt{z_1^2 + x_1^2} = 1 = g_{11}$ and

$$\mathbf{N} = (z_1 c, z_1 s, -x_1).$$

The second fundamental coefficients are

$$b_{ij} = \mathbf{x}_{ij} \cdot \mathbf{N} = \begin{pmatrix} x_{11} z_1 - x_1 z_{11} & 0 \\ 0 & -x z_1 \end{pmatrix}.$$

Since $g_{12} = b_{12} = 0$ the principal curvatures of a surface of revolution are

$$k_1 = b_{11}/g_{11} = x_{11}z_1 - x_1z_{11}$$
$$k_2 = b_{22}/g_{22} = -z_1/x.$$

The expression for k_1 is identical to the expression for the curvature along α. In fact the meridians (the various positions of α on S) are lines of curvature, as are the parallels. The curvature along the meridians is given by the expression for k_1 and the curvature along the parallel is given by the expression for k_2. The expression for k_2 is simply the curvature of a circle of radius x multiplied by the cosine of the angle that the tangent to α makes with the axis of rotation.

Observe that the expressions for k_1 and k_2 depend only upon the parameter u^1, not u^2. In particular, since k_2 is independent of u^2 there are no extrema or inflections of the normal curvature along the parallels. The parallels are circles. Consequently no segmentation contours arise from the lines of curvature associated with k_2. Only the minima of k_1 along the meridians are used for segmentation. Fig. 16 shows several surfaces of revolution with the

Figure 16. *Partitions on surfaces of revolution.*

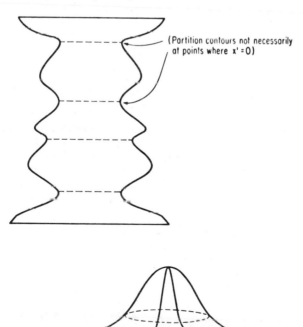

(Partition contours not necessarily at points where x' = 0)

minima of curvature along the meridians marked. The resulting segmentation contours appear quite natural to human observers.

As a surface of revolution is flattened along one axis, the partitioning contours which are at first circles become, in general, more elliptical and bow slightly up or down.

Appendix 2

Inferring part boundaries from image singularities

In general, a concave discontinuity in a silhouette indicates a part boundary (as defined by the minima rule) on the imaged surface. This appendix makes this statement more precise and then examines a special case.

Only two types of singularity can arise in the projection from the world to the retina (Whitney, 1955). These two types are *folds* and *spines* (see Fig. 17). Intuitively, folds are the contours on a surface where the viewer's line of sight would just graze the surface, and a spine separates the visible portion of a fold from the invisible. A contour on the retina corresponding to a fold on a surface is called an *outline* (Koenderink and van Doorn, 1976, 1982b). A *termination* is a point on the retina corresponding to a spine on a surface. A *T-junction* (see Fig. 17) occurs where two outlines cut each other.

We wish to determine the conditions in which a T-junction indicates the presence of a part boundary. Two results are useful here. First, the sign of curvature of a point on an outline (projection of a fold) is the sign of the Gaussian curvature at the corresponding surface point (Koenderink and van Doorn, 1976, 1982b). Convex portions of the outline indicate positive Gaussian curvature, concave portions indicate negative Gaussian curvature, and inflections indicate zero Gaussian curvature. Second, the spine always occurs

Figure 17. *Singularities of the retinal projection.*

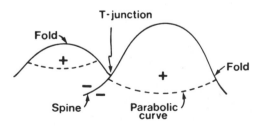

at a point of negative Gaussian curvature. That is, the visible portion of a fold always ends in a segment whose projected image is concave (Koenderink and van Doorn, 1982b).

The scheme of the proof is the following. Suppose that the folds on both sides of a T-junction have convex regions, as shown in Fig. 17. Then the sign of the Gaussian curvature is positive, and in fact both principal curvatures are positive, in these two regions. Now the presence of a spine indicates that these regions of positive Gaussian curvature are separated by a region of negative Gaussian curvature. This implies that the principal curvature associated with one family of lines of curvature is negative in this region. But then the principal curvature along this family of lines of curvature must go from positive to negative and back to positive as the lines of curvature go from one hill into the valley and back up the other hill. If this is true, then in the generic case the principal curvature will go through a negative minimum somewhere in the valley—and we have a part boundary.

There are two cases to consider. In the first the loci where one principal curvature goes from positive to negative (parabolic curves) surround each hill. In the second case the parabolic curve surrounds the valley between the two hills. We consider only the first case.

In the first case there are two ways that the lines of curvature entering the valley from one parabolic curve might fail to connect smoothly with lines of curvature entering the valley from the other parabolic curve: they might intersect orthogonally or not at all. If they intersect orthogonally then the two principal curvatures must both be negative, and the Gaussian curvature, which is the product of the two principal curvatures, must be positive. But the valley between the parabolic contours has negative Gaussian curvature, a contradiction.

If the lines of curvature fail to intersect then there must be a singularity in the lines of curvature somewhere in the region having negative Gaussian curvature. However, "The net of lines of curvature may have singular properties at umbilical points, and at them only." (Hilbert and Cohn-Vossen, 1952, p. 187). Umbilical points, points where the two principal curvatures are equal, can only occur in regions of positive Gaussian curvature—again a contradiction. (Here we assume the surface is smooth. A singularity could also occur if the surface were not smooth at one point in the valley. But in the generic case part boundaries would still occur.)

This proof requires that the two folds of a T-junction each have a convex region. The two folds of T-junctions on a torus do not satisfy this condition—they are always concave. Thus it is a simple matter to determine from an image when a T-junction warrants the inference of a part boundary.

The proof outlined here is a special case. A general proof is needed which specifies when a concave cusp in a silhouette indicates the presence of a part boundary or two different objects. The more general proof would not use the relation between spine points and Gaussian curvature. The proof might run roughly as follows: a concave cusp is a double point in the projection. A line connecting the two points on the surface which project to the cusp necessarily lies outside the surface between the two points. But then the surface is not convex everywhere between these two points. Consequently there is a concave discontinuity (part boundary) between the points or the Gaussian curvature must go negative. If the Gaussian curvature goes from positive (convex) to negative and then back to positive (convex), one of the principal curvatures must also. But this implies it has a negative minimum, in the general case, and so we have a smooth part boundary.

References

Attneave, F. (1974) Multistability in perception, *Scient. Am., 225*, 63–71.
Badler, N. and Bajcsy, R. (1978) Three-dimensional representations for computer graphics and computer vision. *Comp. Graph., 12*, 153–160.
Ballard, D. and Brown, C. (1982) *Computer Vision*, Englewood Cliffs, N.J., Prentice-Hall.
Baumgart, B. (1972) *Winged edge polyhedron representation*. STAN-CS-320, AIM-179, Stanford AI Lab.
Binford, T. (1971) Visual perception by computer. IEEE Conf. Syst. Cont., Miami.
Binford, T. (1981) Inferring surfaces from images. *Art. Intell., 17*, 205–244.
Bobick, A. (1983) A hybrid approach to structure-from-motion. Association for Computing Machinery Workshop on Motion: Representation and Perception.
Brady, J.M. (1982a) Parts description and acquisition using vision. *Proc. Soc. Photo-opt. Instrument. Eng.*
Brady, J.M. (1982b) Criteria for representations of shape. In A. Rosenfeld and J. Beck (eds.), *Human and Machine Vision*.
Brady, J.M. (1982c) Describing visible surfaces. In A. Hanson and E. Riseman (eds.), *Computer Vision Systems*.
Brooks, R., Greiner Russell, and Binford, T. (1979) The ACRONYM model based vision system. *Proc. Int. Joint Conf. Art. Intell., 6*, 105–113.
Clowes M. (1971) On seeing things. *Art. Intell., 2*, 79–116.
Dennett, D. (1978) Intentional systems. In *Brainstorms*. Montgomery, VT, Bradford.
Do Carmo, M. (1976) *Differential Geometry of Curves and Surfaces*. Englewood Cliffs, NJ, Prentice-Hall.
Dodson, D. and Poston, T. (1977) *Tensor Geometry*. London, Pitman.
Duda, R. and Hart, P. (1973) *Pattern Classification and Scene Analysis*. New York, Wiley.
Fodor, J. (1975) *The Language of Thought*, Cambridge, MA, Harvard University Press.
Fodor, J. (1983) *The Modularity of Mind*, Cambridge, MA, MIT Press.
Fodor, J. and Pylyshyn, Z. (1981) How direct is visual perception?: Some reflections on Gibson's "Ecological Approach". *Cog., 9*, 139–196.
Goodman, N. (1955) *Fact, Fiction and Forecast*. Cambridge, MA, Harvard University Press.
Gregory, R. (1970) *The Intelligent Eye*. New York, McGraw-Hill.
Guillemin, V. and Pollack, A. (1974) *Differential Topology*. Englewood Cliffs, NJ, Prentice-Hall.
Guzman, A. (1969) Decomposition of a visual scene into three-dimensional bodies. In A. Grasseli (ed.), *Automatic Interpretation and Classification of Images*, New York, Academic Press.

Helmholtz, H. (1962) *Treatise on Physiological Optics, Volume 3*, Dover reprint.

Hilbert, D. and Cohn-Vossen, S. (1952) *Geometry and the Imagination*, New York, Chelsea.

Hoffman, D. (1983a) Representing Shapes for Visual Recognition. MIT Ph.D. thesis.

Hoffman, D. (1983b) The interpretation of visual illusions, *Scient. Am., 249*, 154–162.

Hoffman D. and Flinchbaugh, B. (1982) The interpretation of biological motivation, *Biol. Cybernet., 42*, 195–204.

Hoffman, D. and Richards, W. (1982) Representing smooth plane curves for visual recognition: Implications for figure–ground reversal. *Proc. Am. Ass. Art. Intell.*, 5–8.

Hollerbach, J. (1975) *Hierarchical Shape Description of Objects by Selection and Modification of Prototypes*, MIT AI-TR-346.

Huffman, D. (1971) Impossible objects as nonsense sentences. *Mach. Intell., 6.*

Koenderink, J. and van Doorn, A. (1976) The singularities of the visual mapping. *Biol. Cybernet., 24*, 51–59.

Koenderink, J. and van Doorn, A. (1979) The internal representation of solid shape with respect to vision. *Biol. Cybernet., 32*, 211–216.

Koenderink, J. and van Doorn, A. (1980) Photometric invariants related to solid shape. *Optica Acta, 7*, 981–996.

Koenderink, J. and van Doorn, A. (1982a) Perception of solid shape and spatial lay-out through photometric invariants. In R. Trappl (ed.), *Cybernetics and Systems Research*, Amsterdam, North-Holland.

Koenderink, J. and van Doorn, A. (1982b) The shape of smooth objects and the way contours end. *Perception, 11*, 129–137.

Levi, I. (1980) *The Enterprise of Knowledge*, Cambridge, MA, MIT Press.

Liberman, A., Cooper, F., Shankweiler, D., and Studdert-Kennedy, M. (1967) The perception of the speech code. *Psychol. Rev., 74*, 431–461.

Lipschutz, M. (1969) *Differential Geometry*, (Schaum's Outline), New York, McGraw Hill.

Longuet-Higgins, H.C. and Prazdny, K. (1981) The interpretation of a moving retinal image. *Proc. R. Soc. Lond., B208*, 385–397.

Mackworth, A. (1973) Interpreting pictures of polyhedral scenes. *Art. Intell., 4*, 121–137.

Mandelbrot, B. (1982) *The Fractal Geometry of Nature*. San Francisco, Freeman

Marr, D. (1977) Analysis of occluding countour. *Proc. R. Soc. Lond., B197*, 441–475.

Marr, D. (1982) *Vision*. San Francisco, Freeman.

Marr, D. and Nishihara, H.K. (1978) Representation and recognition of the spatial organization of three-dimensional shapes. *Proc. R. Soc. Lond., B200*, 269–294.

Marr, D. and Poggio, T. (1977) From understanding computation to understanding neural circuitry, *Neurosci. Res. Prog. Bull., 15*, 470–488.

Nicod, J. (1968) *Geometry and Induction*, Berkeley, University of California Press.

Nishihara, H.K. (1981) Intensity, visible-surface, and volumetric representations. *Art. Intell., 17*, 265–284.

O'Rourke, J. and Badler, N. (1979) Decomposition of three-dimensional objects into spheres. *IEEE Trans. Pattern Anal. Mach. Intell., 1.*

Pentland, A. (1983) Fractal-based description. *Proc. Int. Joint Conf. Art. Intell.*

Peirce, C. (1931) *Collected Papers*, Cambridge, MA, Harvard University Press.

Richards, W., Rubin, J.M. and Hoffman, D.D. (1983) Equation counting and the interpretation of sensory data. *Perception, 11*, 557–576, and MIT AI Memo 618 (1981).

Rock, I. (1974) The perception of disoriented figures. *Scient. Am. 230*, 78–85.

Skyrms, B. (1975) *Choice and Chance*. Belmont, Wadsworth Publishing Co.

Soroka, B. (1979) Generalized cylinders from parallel slices. *Proc. Pattern Recognition and Image processing*, 421–426.

Spivak, M. (1970) *Differential Geometry, Volume 2*, Berkeley, Publish or Perish.

Sutherland, N.S. (1968) Outlines of a theory of visual pattern recognition in animals and man. *Proc. R. Soc. Lond., B171*, 297-317.

Thompson, D'Arcy (1968) *On Growth and Form*, Cambridge, University of Cambridge Press.

Turton, W. (1819) *A Conchological Dictionary of the British Islands*, (frontispiece), printed for John Booth, London. [This early reference was kindly pointed out to us by J.F.W. McOmie.]

Ullman, S. (1979) *The Interpretation of Visual Motion*. Cambridge, MA, MIT Press.

Waltz, D. (1975) Understanding line drawings of scenes with shadows. In P. Winston (ed.), *The Psychology of Computer Vision*, New York, McGraw-Hill.

Whitney, H. (1955) On singularities of mappings of Euclidean spaces. I. Mappings of the plane into the plane. *Ann. Math., 62*, 374-410.

Witkin, A.P. (1983) Scale-space filtering. *Proc. Int. Joint Conf. Artificial Intelligence.*

Yin, R. (1970) Face recognition by brain-injured patients: A dissociable ability? *Neuropsychologia, 8*, 395-402.

Yuille, A. (1983) *Scaling theorems for zero-crossings*. MIT AI Memo 722.

3

Visual routines*

SHIMON ULLMAN

Massachusetts Institute of Technology

Abstract

This paper examines the processing of visual information beyond the creation of the early representations. A fundamental requirement at this level is the capacity to establish visually abstract shape properties and spatial relations. This capacity plays a major role in object recognition, visually guided manipulation, and more abstract visual thinking.

For the human visual system, the perception of spatial properties and relations that are complex from a computational standpoint nevertheless often appears deceivingly immediate and effortless. The proficiency of the human system in analyzing spatial information far surpasses the capacities of current artificial systems. The study of the computations that underlie this competence may therefore lead to the development of new more efficient methods for the spatial analysis of visual information.

The perception of abstract shape properties and spatial relations raises fundamental difficulties with major implications for the overall processing of visual information. It will be argued that the computation of spatial relations divides the analysis of visual information into two main stages. The first is the bottom-up creation of certain representations of the visible environment. The second stage involves the application of processes called 'visual routines' to the representations constructed in the first stage. These routines can establish properties and relations that cannot be represented explicitly in the initial representations.

Visual routines are composed of sequences of elemental operations. Routines for different properties and relations share elemental operations. Using a fixed set of basic operations, the visual system can assemble different routines to extract an unbounded variety of shape properties and spatial relations.

*This report describes research done at the Artificial Intelligence Laboratory of the Massachusetts Institute of Technology. Support for the laboratory's artificial intelligence research is provided in part by the Advanced Research Projects Agency of the Department of Defense under Office of Naval Research contract N00014-80-C-0505 and in part by National Science Foundation Grant 79-23110MCS. Reprint requests should be sent to Shimon Ullman Department of Psychology and Artificial Intelligence Laboratory, M.I.T., Cambridge, MA 02139, U.S.A.

At a more detailed level, a number of plausible basic operations are suggested, based primarily on their potential usefulness, and supported in part by empirical evidence. The operations discussed include shifting of the processing focus, indexing to an odd-man-out location, bounded activation, boundary tracing, and marking. The problem of assembling such elemental operations into meaningful visual routines is discussed briefly.

1. The perception of spatial relations

1.1. Introduction

Visual perception requires the capacity to extract shape properties and spatial relations among objects and objects' parts. This capacity is fundamental to visual recognition, since objects are often defined visually by abstract shape properties and spatial relations among their components.

A simple example is illustrated in Fig. 1a, which is readily perceived as representing a face. The shapes of the individual constituents, the eyes, nose, and mouth, in this drawing are highly schematized; it is primarily the spatial arrangement of the constituents that defines the face. In Fig. 1b, the same components are rearranged, and the figure is no longer interpreted as a face. Clearly, the recognition of objects depends not only on the presence of certain features, but also on their spatial arrangement.

The role of establishing properties and relations visually is not confined to the task of visual recognition. In the course of manipulating objects we often rely on our visual perception to obtain answers to such questions as "is *A* longer than *B*", "does *A* fit inside *B*", etc. Problems of this type can be solved without necessarily implicating object recognition. They do require, however,

Figure 1.   *Schematic drawings of normally-arranged (a) and scrambled (b) faces. Figure 1a is readily recognized as representing a face although the individual features are meaningless. In 1b, the same constituents are rearranged, and the figure is no longer perceived as a face.*

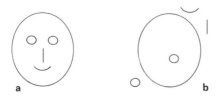

a   b

the visual analysis of shape and spatial relations among parts.[1] Spatial relations in three-dimensional space therefore play an important role in visual perception.

In view of the fundamental importance of the task, it is not surprising that our visual system is indeed remarkably adept at establishing a variety of spatial relations among items in the visual input. This proficiency is evidenced by the fact that the perception of spatial properties and relations that are complex from a computational standpoint, nevertheless often appears immediate and effortless. It also appears that some of the capacity to establish spatial relations is manifested by the visual system from a very early age. For example, infants of 1–15 weeks of age are reported to respond preferentially to schematic face-like figures, and to prefer normally arranged face figures over 'scrambled' face patterns (Fantz, 1961).

The apparent immediateness and ease of perceiving spatial relations is deceiving. As we shall see, it conceals in fact a complex array of processes that have evolved to establish certain spatial relations with considerable efficiency. The processes underlying the perception of spatial relations are still unknown even in the case of simple elementary relations. Consider, for instance, the task of comparing the lengths of two line segments. Faced with this simple task, a draftsman may measure the length of the first line, record the result, measure the second line, and compare the resulting measurements. When the two lines are present simultaneously in the field of view, it is often possible to compare their lengths by 'merely looking'. This capacity raises the problem of how the 'draftsman in our head' operates, without the benefit of a ruler and a scratchpad. More generally, a theory of the perception of spatial relations should aim at unraveling the processes that take place within our visual system when we establish shape properties of objects and their spatial relations by 'merely looking' at them.

The perception of abstract shape properties and spatial relations raises fundamental difficulties with major implications for the overall processing of visual information. The purpose of this paper is to examine these problems and implications. Briefly, it will be argued that the computation of spatial relations divides the analysis of visual information into two main stages. The first is the bottom up creation of certain representations of the visible environment. Examples of such representations are the primal sketch (Marr, 1976) and the 2½-D sketch (Marr and Nishihara, 1978). The second stage involves the top–down application of visual routines to the representations constructed

---

[1]Shape properties (such as overall orientation, area, etc.) refer to a single item, while spatial relations (such as above, inside, longer–than, etc.) involve two or more items. For brevity, the term spatial relations used in the discussion would refer to both shape properties and spatial relations.

in the first stage. These routines can establish properties and relations that cannot be represented explicitly in the initial base representations. Underlying the visual routines there exists a fixed set of elemental operations that constitute the basic 'instruction set' for more complicated processes. The perception of a large variety of properties and relations is obtained by assembling appropriate routines based on this set of elemental operations.

The paper is divided into three parts. The first introduces the notion of visual routines. The second examines the role of visual routines within the overall scheme of processing visual information. The third (Sections 3 and 4) examines the elemental operations out of which visual routines are constructed.

1.2. An example: The perception of inside/outside relations

The perception of inside/outside relationships is performed by the human perceptual system with intriguing efficiency. To take a concrete example, suppose that the visual input consists of a single closed curve, and a small 'X' figure (see Fig. 2), and one is required to determine visually whether the X lies inside or outside the closed curve. The correct answers in Fig. 2a and 2b appear to be immediate and effortless, and the response would be fast and accurate.[2]

Figure 2. *Perceiving inside and outside. In 2a and 2b, the perception is immediate and effortless; in 2c, it is not.*

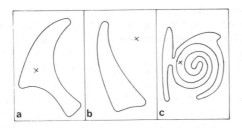

---

[2]For simple figures such as 2a, viewing time of less than 50 msec with moderate intensity, followed by effective masking is sufficient. This is well within the limit of what is considered immediate, effortless perception (e.g., Julesz, 1975). Reaction time of about 500 msec can be obtained in two–choice experiments with simple figures (Varanese, 1981). The response time may vary with the presentation conditions, but the main point is that in/out judgments are fast and reliable and require only a brief presentation.

One possible reason for our proficiency in establishing inside/outside relations is their potential value in visual recognition based on their stability with respect to the viewing position. That is, inside/outside relations tend to remain invariant over considerable variations in viewing position. When viewing a face, for instance, the eyes remain within the head boundary as long as they are visible, regardless of the viewing position (see also Sutherland (1968) on inside/outside relations in perception).

The immediate perception of the inside/outside relation is subject to some limitations (Fig. 2c). These limitations are not very restrictive, however, and the computations performed by the visual system in distinguishing 'inside' from 'outside' exhibit considerable flexibility: the curve can have a variety of shapes, and the positions of the X and the curve do not have to be known in advance.

The processes underlying the perception of insde/outside relations are entirely unknown. In the following section I shall examine two methods for computing 'insideness' and compare them with human perception. The comparison will then serve to introduce the general discussion concerning the notion of visual routines and their role in visual perception.

1.2.1. Computing inside and outside

The ray-intersection method. Shape perception and recognition is often described in terms of a hierarchy of 'feature detectors' (Barlow, 1972; Milner, 1974). According to these hierarchical models, simple feature detecting units such as edge detectors are combined to produce higher order units such as, say, triangle detectors, leading eventually to the detection and recognition of objects. It does not seem possible, however, to construct an 'inside/outside detector' from a combination of elementary feature detectors. Approaches that are more procedural in nature have therefore been suggested instead. A simple procedure that can establish whether a given point lies inside or outside a closed curve is the method of ray-intersections. To use this method, a ray is drawn, emanating from the point in question, and extending to 'infinity'. For practical purposes, 'infinity' is a region that is guaranteed somehow to lie outside the curve. The number of intersections made by the ray with the curve is recorded. (The ray may also happen to be tangential to the curve without crossing it at one or more points. In this case, each tangent point is counted as two intersection points.) If the resulting intersection number is odd, the origin point of the ray lies inside the closed curve. If it is even (including zero), then it must be outside (see Fig. 3a, b).

This procedure has been implemented in computer programs (Evans, 1968; Winston, 1977, Ch. 2), and it may appear rather simple and straightforward. The success of the ray-intersection method is guaranteed, however, only if

Figure 3.   *The ray intersection method for establishing inside/outside relations. When the point lies inside the closed curve, the number of intersections is odd (a); when it lies outside, the number of intersections is even (b).*

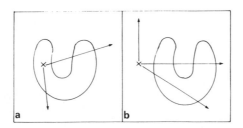

rather restrictive constraints are met. First, it must be assumed that the curve is closed, otherwise an odd number of intersections would not be indicative of an 'inside' relation (see Fig. 4a). Second, it must be assumed that the curve is isolated: in Figs. 4b and 4c, point p lies within the region bounded by the closed curve c, but the number of intersections is even.[3]

These limitations on the ray-intersection method are not shared by the human visual system: in all of the above examples the correct relation is easily established. In addition, some variations of the inside/outside problem pose almost insurmountable difficulties to the ray-intersection procedure, but not to human vision. Suppose that in Fig. 4d the problem is to determine whether any of the points lies inside the curve C. Using the ray-intersection procedure, rays must be constructed from all the points, adding significantly to the complexity of the solution. In Figs. 4e and 4f the problem is to determine whether the two points marked by dots lie inside the same curve. The number of intersections of the connecting line is not helpful in this case in establishing the desired relation. In Fig. 4g the task is to find an innermost point—a point that lies inside all of the three curves. The task is again straightforward, but it poses serious difficulties to the ray-intersection method.

It can be concluded from such considerations that the computations employed by our perceptual system are different from, and often superior to the ray-intersection method.

---

[3]In Fig. 4c region p can also be interpreted as lying inside a hole cut in a planar figure. Under this interpretation the result of the ray–interaction method can be accepted as correct. For the original task, however, which is to determine whether p lies within the region bounded by c, the answer provided by the ray–intersection method is incorrect.

Figure 4.   *Limitations of the ray-intersection method. a, An open curve. The number*
of intersections is odd, but p *does not lie inside* C. *b—c, Additional curves*
may change the number of intersections, leading to errors. d—g, Variations
of the inside/outside problem that render the ray-intersection method in
ineffective. In d *the task is to determine visually whether any of the dots lie*
inside C, *in (—f), whether the two dots lie inside the same curve; in* g *the*
task is to find a point that lies inside all three curves.

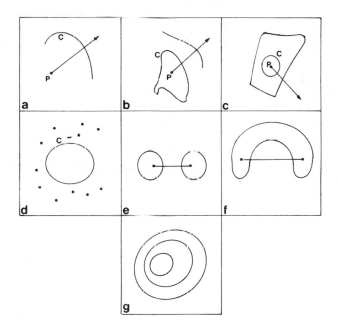

The 'coloring' method. An alternative procedure that avoids some of the limitations inherent in the ray-intersection method uses the operation of activating, or 'coloring' an area. Starting from a given point, the area around it in
the internal representation is somehow activated. This activation spreads outward until a boundary is reached, but it is not allowed to cross the boundary.
Depending on the starting point, either the inside or the outside of the curve,
but not both, will be activated. This can provide a basis for separating inside
from outside. An additional stage is still required, however, to complete the
procedure, and this additional stage will depend on the specific problem at
hand. One can test, for example, whether the region surrounding a 'point at
infinity' has been activated. Since this point lies outside the curve in question,

it will thereby be established whether the activated area constitutes the curve's inside or the outside. In this manner a point can sometimes be determined to lie outside the curve without requiring a detailed analysis of the curve itself. In Fig. 5, most of the curve can be ignored, since activation that starts at the X will soon 'leak out' of the enclosing corridor and spread to 'infinity'. It will thus be determined that the X cannot lie inside the curve, without analyzing the curve and without attempting to separate its inside from the outside.[4]

Alternatively, one may start at an infinity point, using for instance the following procedure: (1) move towards the curve until a boundary is met; (2) mark this meeting point; (3) start to track the boundary, in a clockwise direction, activating the area on the right; (4) stop when the marked position is reached. If a termination of the curve is encountered before the marked position is reached, the curve is open and has no inside or outside. Otherwise, when the marked position is reached again and the activation spread stops, the inside of the curve will be activated. Both routines are possible, but, depending on the shape of the curve and the location of the X, one or the other may become more efficient.

The coloring method avoids some of the main difficulties with the ray-intersection method, but it also falls short of accounting for the performance of human perception in similar tasks. It seems, for example, that for human perception the computation time is to a large extent scale independent. That

Figure 5.   *That the* x *does not lie inside the curve* C *can be established without a detailed analysis of the curve.*

---

[4]In practical applications 'infinity points' can be located if the curve is known in advance not to extend beyond a limited region. In human vision it is not clear what may constitute an 'infinity point', but it seems that we have little difficulty in finding such points. Even for a complex shape, that may not have a well–defined inside and outside, it is easy to determine visually a location that clearly lies outside the region occupied by the shape.

is, the size of the figures can be increased considerably with only a small effect on the computation time.[5] In contrast, in the activation scheme outlined above computation time should increase with the size of the figures.

The basic coloring scheme can be modified to increase its efficiency and endow it with scale independence, for example by performing the computation simultaneously at a number of resolution scales. Even the modified scheme will have difficulties, however, competing with the performance of the human perceptual system. Evidently, elaborate computations will be required to match the efficiency and flexibility exhibited by the human perceptual system in establishing inside/outside relationships.

The goal of the above discussion was not to examine the perception of inside/outside relations in detail, but to introduce the problems associated with the seemingly effortless and immediate perception of spatial relations. I next turn to a more general discussion of the difficulties associated with the perception of spatial relations and shape properties, and the implications of these difficulties to the processing of visual information.

1.3. Spatial analysis by visual routines

In this section, we shall examine the general requirements imposed by the visual analysis of shape properties and spatial relations. The difficulties involved in the analysis of spatial properties and relations are summarized below in terms of three requirements that must be faced by the 'visual processor' that performs such analysis. The three requirements are (i) the capacity to establish abstract properties and relations (abstractness), (ii) the capacity to establish a large variety of relations and properties, including newly defined ones (open-endedness), and (iii) the requirement to cope efficiently with the complexity involved in the computation of spatial relations (complexity).

1.3.1. Abstractness

The perception of inside/outside relations provides an example of the visual system's capacity to analyze abstract spatial relations. In this section the notion of abstract properties and relations and the difficulties raised by their perception will be briefly discussed.

Formally, a shape property P defines a set S of shapes that share this property. The property of closure, for example, divides the set of all curves

---

[5]The dependency of inside/outside judgments on the size of the figure is currently under empirical investigation. There seems to be a slight increase in reaction time as a function of the figure size.

into the set of closed curves that share this property, and the complementary set of open curves. (Similarly, a relation such as 'inside' defines a set of configurations that satisfy this relation.)

Clearly, in many cases the set of shapes S that satisfy a property P can be large and unwieldy. It therefore becomes impossible to test a shape for property P by comparing it against all the members of S stored in memory. The problem lies in fact not simply in the size of the set S, but in what may be called the size of the *support* of S. To illustrate this distinction, suppose that given a plane with one special point X marked on it we wish to identify the black figures containing X. This set of figures is large, but, given an isolated figure, it is simple to test whether it is a member of the set: only a single point, X, need be inspected. In this case the relevant part of the figure, or its support, consists of a single point. In contrast, the set of supports for the property of closure, or the inside/outside relation, is unmanageably large.

When the set of supports is small, the recognition of even a large set of objects can be accomplished by simple template matching. This means that a small number of patterns is stored, and matched against the figure in question.[6] When the set of supports is prohibitively large, a template matching decision scheme will become impossible. The classification task may nevertheless be feasible if the set contains certain regularities. This roughly means that the recognition of a property P can be broken down into a set of operations in such a manner that the overall computation required for establishing P is substantially less demanding than the storing of all the shapes in S. The set of all closed curves, for example, is not just a random collection of shapes, and there are obviously more efficient methods for establishing closure than simple template matching. For a completely random set of shapes containing no regularities, simplified recognition procedures will not be possible. The minimal program required for the recognition of the set would be in this case essentially as large as the set itself (cf. Kolmogorov, 1968).

The above discussion can now serve to define what is meant here by 'abstract' shape properties and spatial relations. This notion refers to properties and relations with a prohibitively large set of supports that can nevertheless be established efficiently by a computation that captures the regularities in the set. Our visual system can clearly establish abstract properties and

---

[6]For the present discussion, template–matching between plane figures can be defined as their cross–correlation. The definition can be extended to symbolic descriptions in the plane. In this case at each location in a plane a number of symbols can be activated, and a pattern is then a subset of activated symbols. Given a pattern P and a template T, their degree of match m is a function that is increasing in $P \cap T$ and decreasing in $P \cup T - P \cap T$ (when P is 'positioned over' T so as to maximize m).

relations. The implication is that it should employ sets of processes for establishing shape properties and spatial relations. The perception of abstract properties such as insideness or closure would then be explained in terms of the computations employed by the visual system to capture the regularities underlying different properties and relations. These computations would be described in terms of their constituent operations and how they are combined to establish different properties and relations.

We have seen in Section 1.2 examples of possible computations for the analysis of inside/outside relations. It is suggested that processes of this general type are performed by the human visual system in perceiving inside/outside relations. The operations employed by the visual system may prove, however, to be different from those considered in Section 1.2. To explain the perception of inside/outside relations it would be necessary, therefore, to unravel the constituent operations employed by the visual system, and how they are used in different judgments.

1.3.2. Open-endedness

As we have seen, the perception of an abstract relation is quite a remarkable feat even for a single relation, such as insideness. Additional complications arise from the requirement to recognize not only one, but a large number of different properties and relations. A reasonable approach to the problem would be to assume that the computations that establish different properties and relations share their underlying elemental operations. In this manner a large variety of abstract shape properties and spatial relations can be established by different processes assembled from a fixed set of elemental operations. The term 'visual routines' will be used to refer to the processes composed out of the set of elemental operations to establish shape properties and spatial relations.

A further implication of the open-endedness requirement is that a mechanism is required by which new combinations of basic operations can be assembled to meet new computational goals. One can impose goals for visual analysis, such as "determine whether the green and red elements lie on the same side of the vertical line". That the visual system can cope effectively with such goals suggests that it has the capacity to create new processes out of the basic set of elemental operations.

1.3.3. Complexity

The open-endedness requirement implied that different processes should share elemental operations. The same conclusion is also suggested by complexity considerations. The complexity of basic operations such as the bounded activation (discussed in more detail in Section 3.4) implies that different routines that establish different properties and relations and use the bounded activation operation would have to share the same mechanism rather than have their own separate mechanisms.

A special case of the complexity consideration arises from the need to apply the same computation at different spatial locations. The ability to perform a given computation at different spatial positions can be obtained by having an independent processing module at each location. For example, the orientation of a line segment at a given location seems to be performed in the primary visual cortex largely independent of other locations. In contrast, the computations of more complex relations such as inside/outside independent of location cannot be explained by assuming a large number of independent 'inside/outside modules', one for each location. Routines that establish a given property or relation at different positions are likely to share some of their machinery, similar to the sharing of elemental operations by different routines.

Certain constraints will be imposed upon the computation of spatial relations by the sharing of elemental operations. For example, the sharing of operations by different routines will restrict the simultaneous perception of different spatial relations. The application of a given routine to different spatial locations will be similarly restricted. In applying visual routines the need will consequently arise for the sequencing of elemental operations, and for selecting the location at which a given operation is applied.

In summary, the three requirements discussed above suggest the following implications.

(1)   Spatial properties and relations are established by the application of visual routines to a set of early visual representations.
(2)   Visual routines are assembled from a fixed set of elemental operations.
(3)   New routines can be assembled to meet newly specified processing goals.
(4)   Different routines share elemental operations.
(5)   A routine can be applied to different spatial locations. The processes that perform the same routine at different locations are not independent.
(6)   In applying visual routines mechanisms are required for sequencing elemental operations and for selecting the locations at which they are applied.

1.4. Conclusions and open problems

The discussion so far suggests that the immediate perception of seemingly simple spatial relations requires in fact complex computations that are difficult to unravel, and difficult to imitate. These computations were termed above 'visual routines'. The general proposal is that using a fixed set of basic operations, the visual system can assemble routines that are applied to the visual representations to extract abstract shape properties and spatial relations.

The use of visual routines to establish shape properties and spatial relations raises fundamental problems at the levels of computational theory, algorithms, and the underlying mechanisms. A general problem on the computational level is which spatial properties and relations are important for object recognition and manipulation. On the algorithmic level, the problem is how these relations are computed. This is a challenging problem, since the processing of spatial relations and properties by the visual system is remarkably flexible and efficient. On the mechanism level, the problem is how visual routines are implemented in neural networks within the visual system.

In concluding this section, major problems raised by the notion of visual routines are listed below under four main categories.

(1) *The elemental operations.* In the examples discussed above the computation of inside/outside relations employed operations such as drawing a ray, counting intersections, boundary tracking, and area activation. The same basic operations can also be used in establishing other properties and relations. In this manner a variety of spatial relations can be computed using a fixed and powerful set of basic operations, together with means for combining them into different routines that are then applied to the base representation. The first problem that arises therefore is the identification of the elemental operations that constitute the basic 'instruction set' in the composition of visual routines.

(2) *Integration.* The second problem that arises is how the elemental operations are integrated into meaningful routines. This problem has two aspects. First, the general principles of the integration process, for example, whether different elemental operations can be applied simultaneously. Second, there is the question of how specific routines are composed in terms of the elemental operations. An account of our perception of a given shape property or relation such as elongation, above, next-to, inside/outside, taller-than etc. should include a description of the routines that are employed in the task in question, and the composition of each of these routines in terms of the elemental operations.

(3) *Control.* The questions in this category are how visual routines are

selected and controlled, for example, what triggers the execution of different routines during visual recognition and other visual tasks, and how the order of their execution is determined.

(4) *Compilation*. How new routines are generated to meet specific needs, and how they are stored and modified with practice.

The remainder of this paper is organized as follows. In Section 2 I shall discuss the role of visual routines within the overall processing of visual information. Section 3 will then examine the first of the problems listed above, the elemental operations problem. Section 4 will conclude with a few brief comments pertaining to the other problems.

2. Visual routines and their role in the processing of visual information

The purpose of this section is to examine how the application of visual routines fits within the overall processing of visual information. The main goal is to elaborate the relations between the initial creation of the early visual representations and the subsequent application of visual routines. The discussion is structured along the following lines.

The first half of this section examines the relation between visual routines and the creation of two types of visual representations: the bare representation (Section 2.1) that precedes the application of visual routines, and the incremental representations that are produced by them (Section 2.2). The second half examines two general problems raised by the nature of visual routines as described in the first half. These problems are: the initial selection of routines (Section 2.3) and the parallel processing of visual information (Section 2.4).

2.1. Visual routines and the base representations

In the scheme suggested above, the processing of visual information can be divided into two main stages. The first is the 'bottom-up' creation of some base representations by the early visual processes (Marr, 1980). The second stage is the application of visual routines. At this stage, procedures are applied to the base representations to define distinct entities within these representations, establish their shape properties, and extract spatial relations among them. In this section we shall examine more closely the distinction between these two stages.

2.1.1. The base representations

The first stage in the analysis of visual information can usefully be described as the creation of certain representations to be used by subsequent visual processes. Marr (1976) and Marr and Nishihara (1978) have suggested a division of these early representations into two types: the primal sketch, which is a representation of the incoming image, and the 2½-D sketch, which is a representation of the visible surfaces in three-dimensional space. The early visual representations share a number of fundamental characteristics: they are unarticulated, viewer-centered, uniform, and bottom-up driven. By 'unarticulated' I mean that they are essentially local descriptions that represent properties such as depth, orientation, color, and direction of motion at a point. The definition of larger more complicated units, and the extraction and description of spatial relationships among their parts, is not achieved at this level.

The base representations are spatially uniform in the sense that, with the exception of a scaling factor, the same properties are extracted and represented across the visual field (or throughout large parts of it). The descriptions of different points (e.g., the depth at a point) in the early representations are all with respect to the viewer, not with respect to one another. Finally, the construction of the base representations proceeds in a bottom-up fashion. This means that the base representations depend on the visual input alone.[7] If the same image is viewed twice, at two different times, the base representations associated with it will be identical.

2.1.2. Applying visual routines to the base representations

Beyond the construction of the base representations, the processing of visual information requires the definition of objects and parts in the scene, and the analysis of spatial properties and relations. The discussion in Section 1.3 concluded that for these tasks the uniform bottom-up computation is no longer possible, and suggested instead the application of visual routines. In contrast with the construction of the base representations, the properties and relations to be extracted are not determined by the input alone: for the same visual input different aspects will be made explicit at different times, depend-

---

[7]Although 'bottom–up' and 'top–down' processing are useful and frequently used terms, they lack a precise, well–accepted definition. As mentioned in the text, the definition I adopt is that bottom–up processing is determined entirely by the input. Top–down processing depends on additional factors, such as the goal of the computation (but not necessarily on object–specific knowledge).

Physiologically, various mechanisms that are likely to be involved in the creation of the base representation appear to be bottom–up: their responses can be predicted from the parameters of the stimulus alone. They also show strong similarity in their responses in the awake, anesthetized, and naturally sleeping animal (e.g., Livingstone and Hubel, 1981).

ing on the goals of the computation. Unlike the base representations, the computations by visual routines are not applied uniformly over the visual field (e.g., not all of the possible inside/outside relations in the scene are computed), but only to selected objects. The objects and parts to which these computations apply are also not determined uniquely by the input alone; that is, there does not seem to be a universal set of primitive elements and relations that can be used for all possible perceptual tasks. The definition of objects and distinct parts in the input, and the relations to be computed among them may change with the situation. I may recognize a particular cat, for instance, using the shape of the white patch on its forehead. This does not imply, however, that the shapes of all the white patches in every possible scene and all the spatial relations in which such patches participate are universally made explicit in some internal representation. More generally, the definition of what constitutes a distinct part, and the relations to be established often depends on the particular object to be recognized. It is therefore unlikely that a fixed set of operations applied uniformly over the base representations would be sufficient to capture all of the properties and relations that may be relevant for subsequent visual analysis.[8] A final distinction between the two stages is that the construction of the base representations is fixed and unchanging, while visual routines are open-ended and permit the extraction of newly defined properties and relations.

In conclusion, it is suggested that the analysis of visual information divides naturally into two distinct successive stages: the creation of the base representations, followed by the application of visual routines to these representations. The application of visual routines can define objects within the base representations and establish properties and spatial relations that cannot be established within the base representations.

It should be noted that many of the relations that are established at this stage are defined not in the image but in three-dimensional space. Since the base representations already contain three-dimensional information, the visual routines applied to them can also establish properties and relations in three-dimensional space.[9]

---

[8]The argument does not preclude the possibility that some grouping processes that help to define distinct parts and some local shape descriptions take place within the basic representations.

[9]Many spatial judgments we make depend primarily on three dimensional relations rather than on projected, two–dimensional ones (see e.g., Joynson and Kirk, 1960; Kappin and Fuqua, 1983). The implication is that various visual routines such as those used in comparing distances, operate upon a three–dimensional representation, rather than a representation that resembles the two–dimensional image.

2.2. The incremental representations

The creation of visual representations does not stop at the base representations. It is reasonable to expect that results established by visual routines are retained temporarily for further use. This means that in addition to the base representations to which routines are applied initially representations are also being created and modified in the course of executing visual routines. I shall refer to these additional structures as 'incremental representations', since their content is modified incrementally in the course of applying visual routines. Unlike the base representations, the incremental representations are not created in a uniform and unguided manner: the same input can give rise to different incremental representations, depending on the routines that have been applied.

The role of the incremental representations can be illustrated using the inside/outside judgments considered in Section 1. Suppose that following the response to an inside/outside display using a fairly complex figure, an additional point is lit up. The task is now to determine whether this second point lies inside or outside the closed figure. If the results of previous computations are already summarized in the incremental representation of the figure in question, the judgment in the second task would be expected to be considerably faster than the first, and the effects of the figure's complexity might be reduced.[10] Such facilitation effects would provide evidence for the creation of some internal structure in the course of reaching a decision in the first task that is subsequently used to reach a faster decision in the second task. For example, if area activation or 'coloring' is used to separate inside from outside, then following the first task the inside of the figure may be already 'colored'. If, in addition, this coloring is preserved in the incremental representation, then subsequent inside/outside judgments with respect to the same figure would require considerably less processing, and may depend less on the complexity of the figure.

This example also serves to illustrate the distinction between the base representations and the incremental representations. The 'coloring' of the curve in question will depend on the particular routines that happened to be employed. Given the same visual input but a different visual task, or the same task but applied to a different part of the input, the same curve will not be 'colored' and a similar saving in computation time will not be obtained. The general point illustrated by this example is that for a given visual stimulus but different computational goals the base representations remain the same,

---

[10]This example is due to Steve Kosslyn. It is currently under empirical investigations.

while the incremental representations would vary.

Various other perceptual phenomena can be interpreted in a similar manner in light of the distinction between the base and the incremental representations. I shall mention here only one recent example from a study by Rock and Gutman (1981). Their subjects were presented with pairs of overlapping red and green figures. When they were instructed to attend selectively to the green or red member of the pair, they were later able to recognize the 'attended' but not the 'unattended' figure. This result can be interpreted in terms of the distinction between the base and the incremental representations. The creation of the base representations is assumed to be a bottom-up process, unaffected by the goal of the computation. Consequently, the two figures would not be treated differently within these representations. Attempts to attend selectively to one sub-figure resulted in visual routines being applied preferentially to it. A detailed description of this sub-figure is consequently created in the incremental representations. This detailed description can then be used by subsequent routines subserving comparison and recognition tasks.

The creation and use of incremental representations imply that visual routines should not be thought of merely as predicates, or decision processes that supply 'yes' or 'no' answers. For example, an inside/outside routine does not merely signal 'yes' if an inside relation is established, and 'no' otherwise. In addition to the decision process, certain structures are being created during the execution of the routine. These structures are maintained in the incremental representation, and can be used in subsequent visual tasks. The study of a given routine is therefore not confined to the problem of how a certain decision is reached, but also includes the structures constructed by the routine in question in the incremental representations.

In summary, the use of visual routines introduces a distinction between two different types of visual representations: the base representations and incremental representations. The base representations provide the initial data structures on which the routines operate, and the incremental representations maintain results obtained by the application of visual routines.

The second half of Section 2 examines two general issues raised by the nature of visual routines as introduced so far. Visual routines were described above as sequences of elementary operations that are assembled to meet specific computational goals. A major problem that arises is the initial selection of routines to be applied. This problem is examined briefly in Section 2.3. Finally, sequential application of elementary operations seems to stand in contrast with the notion of parallel processing in visual perception. (Biederman et al., 1973; Donderi and Zelnicker, 1969; Egeth et al., 1972; Jonides and Gleitman, 1972; Neisser et al., 1963). Section 2.4 examines the distinction between sequential and parallel processing, its significance to the processing of visual information, and its relation to visual routines.

2.3. Universal routines and the initial access problem

The act of perception requires more than the passive existence of a set of representations. Beyond the creation of the base representations, the perceptual process depends upon the current computational goal. At the level of applying visual routines, the perceptual activity is required to provide answers to queries, generated either externally or internally, such as: "is this my cat?" or, at a lower level, "is A longer than B?" Such queries arise naturally in the course of using visual information in recognition, manipulation, and more abstract visual thinking. In response to these queries routines are executed to provide the answers. The process of applying the appropriate routines is apparently efficient and smooth, thereby contributing to the impression that we perceive the entire image at a glance, when in fact we process only limited aspects of it at any given time. We may not be aware of the restricted processing since whenever we wish to establish new facts about the scene, that is, whenever an internal query is posed, an answer is provided by the execution of an appropriate routine.

Such application of visual routines raises the problem of guiding the perceptual activity and selecting the appropriate routines at any given instant. In dealing with this problem, several theories of perception have used the notion of schemata (Bartlett, 1932; Biederman et al., 1973; Neisser, 1967) or frames (Minsky, 1975) to emphasize the role of expectations in guiding perceptual activity. According to these theories, at any given instant we maintain detailed expectations regarding the objects in view. Our perceptual activity can be viewed according to such theories as hypothesizing a specific object and then using detailed prior knowledge about this object in an attempt to confirm or refute the current hypothesis.

The emphasis on detailed expectations does not seem to me to provide a satisfactory answer to the problem of guiding perceptual activity and selecting the appropriate routines. Consider for example the 'slide show' situation in which an observer is presented with a sequence of unrelated pictures flashed briefly on a screen. The sequence may contain arbitrary ordinary objects, say, a horse, a beachball, a printed letter, etc. Although the observer can have no expectations regarding the next picture in the sequence, he will experience little difficulty identifying the viewed objects. Furthermore, suppose that an observer does have some clear expectations, e.g., he opens a door expecting to find his familiar office, but finds an ocean beach instead. The contradiction to the expected scene will surely cause a surprise, but no major perceptual difficulties. Although expectations can under some conditions facilitate perceptual processes significantly (e.g. Potter, 1975), their role is not indispensable. Perception can usually proceed in the absence of prior specific expectations and even when expectations are contradicted.

The selection of appropriate routines therefore raises a difficult problem. On the one hand, routines that establish properties and relations are situation-dependent. For example, the white patch on the cat's forehead is analyzed in the course of recognizing the cat, but white patches are not analyzed invariably in every scene. On the other hand, the recognition process should not depend entirely on prior knowledge or detailed expectations about the scene being viewed. How then are the appropriate routines selected?

It seems to me that this problem can be best approached by dividing the process of routine selection into two stages. The first stage is the application of what may be called *universal routines*. These are routines that can be usefully applied to any scene to provide some initial analysis. They may be able, for instance, to isolate some prominent parts in the scene and describe, perhaps crudely, some general aspects of their shape, motion, color, the spatial relations among them etc. These universal routines will provide sufficient information to allow initial indexing to a recognition memory, which then serves to guide the application of more specialized routines.

To make the motion of universal routines more concrete, I shall cite one example in which universal routines probably play a role. Studying the comparison of shapes presented sequentially, Rock *et al.* (1972) found that some parts of the presented shapes can be compared reliably while others cannot. When a shape was composed, for example, of a bounding contour and internal lines, in the absence of any specific instructions only the bounding contour was used reliably in the successive comparison task, even if the first figure was viewed for a long period (5 sec). This result would be surprising if only the base representations were used in the comparison task, since there is no reason to assume that in these representations the bounding contours of such line drawings enjoy a special status. It seems reasonable, however, that the bounding contour is special from the point of view of the universal routines, and is therefore analyzed first. If successive comparisons use the incremental representation as suggested above, then performance would be superior on those parts that have been already analyzed by visual routines. It is suggested, therefore, that in the absence of specific instructions, universal routines were applied first to the bounding contour. Furthermore, it appears that in the absence of specific goals, no detailed descriptions of the entire figure are generated even under long viewing periods. Only those aspects analyzed by the universal routines are summarized in the incremental representation. As a result, a description of the outside boundary alone has been created in the incremental representation. This description could then be compared against the second figure. It is of interest to note that the description generated in this task appears to be not just a coarse structural description of the figure, but has template-like quality that enable fine judgments of shape similarity.

These results can be contrasted with the study mentioned earlier by Rock and Gutman (1981) using pairs of overlapping and green figures. When subjects were instructed to "attend" selectively to one of the subfigures, they were subsequently able to make reliable shape comparisons to this, but not the other, subfigure. Specific requirements can therefore bias the selection and application of visual routines. Universal routines are meant to fill the void when no specific requirements are set. They are intended to acquire sufficient information to then determine the application of more specific routines.

For such a scheme to be of value in visual recognition, two interrelated requirements must be met. The first is that with universal routines alone it should be possible to gather sufficiently useful information to allow initial classification. The second requirement has to do with the organization of the memory used in visual recognition. It should contain intermediate constructs of categories that are accessible using the information gathered by the universal routines, and the access to such a category should provide the means for selecting specialized routines for refining the recognition process. The first requirement raises the question of whether universal routines, unaided by specific knowledge regarding the viewed objects, can reasonably be expected to supply sufficiently useful information about any viewed scene. The question is difficult to address in detail, since it is intimately related to problems regarding the structure of the memory used in visual recognition. It nonetheless seems plausible that universal routines may be sufficient to analyze the scene in enough detail to allow the application of specialized routines.

The potential usefulness of universal routines in the initial phases of the recognition process is supported in part by Marr and Nishihara's (1978) study of shape recognition. This work has demonstrated that at least for certain classes of shapes crude overall shape descriptions, which can be obtained by universal routines without prior knowledge regarding the viewed objects, can provide a powerful initial categorization. Similarly, the "perceptual 20 question game" of W. Richards (1982) suggests that a small fixed set of visual attributes (such as direction and type of motion, color, etc.) is often sufficient to form a good idea of what the object is (e.g., a walking person) although identifying a specific object (e.g., who the person is) may be considerably more difficult [cf. Milner, 1974]. These examples serve to illustrate the dis-

Figure 6.   *The routine processor acts as an intermediary between the visual representations and higher level components of the system.*

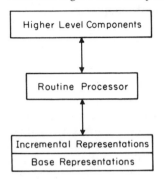

tinction in visual recognition between universal and specific stages. In the first, universal routines can supply sufficient information for accessing a useful general category. In the second, specific routines associated with this category can be applied.

The relations between the different representations and routines can now be summarized as follows. The first stage in the analysis of the incoming visual input is the creation of the base representations. Next, visual routines are applied to the base representations. In the absence of specific expectations or prior knowledge universal routines are applied first, followed by the selective application of specific routines. Intermediate results obtained by visual routines are summarized in the incremental representation and can be used by subsequent routines.

2.3.1. Routines as intermediary between the base representations and higher-level components

The general role of visual routines in the overall processing of visual information as discussed so far is illustrated schematically in Fig. 6. The processes that assemble and execute visual routines (the 'routines processor' module in the figure) serve as an intermediary between the visual representations and higher level components of the system, such as recognition memory. Communication required between the higher level components and the visual representations for the analysis of shape and spatial relations are channeled via the routine processor.[11]

---

[11]Responses to certain visual stimuli that do not require abstract spatial analysis could bypass the routine processor. For example, a looming object may initiate an immediate avoidance response (Regan and Beverly, 1978). Such 'visual reflexes' do not require the application of visual routines. The visual system of lower animals such as insects or the frog, although remarkably sophisticated, probably lack routine mechanisms, and can perhaps be described as collections of 'visual reflexes'.

Visual routines operate in the middle ground that, unlike the bottom-up creation of the base representations, is a part of the top-down processing and yet is independent of object-specific knowledge. Their study therefore has the advantage of going beyond the base representations while avoiding many of the additional complications associated with higher level components of the system. The recognition of familiar objects, for example, often requires the use of knowledge specific to these objects. What we know about telephones or elephants can enter into the recognition process of these objects. In contrast, the extraction of spatial relations, while important for object recognition, is independent of object-specific knowledge. Such knowledge can determine the routine to be applied: the recognition of a particular object may require, for instance, the application of inside/outside routines. When a routine is applied, however, the processing is no longer dependent on object-specific knowledge.

It is suggested, therefore, that in studying the processing of visual information beyond the creation of the early representations, a useful distinction can be drawn between two problem areas. One can approach first the study of visual routines almost independently of the higher level components of the system. A full understanding of problems such as visually guided manipulation and object recognition would require, in addition, the study of higher level components, how they determine the application of visual routines, and how they are affected by the results of applying visual routines.

2.4. Routines and the parallel processing of visual information

A popular controversy in theories of visual perception is whether the processing of visual information proceeds in parallel or sequentially. Since visual routines are composed of sequences of elementary operations, they may seem to side strongly with the point of view of sequential processing in perception. In this section I shall examine two related questions that bear on this issue. First, whether the application of visual routines implies sequential processing. Second, what is the significance of the distinction between the parallel and sequential processing of visual information.

2.4.1. Three types of parallelism

The notion of processing visual information 'in parallel' does not have a unique, well-defined meaning. At least three types of parallelism can be distinguished in this processing: spatial, functional, and temporal. Spatial parallelism means that the same or similar operations are applied simultaneously to different spatial locations. The operations performed by the retina and the primary visual cortext, for example, fall under this category. Functional parallelism means that different computations are applied simultaneously to the same location. Current views of the visual cortex (e.g., Zeki, 1978a, b) suggest that different visual areas in the extra-striate cortex process different aspects of the input (such as color, motion, and stereoscopic disparity) at the same location simultaneously, thereby achieving functional parallelism.[12] Temporal parallelism is the simultaneous application of different processing stages to different inputs (this type of parallelism is also called 'pipelining'.[13]

Visual routines can in principle employ all three types of parallelism. Suppose that a given routine is composed of a sequence of operations O_1, O_2, ... O_n. Spatial parallelism can be obtained if a given operation O_i is applied simultaneously to various locations. Temporal parallelism can be obtained by applying different operations O_i simultaneously to successive inputs. Finally, functional parallelism can be obtained by the concurrent application of different routines.

The application of visual routines is thus compatible in principle with all three notions of parallelism. It seems, however, that in visual routines the use of spatial parallelism is more restricted than in the construction of the base representations.[14] At least some of the basic operations do not employ extensive spatial parallelism. The internal tracking of a discontinuity boundary in the base representation, for instance, is sequential in nature and does not apply to all locations simultaneously. Possible reasons for the limited spatial parallelism in visual routines are discussed in the next section.

2.4.2. Essential and non-essential sequential processing

When considering sequential *versus* spatially parallel processing, it is useful to distinguish between essential and non-essential sequentially. Suppose, for example, that O_1 and O_2 are two independent operations that can, in principle, be applied simultaneously. It is nevertheless still possible to apply them in sequence, but such sequentiality would be non-essential. The total computation required in this case will be the same regardless of whether the operations are performed in parallel or sequentially. Essential sequentiality, on the other hand, arises when the nature of the task makes parallel processing impossible or highly wasteful in terms of the overall computation required.

---

[12]Disagreements exist regarding this view, in particular, the role of area V4 in the rhesus monkey i processing color (Schein *et al.*, 1982). Although the notion o "one cortical area for each function" is too simplistic, the physiological data support in general the notion of functional parallelism.

[13]Suppose that a sequence of operations O_1, O_2 ... O_k applied to each input in a temporal sequence I_1. I_2, I_3 .... First, O_1 is applied to I_1. Next, as O_2 is applied to I_1, O_1 can be applied to I_2. In general O_i, $1 < i < k$ can be applied simultaneously to I_{n-i}. Such a simultaneous application constitute temporal parallelism.

[14]The general notion of an extensively parallel stage followed by a more sequential one is in agreement with various findings and theories of visual perception (e.g., Estes, 1972; Neisser, 1967; Shiffrin *et al.*, 1976).

Problems pertaining to the use of spatial parallelism in the computation of spatial properties and relations were studied extensively by Minsky and Papert (1969) within the perceptrons model.[15] Minsky and Paper have established that certain relations, including the inside/outside relation, cannot be computed at all in parallel by any diamater-limited or order-limited perceptrons. This limitation does not seem to depend critically upon the perceptron-like decision scheme. It may be conjectured, therefore, that certain relations are inherently sequential in the sense that it is impossible or highly wasteful to employ extensive spatial parallelism in their computation. In this case sequentiality is essential, as it is imposed by the nature of the task, not by particular properties of the underlying mechanisms. Essential sequentiality is theoretically more interesting, and has more significant ramifications, than non-essential sequential ordering. In non-essential sequential processing the ordering has no particular importance, and no fundamentally new problems are introduced. Essential sequentiality, on the other hand, requires mechanisms for controlling the appropriate sequencing of the computation.

It has been suggested by various theories of visual attention that sequential ordering in perception is non-essential, arising primarily from a capacity limitation of the system (see, e.g., Holtzman and Gazzaniga, 1982; Kahneman, 1973; Rumelhart, 1970). In this view only a limited region of the visual scene (1 degree, Eriksen and Hoffman, 1972; see also Humphreys, 1981; Mackworth, 1965) is processed at any given time because the system is capacity-limited and would be overloaded by excessive information unless a spatial restriction is employed. The discussion above suggests, in contrast, that sequential ordering may in fact be essential, imposed by the inherently sequential nature of various visual tasks. This sequential ordering has substantial implications since it requires perceptual mechanisms for directing the processing and for concatenating and controlling sequences of basic operations.

Although the elemental operations are sequenced, some of them, such as the bounded activation, employ spatial parallelism and are not confined to a limited region. This spatial parallelism plays an important role in the inside/outside routines. To appreciate the difficulties in computing inside/outside relations without the benefit of spatial parallelism, consider solving a tactile

---

[15]In the perceptron scheme the computation is performed in parallel by a large number of units ϕ_i. Each unit examine a restricted part of the 'retina' R. In a diamater–limited perceptron, for instance, the region examined by each unit is restricted to lie within a circle whose diameter is small compared to the size of R. The computation performed by each unit is a predicate of its inputs (i.e., $\phi_i = 0$ or $\phi_i = 1$). For example, a unit may be a 'corner detector' at a particular location, signalling 1 in the presence of a corner and 0 otherwise. All the local units then feed a final decision stage, assumed to be a linear threshold device. That is, it tests whether the weighted sum of the inputs $\Sigma_i \, \omega_i \, \phi_i$ exceeds a predetermined threshold θ.

version of the same problem by moving a cane or a fingertip over a relief surface. Clearly, when the processing is always limited to a small region of space, the task becomes considerably more difficult. Spatial parallelism must therefore play an important role in visual routines.

In summary, visual routines are compatible in principle with spatial, temporal, and functional parallelism. The degree of spatial parallelism employed by the basic operations seems nevertheless limited. It is conjectured that this reflects primarily essential sequentiality, imposed by the nature of the computations.

3. The elemental operations

3.1. Methodological considerations

In this section, we examine the set of basic operations that may be used in the construction of visual routines. In trying to explore this set of internal operations, at least two types of approaches can be followed. The first is the use of empirical psychological and physiological evidence. The second is computational: one can examine, for instance, the types of basic operations that would be useful in principle for establishing a large variety of relevant properties and relations. In particular, it would be useful to examine complex tasks in which we exhibit a high degree of proficiency. For such tasks, processes that match in performance the human system are difficult to devise. Consequently, their examination is likely to provide useful constraints on the nature of the underlying computations.

In exploring such tasks, the examples I shall use will employ schematic drawings rather than natural scenes. The reason is that simplified artificial stimuli allow more flexibility in adapting the stimulus to the operation under investigation. It seems to me that insofar as we examine visual tasks for which our proficiency is difficult to account for, we are likely to be exploring useful basic operations even if the stimuli employed are artificially constructed. In fact, this ability to cope efficiently with artificially imposed visual tasks underscores two essential capacities in the computation of spatial relations. First, that the computation of spatial relations is flexible and open-ended: new relations can be defined and computed efficiently. Second, it demonstrates our capacity to accept non-visual specification of a task and immediately produce a visual routine to meet these specifications.

The empirical and computational studies can then be combined. For example, the complexity of various visual tasks can be compared. That is, the theoretical studies can be used to predict how different tasks should vary in complexity, and the predicted complexity measure can be gauged against human performance. We have seen in Section 1.2 an example along this line, in the discussion of the inside/outside computation. Predictions regarding relative complexity, success, and failure, based upon the ray-intersection method prove largely incompatible with human performance, and consequently the employment of this method by the human perceptual system can be ruled out. In this case, the refutation is also supported by theoretical considerations exposing the inherent limitations of the ray-intersection method.

In this section, only some initial steps towards examining the basic operations problem will be taken. I shall examine a number of plausible candidates for basic operations, discuss the available evidence, and raise problems for further study. Only a few operations will be examined; they are not intended to form a comprehensive list. Since the available empirical evidence is scant, the emphasis will be on computational considerations of usefulness. Finally, some of the problems associated with the assembly of basic operations into visual routines will be briefly discussed.

3.2. Shifting the processing focus

A fundamental requirement for the execution of visual routines is the capacity to control the location at which certain operations take place. For example, the operation of area activation suggested in Section 1.2 will be of little use if the activation starts simultaneously everywhere. To be of use, it must start at a selected location, or along a selected contour. More generally, in applying visual routines it would be useful to have a 'directing mechanism' that will allow the application of the same operation at different spatial locations. It is natural, therefore, to start the discussion of the elemental operations by examining the processes that control the locations at which these operations are applied.

Directing the processing focus (that is, the location to which an operation is applied) may be achieved in part by moving the eyes (Noton and Stark, 1971). But this is clearly insufficient: many relations, including, for instance, the inside/outside relation examined in Section 1.2, can be established without eye movements. A capacity to shift the processing focus internally is therefore required.

Problems related to the possible shift of internal operations have been studied empirically, both psychophysically and physiologically. These diverse studies still do not provide a complete picture of the shift operations and their use in the analysis of visual information. They do provide, however, strong support for the notion that shifts of the processing focus play an important role in visual information processing, starting from early processing stages. The main directions of studies that have been pursued are reviewed briefly in the next two sections.

3.2.1. Psychological evidence

A number of psychological studies have suggested that the focus of visual processing can be directed, either voluntarily or by manipulating the visual stimulus, to different spatial location in the visual input. They are listed below under three main categories.

The first line of evidence comes from reaction time studies suggesting that it takes some measurable time to shift the processing focus from one location to another. In a study by Eriksen and Schultz (1977), for instance, it was found that the time required to identify a letter increased linearly with the eccentricity of the target letter, the difference being on the order of 100 msec at 3° from the fovea center. Such a result may reflect the effect of shift time, but, as pointed out by Eriksen and Schultz, alternative explanations are possible.

More direct evidence comes from a study by Posner et al. (1978). In this study a target was presented seven degrees to the left or right of fixation. It was shown that if the subjects correctly anticipated the location at which the target will appear using prior cueing (an arrow at fixation), then their reaction time to the target in both detection and identification tasks were consistently lower (without eye movements). For simple detection tasks, the gain in detection time for a target at 70 eccentricity was on the order of 30 msec.

A related study by Tsal (1983) employed peripheral rather than central cueing. In his study a target letter could appear at different eccentricities, preceded by a brief presentation of a dot at the same location. The results were consistent with the assumption that the dot initiated a shift towards the cued location. If a shift to the location of the letter is required for its identification, the cue should reduce the time between the letter presentation and its identification. If the cue precedes the target letter by k msec, then by the time the letter appears the shift operation is already k msec under way, and the response time should decrease by this amount. The facilitation should therefore increase linearly with the temporal delay between the cue and target until the delay equals the total shift time. Further increase of the delay should have no additional effect. This is exactly what the experimental results indicated. It was further found that the delay at which facilitation saturates (presumably the total shift time) increases with eccentricity, by about 8 msec on the average per 1° of visual angle.

A second line of evidence comes from experiments suggesting that visual sensitivity at different locations can be somewhat modified with a fixed eye position. Experiments by Shulman *et al.* (1979) can be interpreted as indicating that a region of somewhat increased sensitivity can be shifted across the visual field. A related experiment by Remington (1978, described in Posner, 1980), showed an increase in sensitivity at a distance of 8° from the fixation point 50–100 msec after the location has been cued.

A third line of evidence that may bear on the internal shift operations comes from experiments exploring the selective readout from some form of short term visual memory (e.g., Shiffrin *et al.*, 1976; Sperling, 1960). These experiments suggest that some internal scanning can be directed to different locations a short time after the presentation of a visual stimulus.

The shift operation and selective visual attention. Many of the experiments mentioned above were aimed at exploring the concept of 'selective attention'. This concept has a variety of meanings and connotations (cf. Estes, 1972), many of which are not related directly to the proposed shift of processing focus in visual routines. The notion of selective visual attention often implies that the processing of visual information is restricted to small region of space, to avoid 'overloading' the system with excessive information. Certain processing stages have, according to this description, a limited total 'capacity' to invest in the processing, and this capacity can be concentrated in a spatially restricted region. Attempts to process additional information would detract from this capacity, causing interference effects and deterioration of performance. Processes that do not draw upon this general capacity are, by definition, pre-attentive. In contrast, the notion of processing shift discussed above stems from the need for spatially-structured processes, and it does not necessarily imply such notions as general capacity or protection from overload. For example, the 'coloring' operation used in Section 1.2 for separating inside from outside started from a selected point or contour. Even with no capacity limitations such coloring would not start simultaneously everywhere, since a simultaneous activation will defy the purpose of the coloring operation. The main problem in this case is in coordinating the process, rather than excessive capacity demands. As a result, the process is spatially structured, but not in a simple manner as in the 'spotlight model' of selective attention. In the course of applying a visual routine, both the locations and the operations performed at the selected locations are controlled and coordinated according to the requirement of the routine in question.

Many of the results mentioned above are nevertheless in agreement with the possible existence of a directable processing focus. They suggest that the redirection of the processing focus to a new location may be achieved in two ways. The experiments of Posner and Shulman *et al.* suggest that it can be 'programmed' to move along a straight path using central cueing. In other experiments, such as Remmington's and Tsal's, the processing focus is shifted by being attracted to a peripheral cue.

3.2.2. Physiological evidence

Shift-related mechanisms have been explored physiologically in the monkey in a number of different visual areas: the superior colliculus, the posterior parietal lobe (area 7) the frontal eye fields, areas V1, V2, V4, MT, MST, and the inferior temporal lobe.

In the superficial layers of the superior colliculus of the monkey, many cells have been found to have an enhanced response to a stimulus when the monkey uses the stimulus as a target for a saccadic eye movement (Goldberg and Wurtz, 1972). This enhancement is not strictly sensory in the sense that it is not produced if the stimulus is not followed by a saccade. It also does not seem strictly associated with a motor response, since the temporal delay between the enhanced response and the saccade can vary considerably (Wurtz and Mohler, 1976a). The enhancement phenomenon was suggested as a neural correlate of "directing visual attention", since it modifies the visual input and enhances it at selective locations when the sensory input remains constant (Goldberg and Wurtz, op. cit.). The intimate relation of the enhancement to eye movements, and its absence when the saccade is replaced by other responses (Wurtz and Mohler, op. cit., Wurtz et al., 1982) suggest, however, that this mechanism is specifically related to saccadic eye movements rather than to operations associated with the shifting of an internal processing focus. Similar enhancement that depends on saccade initiation to a visual target has also been described in the frontal eye fields (Wurtz and Mohler, 1976b) and in prestriate cortex, probably area V4 (Fischer and Boch, 1981).

Another area that exhibits similar enhancement phenomena, but not exclusively to saccades, is area 7 of the posterior parietal lobe of the monkey. Using recordings from behaving monkeys, Mountcastle and his collaborators (Mountcastle, 1976, Mountcastle et al., 1975) found three populations of cells in area 7 that respond selectively (i) when the monkey fixates an object of interest within its immediate surrounding (fixation neurons), (ii) when it tracks an object of interest (tracking neurons), and (iii) when it saccades to an object of interest (saccade neurons). (Tracking neurons were also described in area MST (Newsome and Wurtz, 1982).) Studies by Robinson et al. (1978) indicated that all of these neurons can also be driven by passive sensory stimulation, but their response is considerably enhanced when the stimulation is 'selected' by the monkey to initiate a response. On the basis of such findings it was suggested by Mountcastle (as well as by Posner, 1980; Robinson et al., 1978; Wurtz et al., 1982) that mechanisms in area 7 are responsible for "directing visual attention" to selected stimuli. These mechanisms may be primarily related, however, to tasks requiring hand-eye coordination for manipulation in the reachable space (Mountcastle, 1976), and there is at present no direct evidence to link them with visual routines and the shift of processing focus discussed above.[16]

In area TE of the inferotemporal cortex units were found whose responses depend strongly upon the visual task performed by the animal. Fuster and Jervey (1981) described units that responded strongly to the stimulus' color, but only when color was the relevant parameter in a matching task. Richmond and Sato (1982) found units whose responses to a given stimulus were enhanced when the stimulus was used in a pattern discrimination task, but not in other tasks (e.g., when the stimulus was monitored to detect its dimming).

In a number of visual areas, including V1, V2, and MT, enhanced responses associated with performing specific visual tasks were not found (Newsome and Wurtz, 1982; Wurtz *et al.*, 1982). It remains possible, however, that task-specific modulation would be observed when employing different visual tasks. Finally, responses in the pulvinar (Gattas *et al.*, 1979) were shown to be strongly modulated by attentional and situational variables. It remains unclear, however, whether these modulations are localized (i.e., if they are restricted to a particular location in the visual field) and whether they are task-specific.

Physiological evidence of a different kind comes from visual evoked potential (VEP) studies. With fixed visual input and in the absence of eye movements, changes in VEP can be induced, for example, by instructing the subject to "attend" to different spatial locations (e.g., van Voorhis and Hillyard, 1977). This evidence may not be of direct relevance to visual routines, since it is not clear whether there is a relation between the voluntary 'direction of visual attention' used in these experiments and the shift of processing focus in visual routines. VEP studies may nonetheless provide at least some evidence regarding the possibility of internal shift operations.

In assessing the relevance of these physiological findings to the shifting of the processing focus it would be useful to distinguish three types of interactions between the physiological responses and the visual task performed by the experimental animal. The three types are task-dependent, task-location dependent, and location-dependent responses.

---

[16]A possible exception is some preliminary evidence by Robinson *et al.* (1978) suggesting that, unlike the superior colliculus, enhancement effects in the parietal cortex may be dissociated from movement. That is, a response of a cell may be facilitated when the animal is required to attend to a stimulus even when the stimulus is not used as a target for hand or eye movement.

A response is task-dependent if, for a given visual stimulus, it depends upon the visual task being performed. Some of the units described in area TE, for instance, are clearly task-dependent in this sense. In contrast, units in area V1 for example, appear to be task-independent. Task-dependent responses suggest that the units do not belong to the bottom-up generation of the early visual representations, and that they may participate in the application of visual routines. Task-dependence by itself does not necessarily imply, however, the existence of shift operations. Of more direct relevance to shift operations are responses that are both task- and location-dependent. A task-location dependent unit would respond preferentially to a stimulus when a given task is performed at a given location. Unlike task-dependent units, it would show a different response to the same stimulus when an identical task is applied to a different location. Unlike the spotlight metaphor of visual attention, it would show different responses when different tasks are performed at the same locations.

There is at least some evidence for the existence of such task-location dependent responses. The response of a saccade neuron in the superior colliculus, for example, is enhanced only when a saccade is initiated in the general direction of the unit's receptive field. A saccade towards a different location would not produce the same enhancement. The response is thus enhanced only when a specific location is selected for a specific task.

Unfortunately, many of the other task-dependent responses have not been tested for location specificity. It would be of interest to examine similar task-location dependence in tasks other than eye movement, and in the visual cortex rather than the superior colliculus. For example, the units described by Fuster and Jervey (1981) showed task-dependent response (responded strongly during a color matching task, but not during a form matching task). It would be interesting to know whether the enhanced response is also location specific. For example, if during a color matching task, when several stimuli are presented simultaneously, the response would be enhanced only at the location used for the matching task.

Finally, of particular interest would be units referred to above as location-dependent (but task-independent). Such a unit would respond preferentially to a stimulus when it is used not in a single task but in a variety of different visual tasks. Such units may be a part of a general 'shift controller' that selects a location for processing independent of the specific operation to be applied. Of the areas discussed above, the responses in area 7, the superior colliculus, and TE, do not seem appropriate for such a 'shift controller'. The pulvinar remains a possibility worthy of further exploration in view of its rich pattern of reciprocal and orderly connections with a variety of visual areas (Beneveneto and Davis, 1977; Rezak and Beneveneto, 1979).

3.3. Indexing

Computational considerations strongly suggest the use of internal shifts of the processing focus. This notion is supported by psychological evidence, and to some degree by physiological data.

The next issue to be considered is the selection problem: how specific locations are selected for further processing. There are various manners in which such a selection process could be realized. On a digital computer, for instance, the selection can take place by providing the coordinates of the next location to be processed. The content of the specified address can then be inspected and processed. This is probably not how locations are being selected for processing in the human visual system. What determines, then, the next location to be processed, and how is the processing focus moved from one location to the next?

In this section we shall consider one operation which seems to be used by the visual system in shifting the processing focus. This operation is called 'indexing'. It can be described as a shift of the processing focus to special 'odd-man-out' locations. These locations are detected in parallel across the base representations, and can serve as 'anchor points' for the application of visual routines.

As an example of indexing, suppose that a page of printed text is to be inspected for the occurrence of the letter 'A'. In a background of similar letters, the 'A' will not stand out, and considerable scanning will be required for its detection (Nickerson, 1966). If, however, all the letters remain stationary with the exception of one which is jiggled, or if all the letters are red with the exception of one green letter, the odd-man-out will be immediately identified.

The identification of the odd-man-out items proceeds in this case in several stages.[17] First the odd-man-out location is detected on the basis of its unique motion or color properties. Next, the processing focus is shifted to this odd-man-out location. This is the indexing stage. As a result of this stage, visual routines can be applied to the figure. By applying the appropriate routines, the figure is identified.

Indexing also played a role in the inside/outside example examined in Section 1.2. It was noted that one plausible strategy is to start the processing at the location marked by the X figure. This raises a problem, since the location of the X and of the closed curve were not known in advance. If the X can define an indexable location, that is, if it can serve to attract the

---

[17]The reasons for assuming several stages are both theoretical and empirical. On the empirical side, the experiments by Posner, Treisman, and Tsal provide support for this view.

processing focus, then the execution of the routine can start at that location. More generally, indexable locations can serve as starting points or 'anchors' for visual routines. In a novel scene, it would be possible to direct the processing focus immediately to a salient indexable item, and start the processing at that location. This will be particularly valuable in the execution of universal routines that are to be applied prior to any analysis of the viewed objects.

The indexing operation can be further subdivided into three successive stages. First, properties used for indexing, such as motion, orientation, and color, must be computed across the base representations. Second, an 'odd-man-out operation' is required to define locations that are sufficiently different from their surroundings. The third and final stage is the shift of the processing focus to the indexed location. These three stages are examined in turn in the next three subsections.

3.3.1. Indexable properties

Certain odd-man-out items can serve for immediate indexing, while others cannot. For example, orientation and direction of motion are indexable, while a single occurrence of the letter 'A' among similar letters does not define an indexable location. This is to be expected, since the recognition of letters requires the application of visual routines while indexing must precede their application. The first question that arises, therefore, is what the set of elemental properties is that can be computed everywhere across the base representations prior to the application of visual routines.

One method of exploring indexable properties empirically is by employing an odd-man-out test. If an item is singled out in the visual field by an indexable property, then its detection is expected to be immediate. The ability to index an item by its color, for instance, implies that a red item in a field of green items should be detected in roughly constant time, independent of the number of green distractors.

Using this and other techniques, A. Treisman and her collaborators (Treisman, 1977; Treisman and Gelade, 1980; see also Beck and Ambler, 1972, 1973; Pomerantz et al., 1977) have shown that color and simple shape parameters can serve for immediate indexing. For example, the time to detect a target blue X in a field of brown T's and green X's does not change significantly as the number of distractors is increased (up to 30 in these experiments). The target is immediately indexable by its unique color. Similarly, a target green S letter is detectable in a field of brown T's and green X's in constant time. In this case it is probably indexable by certain shape parameters, although it cannot be determined from the experiments what the relevant parameters are. Possible candidates include (i) curvature, (ii) orientation, since the S contains some orientations that are missing in the X and

T, and (iii) the number of terminators, which is two for the S, but higher for the X and T. It would be of interest to explore the indexability of these and other properties in an attempt to discover the complete set of indexable properties.

The notion of a severely limited set of properties that can be processed 'pre-attentively' agrees well with Julesz' studies of texture perception (see Julesz (1981) for a review). In detailed studies, Julesz and his collaborators have found that only a limited set of features, which he termed 'textons', can mediate immediate texture discrimination. These textons include color, elongated blobs of specific sizes, orientations, and aspect ratios, and the terminations of these elongated blobs.

These psychological studies are also in general agreement with physiological evidence. Properties such as motion, orientation, and color, were found to be extracted in parallel by units that cover the visual field. On physiological grounds these properties are suitable, therefore, for immediate indexing.

The emerging picture is, in conclusion, that a small number of properties are computed in parallel over the base representations prior to the application of visual routines, and represented in ordered retinotopic maps. Several of these properties are known, but a complete list is yet to be established. The results are then used in a number of visual tasks including, probably, texture discrimination, motion correspondence, stereo, and indexing.

3.3.2. Defining an indexable location

Following the initial computation of the elementary properties, the next stage in the indexing operation requires comparisons among properties computed at different locations to define the odd-man-out indexable locations.

Psychological evidence suggests that only simple comparisons are used at this stage. Several studies by Treisman and her collaborators examined the problem of whether different properties measured at a given location can be combined prior to the indexing operation.[18] They have tested, for instance, whether a green T could be detected in a field of brown T's and Green X's. The target in this case matches half the distractors in color, and the other half in shape. It is the combination of shape and color that makes it distinct. Earlier experiments have established that such a target is indexable if it has a unique color or shape. The question now was whether the conjunction of two indexable properties is also immediately indexable. The empirical evidence indicates that items cannot be indexed by a conjunction of properties: the time to detect the target increases linearly in the conjunction task with the number of distractors. The results obtained by Treisman *et al.* were con-

---

[18]Triesman's own approach to the problem was somewhat different from the one discussed here.

sistent with a serial self-terminating search in which the items are examined sequentially until the target is reached.

The difference between single and double indexing supports the view that the computations performed in parallel by the distributed local units are severely limited. In particular, these units cannot combine two indexable properties to define a new indexable property. In a scheme where most of the computation is performed by a directable central processor, these results also place constraints on the communication between the local units and the central processor. The central processor is assumed to be computationally powerful, and consequently it can also be assumed that if the signals relayed to it from the local units contained sufficient information for double indexing, this information could have been put to use by the central processor. Since it is not, the information relayed to the central processor must be limited.

The results regarding single and double indexing can be explained by assuming that the local computation that precedes indexing is limited to simple local comparisons. For example, the color in a small neighborhood may be compared with the color in a surrounding area, employing, perhaps, lateral inhibition between similar detectors (Estes, 1972; Andriessen and Bouma, 1976; Pomerantz et al., 1977). If the item differs significantly from its surround, the difference signal can be used in shifting the processing focus to that location. If an item is distinguishable from its surround by the conjunction of two properties such as color and orientation, then no difference signal will be generated by either the color or the orientation comparisons, and direct indexing will not be possible. Such a local comparison will also allow the indexing of a local, rather than a global, odd-man-out. Suppose, for example, that the visual field contains green and red elements in equal numbers, but one and only one of the green elements is completely surrounded by a large region of red elements. If the local elements signaled not their colors but the results of local color comparisons, then the odd-man-out alone would produce a difference signal and would therefore be indexable. To explore the computations performed at the distributed stage it would be of interest, therefore, to examine the indexability of local odd-men-out. Various properties can be tested, while manipulating the size and shape of the surrounding region.

3.3.3. Shifting the processing focus to an indexable location

The discussion so far suggests the following indexing scheme. A number of elementary properties are computed in parallel across the visual field. For each property, local comparisons are performed everywhere. The resulting difference signals are combined somehow to produce a final odd-man-out signal at each location. The processing focus then shifts to the location of the strongest signal. This final shift operation will be examined next.

Several studies of selective visual attention likened the internal shift operation to the directing of a spotlight. A directable spotlight is used to 'illuminate' a restricted region of the visual field, and only the information within the region can be inspected. This is, of course, only a metaphor that still requires an agent to direct the spotlight and observe the illuminated region. The goal of this section is to give a more concrete notion of the shift in processing focus, and, using a simple example, to show what it means and how it may be implemented.

The example we shall examine is a version of the property-conjunction problem mentioned in the previous section. Suppose that small colored bars are scattered over the visual field. One of them is red, all the others are green. The task is to report the orientation of the red bar. We would like therefore to 'shift' the processing focus to the red bar and 'read out' its orientation.

A simplified scheme for handling this task is illustrated schematically in Fig. 7. This scheme incorporates the first two stages in the indexing operation discussed above. In the first stage ($S1$ in the figure) a number of different properties (denoted by P_1, P_2, P_3 in the figure) are being detected at each location. The existence of a horizontal green bar, for example, at a given location, will be reflected by the activity of the color- and orientation-detecting units at that location. In addition to these local units there is also a central common representation of the various properties, denoted by CP_1, CP_2, CP_3,

Figure 7. *A simplified scheme that can serve as a basis for the indexing operation. In the first stage (S_1), a number of properties (P_1, P_2, P_3 in figure) are detected everywhere. In the subsequent stage (S_2), local comparisons generate difference signals. The element generating the strongest signal is mapped onto the central common representations (CP_1, CP_2, CP_3).*

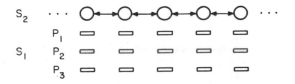

in the figure. For simplicity, we shall assume that all of the local detectors are connected to the corresponding unit in the central representation. There is, for instance, a common central unit to which all of the local units that signal vertical orientation are connected.

It is suggested that to perform the task defined above and determine the orientation of the red bar, this orientation must be represented in the central common representation. Subsequent processing stages have access to this common representation, but not to all of the local detectors. To answer the question, "what is the orientation of the red element", this orientation alone must therefore be mapped somehow into the common representation.

In section 3.3.2, it was suggested that the initial detection of the various local properties is followed by local comparisons that generate difference signals. These comparisons take place in stage $S2$ in Fig. 7, where the odd-man-out item will end up with the strongest signal. Following these two initial stages, it is not too difficult to conceive of mechanisms by which the most active unit in $S2$ would inhibit all the others, and as a result the properties of all but the odd-man-out location would be inhibited from reaching the central representation.[19] The central representations would then represent faithfully the properties of the odd-man-out item, the red bar in our example. At this stage the processing is focused on the red element and its properties are consequently represented explicitly in the central representation, accessible to subsequent processing stages. The initial question is thereby answered, without the use of a specialized vertical red line detector.

In this scheme, only the properties of the odd-man-out item can be detected immediately. Other items will have to await additional processing stages. The above scheme can be easily extended to generate successive 'shifts of the processing focus' from one element to another, in an order that depends on the strength of their signals in $S2$. These successive shifts mean that the properties of different elements will be mapped successively onto the common representations.

Possible mechanisms for performing indexing and processing focus shifts would not be considered here beyond the simple scheme discussed so far. But even this simplified scheme illustrates a number of points regarding shift and indexing. First, it provides an example for what it means to shift the processing focus to a given location. In this case, the shift entailed a selective

---

[19]Models for this stage are being tested by C. Koch at the M.I.T. A.I. Lab. One interesting result from this modeling is that a realization of the inhibition among units leads naturally to the processing focus being shifted continuously from item to item rather than 'leaping', disappearing at one location and reappearing at another. The models also account for the phenomenon that being an odd–man–out is not a simple all or none property (Engel, 1974). With increased dissimilarity, a target item can be detected immediately over a larger area.

readout to the central common representations. Second, it illustrates that shift of the processing focus can be achieved in a simple manner without physical shifts or an internal 'spotlight'. Third, it raises the point that the shift of the processing focus is not a single elementary operation but a family of operations, only some of which were discussed above. There is, for example, some evidence for the use of 'similarity enhancement': when the processing focus is centered on a given item, similar items nearby become more likely to be processed next. There is also some degree of 'central control' over the processing focus. Although the shift appears to be determined primarily by the visual input, there is also a possibility of directing the processing focus voluntarily, for example to the right or to the left of fixation (van Voorhis and Hillyard, 1977).

Finally, it suggests that psychophysical experiments of the type used by Julesz, Treisman and others, combined with physiological studies of the kind described in Section 3.2, can provide guidance for developing detailed testable models for the shift operations and their implementation in the visual system.

In summary, the execution of visual routines requires a capacity to control the locations at which elemental operations are applied. Psychological evidence, and to some degree physiological evidence, are in agreement with the general notion of an internal shift of the processing focus. This shift is obtained by a family of related processes. One of them is the indexing operation, which directs the processing focus towards certain odd-man-out locations. Indexing requires three successive stages. First, a set of properties that can be used for indexing, such as orientation, motion, and color, are computed in parallel across the base representation. Second, a location that differs significantly from its surroundings in one of these properties (but not their combinations) can be singled out as an indexed location. Finally, the processing focus is redirected towards the indexed location. This redirection can be achieved by simple schemes of interactions among the initial detecting units and central common representations that lead to a selective mapping from the initial detectors to the common representations.

3.4. Bounded activation (coloring)

The bounded activation, or 'coloring' operation, was suggested in Section 1.2. in examining the inside/outside relation. It consisted of the spread of activation over a surface in the base representation emanating from a given location or contour, and stopping at discontinuity boundaries.

The results of the coloring operation may be retained in the incremental representation for further use by additional routines. Coloring provides in this manner one method for defining larger units in the unarticulated base representations: the 'colored' region becomes a unit to which routines can be applied selectively. A simple example of this possible role of the coloring operation was mentioned in Section 2.2: the initial 'coloring' could facilitate subsequent inside/outside judgments.

A more complicated example along the same line is illustrated in Fig. 8. The visual task here is to identify the sub-figure marked by the black dot. One may have the subjective feeling of being able to concentrate on this sub-figure, and 'pull it out' from its complicated background. This capacity to 'pull out' the figure of interest can also be tested objectively, for example, by testing how well the sub-figure can be identified. It is easily seen in Fig. 8 that the marked sub-figure has the shape of the letter G. The area surrounding the sub-figure in close proximity contains a myriad of irrelevant features, and therefore identification would be difficult, unless processing can be directed to this sub-figure.

The sub-figure of interest in Fig. 8 is the region inside which the black dot resides. This region could be defined and separated from its surroundings by using the area activation operation. Recognition routines could then concentrate on the activated region, ignoring the irrelevant contours. This examples uses an artificial stimulus, but the ability to identify a region and process it selectively seems equally useful for the recognition of objects in natural scenes.

3.4.1. Discontinuity boundaries for the coloring operation
The activation operation is supposed to spread until a discontinuity bound-

Figure 8.   *The visual task here is to identify the subfigure containing the black dot. This figure (the letter 'G') can be recognized despite the presence of confounding features in close proximity to its contours, the capacity to 'pull out' the figure from the irrelevant background may involve the bounded activation operation.*

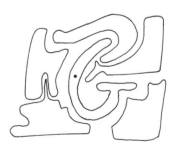

ary is reached. This raises the question of what constitutes a discontinuity boundary for the activation operation. In Fig. 8, lines in the two-dimensional drawing served for this task. If activation is applied to the base representations discussed in Section 2, it is expected that discontinuities in depth, surface orientation, and texture, will all serve a similar role. The use of boundaries to check the activation spread is not straightforward. It appears that in certain situations the boundaries do not have to be entirely continuous in order to block the coloring spread. In Fig. 9, a curve is defined by a fragmented line, but it is still immediately clear that the X lies inside and the black dot outside this curve.[20] If activation is to be used in this situation as well, then incomplete boundaries should have the capacity to block the activation spread. Finally, the activation is sometimes required to spread across certain boundaries. For example, in Fig. 10, which is similar to Fig. 8, the letter G is still recognizable, in spite of the internal bounding contours. To allow the coloring of the entire sub-figure in this case, the activation must spread across internal boundaries.

In conclusion, the bounded activation, and in particular, its interactions with different contours, is a complicated process. It is possible that as far as the activation operation is concerned, boundaries are not defined universally, but may be defined somewhat differently in different routines.

3.4.2. A mechanism for bounded activation and its implications

The 'coloring' spread can be realized by using only simple, local operations. The activation can spread in a network in which each element excites all of its neighbors.

Figure 9.   *Fragmented boundaries. The curve is defined by a dashed line, but inside/ outside judgments are still immediate.*

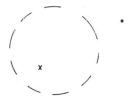

[20]Empirical results show that inside/outside judgments using dashed boundaries require somewhat longer times compared with continuous curves, suggesting that fragmented boundaries may require additional processing. The extra cost associated with fragmental boundaries is small. In a series of experiments performed by J. Varanese at Harvard University this cost averaged about 20 msec. The mean response time was about 540 msec (Varanese, 1983).

Figure 10. *Additional internal lines are introduced into the G-shaped subfigure. If bounded activation is used to 'color' this figure, it must spread across the internal contours.*

A second network containing a map of the discontinuity boundaries will be used to check the activation spread. An element in the activation network will be activated if any of its neighbors is turned on, provided that the corresponding location in the second, control network, does not contain a boundary. The turning on of a single element in the activation network will thus initiate an activation spread from the selected point outwards, that will fill the area bounded by the surrounding contours. (Each element may also have neighborhoods of different sizes, to allow a more efficient, multi-resolution implementation.)

In this scheme, an 'activity layer' serves for the execution of the basic operation, subject to the constraints in a second 'control layer'. The control layer may receive its content (the discontinuity boundaries) from a variety of sources, which thereby affect the execution of the operation.

An interesting question to consider is whether the visual system incorporates mechanisms of this general sort. If this were the case, the interconnected network of cells in cortical visual areas may contain distinct subnetworks for carrying out the different elementary operations. Some layers of cells within the retinotopically organized visual areas would then be best understood as serving for the execution of basic operations. Other layers receiving their inputs from different visual areas may serve in this scheme for the control of these operations.

If such networks for executing and controlling basic operations are incorporated in the visual system, they will have important implications for the interpretation of physiological data. In exploring such networks, physiological studies that attempt to characterize units in terms of their optimal stimuli would run into difficulties. The activity of units in such networks would be better understood not in terms of high-order features extracted by the units, but in terms of the basic operations performed by the networks. Elucidating the basic operations would therefore provide clues for understanding the activity in such networks and their patterns of interconnections.

3.5. *Boundary tracing and activation*

Since contours and boundaries of different types are fundamental entities in visual perception, a basic operation that could serve a useful role in visual routines is the tracking of contours in the base representation. This section examines the tracing operation in two parts. The first shows examples of boundary tracing and activation and their use in visual routines. The second examines the requirements imposed by the goal of having a useful, flexible, tracing operation.

3.5.1. *Examples of tracing and activation*

A simple example that will benefit from the operation of contour tracing is the problem of determining whether a contour is open or closed. If the contour is isolated in the visual field, an answer can be obtained by detecting the presence or absence of contour terminators. This strategy would not apply, however, in the presence of additional contours. This is an example of the 'figure in a context' problem (Minsky and Papert, 1969): figural properties are often substantially more difficult to establish in the presence of additional context. In the case of open and closed curves, it becomes necessary to relate the terminations to the contour in question. The problem can be solved by tracing the contour and testing for the presence of termination points on that contour.

Another simple example which illustrates the role of boundary tracing is shown in Fig. 11. The question here is whether there are two X's lying on a common curve. The answer seems immediate and effortless, but how is it achieved? Unlike the detection of single indexable items, it cannot be mediated by a fixed array of two-X's-on-a-curve detectors. Instead, I suggest that this simple perception conceals, in fact, an elaborate chain of events. In response to the question, a routine has been compiled and executed. An appropriate routine can be constructed if the repertoire of basic operations included the indexing of the X's and the tracking of curves. The tracking provides in this task a useful identity, or 'sameness' operator: it serves to verify that the two X figures are marked on the same curve, and not on two disconnected curves.

This task has been investigated recently by Jolicoeur *et al.* (1984, Reference note 1) and the results strongly supported the use of an internal contour tracing operation. Each display in this study contained two separate curves. In all trials there was an X at the fixation point, intersecting one of the curves. A second X could lie either on the same or on the second curve, and the observer's task was to decide as quickly as possible whether the two X's lay on the same or different curves. The physical distance separating the two X's was always 1.8° of visual angle. When the two X's lay on the same curve, their distance along the curve could be changed, however, in increments of 2.2° of visual angle (measured along the curve).

The main result from a number of related experiments was that the time to detect that the two X's lay on the same curve increased monotonically, and roughly linearly, with their separation along the curve. This result suggests the use of a tracing operation, at an average speed of about 24 msec per degree of visual angle. The short presentation time (250 msec) precluded the tracing of the curve using eye movements, hence the tracing operation must be performed internally.

Although the task in this experiment apparently employed a rather elaborate visual routine, it nevertheless appeared immediate and effortless. Response times were relatively short, about 750 msec for the fastest condition. When subjects were asked to describe how they performed the task, the main response was that the two X's were "simply seen" to lie on either the same curve or on different curves. No subject reported any scanning along a curve before making a decision.

The example above employed the tracking of a single contour. In other cases, it would be advantageous to activate a number of contours simultaneously. In Fig. 12a, for instance, the task is to establish visually whether there is a path connecting the center of the figure to the surrounding contour. The solution can be obtained effortlessly by looking at the figure, but again, it must involve in fact a complicated chain of processing. To cope with this

Figure 11. *The task here is to determine visually whether the two X's lie on the same curve. This simple task requires in fact complex processing that probably includes the use of a contour tracing operation.*

Figure 12. *The task in a is to determine visually whether there is a path connecting the center of the figure to the surrounding circle. In b the solution is labeled. The interpretation of such labels relys upon a set of common natural visual routines.*

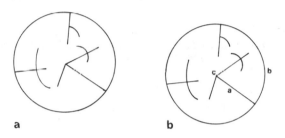

a   b

seemingly simple problem, visual routine must (i) identify the location referred to as "the center of the figure", (ii) identify the outside contour, and (iii) determine whether there is a path connecting the two. (It is also possible to proceed from the outside inwards.) By analogy with the area activation, the solution can be found by activating contours at the center point and examining the activation spread to the periphery. In Fig. 12b, the solution is labeled: the center is marked by the letter c, the surrounding boundary by b, and the connecting path by a. Labeling of this kind is common in describing graphs and figures. A point worth noting is that to be unambiguous, such notations must reply upon the use of common, natural visual routines. The label b, for example, is detached from the figure and does not identify explicitly a complete contour. The labeling notation implicitly assumes that there is a common procedure for identifying a distinct contour associated with the label.[21]

In searching for a connecting contour in Fig. 12, the contours could be activated in parallel, in a manner analogous to area coloring. It seems likely that at least in certain situations, the search for a connecting path is not just an unguided sequential tracking and exploration of all possible paths. A definite answer would require, however, an empirical investigation, for example, by manipulating the number of distracting culy-de-sac paths connected to the center and to the surrounding contour. In a sequential search, detection of the connecting path should be strongly affected by the addition of distracting paths. If, on the other hand, activation can spread along many paths simultaneously, detection will be little affected by the additional paths.

---

[21]It is also of interest to consider how we locate the center of figures. In Noton and Stark's (1971) study of eye movements, there are some indications of an ability to start the scanning of a figure approximately at its center.

Tracking boundaries in the base representations. The examples mentioned above used contours in schematic line drawings. If boundary tracking is indeed a basic operation in establishing properties and spatial relations, it is expected to be applicable not only to such lines, but also to the different types of contours and discontinuity boundaries in the base representations. Exper-

Figure 13. *Certain texture boundaries can delineate effectively shape for recognition (a), while others cannot (b). Micropatterns that are ineffective for delineating shape boundaries can nevertheless give rise to discriminable textures (c). (From Riley, 1981).*

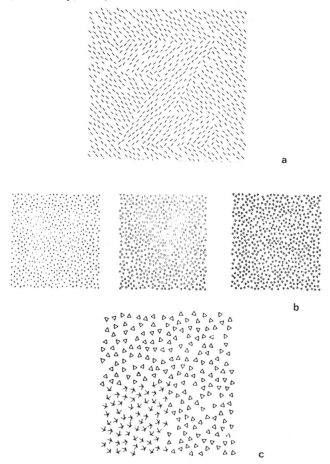

iments with textures, for instance, have demonstrated that texture boundaries can be effective for defining shapes in visual recognition. Figure 13a (reproduced from Riley (1981)) illustrates an easily recognizable Z shape defined by texture boundaries. Not all types of discontinuity can be used for rapid recognition. In Fig. 13b, for example, recognition is difficult. The boundaries defined for instance by a transition between small k-like figures and triangles cannot be used in immediate recognition, although the texture generated by these micropatterns is easily discriminable (Fig. 13c)).

What makes some discontinuities considerably more efficient than others in facilitating recognition? Recognition requires the establishment of spatial properties and relations. It can therefore be expected that recognition is facilitated if the defining boundaries are already represented in the base representations, so that operations such as activation and tracking may be applied to them. Other discontinuities that are not represented in the base representations can be detected by applying appropriate visual routines, but recognition based on these contours will be considerably slower.[22]

3.5.2. Requirements on boundary tracing

The tracing of a contour is a simple operation when the contour is continuous, isolated, and well defined. When these conditions are not met, the tracing operation must cope with a number of challenging requirements. These requirements, and their implications for the tracing operation, are examined in this section.

(a) Tracing incomplete boundaries. The incompleteness of boundaries and contours is a well-known difficulty in image processing systems. Edges and contours produced by such systems often suffer from gaps due to such problems as noise and insufficient contrast. This difficulty is probably not confined to man–made systems alone; boundaries detected by the early processes in the human visual system are also unlikely to be perfect. The boundary tracing operation should not be limited, therefore, to continuous boundaries only. As noted above with respect to inside/outside routines for human perception, fragmented contours can indeed often replace continuous ones.

---

[22]M. Riley (1981) has found a close agreement between texture boundaries that can be used in immediate recognition and boundaries that can be used in long–range apparent motion (cf. Ullman, 1979). Boundaries participating in motion correspondence must be made explicit within the base representations, so that they can be matched over discrete frames. The implication is that the boundaries involved in immediate recognition also preexist in the base representations.

(b) *Tracking across intersections and branches.* In tracing a boundary crossings and branching points can be encountered. It will then become necessary to decide which branch is the natural continuation of the curve. Similarity of color, contrast, motion, etc. may affect this decision. For similar contours, collinearity, or minimal change in direction (and perhaps curvature) seem to be the main criteria for preferring one branch over another.

Tracking a contour through an intersection can often be useful in obtaining a stable description of the contour for recognition purposes. Consider, for example, the two different instances of the numeral '2' in Fig. 14a. There are considerable differences between these two shapes. For example, one contains a hole, while the other does not. Suppose, however, that the contours are traced, and decomposed at places of maxima in curvature. This will lead to the decomposition shown in Fig. 14b. In the resulting descriptions, the

Figure 14. *The tracking of a contour through an intersection is used here in generating a stable description of the contour. a, Two instances of the numeral '2'. b, In spite of the marked difference in their shape, their eventual decomposition and description are highly similar.*

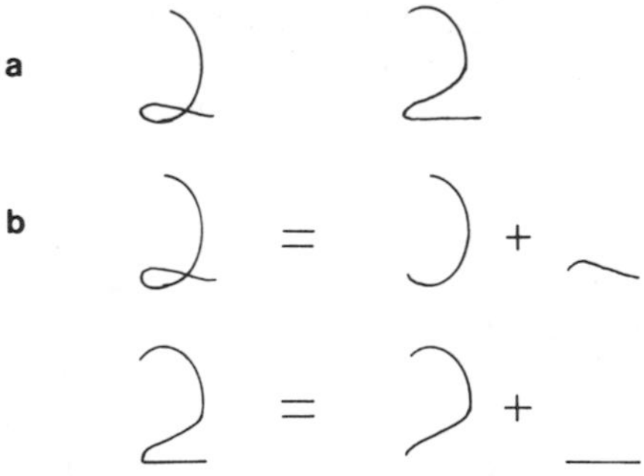

Figure 15. *Tracing a skeleton. The overall figure can be traced and recognized without recognizing first all of the individual components.*

decomposition into strokes, and the shapes of the underlying strokes, are highly similar.

(c) Tracking at different resolutions. Tracking can proceed along the main skeleton of a contour without tracing its individual components. An example is illustrated in Fig. 15, where a figure is constructed from a collection of individual tokens. The overall figure can be traced and recognized without tracing and identifying its components.

Examples similar to Fig. 15 have been used to argue that 'global' or 'holistic' perception precedes the extraction of local features. According to the visual routines scheme, the constituent line elements are in fact extracted by the earliest visual process and represented in the base representations. The constituents are not recognized, since their recognition requires the application of visual routines. The 'forest before the trees' phenomenon (Johnston and McLelland, 1973; Navon, 1977; Pomerantz *et al.*, 1977) is the result of applying appropriate routines that can trace and analyze aggregates without analyzing their individual components, thereby leading to the recognition of the overall figure prior to the recognition of its constituents.

The ability to trace collections of tokens and extract properties of their arrangement raises a question regarding the role of grouping processes in early vision. Our ability to perceive the collinear arrangement of different tokens, as illustrated in Fig. 16, has been used to argue for the existence of sophisticated grouping processes within the early visual representations that detect such arrangements and make them explicit (Marr, 1976). In this view, these grouping processes participate in the construction of the base representations, and consequently collinear arrangements of tokens are detected and represented throughout the base representation prior to the application of visual routines. An alternative possibility is that such arrangements are identified in fact as a result of applying the appropriate routine. This is not to deny the existence of certain grouping processes within the base representations. There is, in fact, strong evidence in support of the existence of such processes.[23] The more complicated and abstract grouping phenomena such as in Fig. 16 may, nevertheless, be the result of applying the appropriate routines, rather than being explicitly represented in the base representations.

Finally, from the point of view of the underlying mechanism, one obvious possibility is that the operation of tracing an overall skeleton is the result of applying tracing routines to a low resolution copy of the image, mediated by low frequency channels within the visual system. This is not the only possibil-

---

[23]For evidence supporting the existence of grouping processes within the early creation of the base representations using dot–interference patterns see Glass (1969), Glass and Perez (1973), Marroquin (1976), Stevens (1978). See also a discussion of grouping in early visual processing in Barlow (1981).

Figure 16. *The collinearity of tokens (items and endpoints) can easily be perceived. This perception may be related to a routine that traces collinear arrangements, rather than to sophisticated grouping processes within the base representations.*

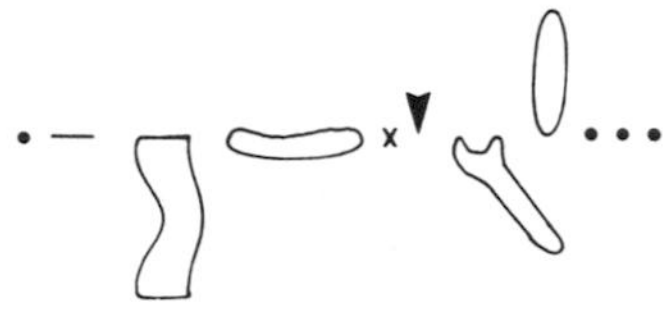

ity, however, and in attempting to investigate this operation further, alternative methods for tracing the overall skeleton of figures should also be considered.

In summary, the tracing and activation of boundaries are useful operations in the analysis of shape and the establishment of spatial relations. This is a complicated operation since flexible, reliable, tracing should be able to cope with breaks, crossings, and branching, and with different resolution requirements.

3.6. Marking

In the course of applying a visual routine, the processing shifts across the base representations from one location to another. To control and coordinate the routine, it would be useful to have the capability to keep at least a partial track of the locations already processed.

A simple operation of this type is the marking of a single location for future reference. This operation can be used, for instance, in establishing the closure of a contour. As noted in the preceding section, closure cannot be tested in general by the presence or absence of terminators, but can be established using a combination of tracing and marking. The starting point of the tracing operation is marked, and if the marked location is reached again the tracing is completed, and the contour is known to be closed.

Figure 17 shows a similar problem, which is a version of a problem examined in the previous section. The task here is to determine visually whether there are two X's on the same curve. Once again, the correct answer is perceived immediately. To establish that only a single X lies on the closed curve *c*, one can use the above strategy of marking the X and tracking the

Figure 17. *The task here is to determine visually whether there are two X's on a common curve. The task could be accomplished by employing marking and tracing operations.*

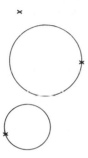

curve. It is suggested that the perceptual system has marking and tracing in its repertoire of basic operations, and that the simple perception of the X on the curve involved the application of visual routines that employ such operations.

Other tasks may benefit from the marking of more than a single location. A simple example is visual counting, that is, the problem of determining as fast as possible the number of distinct items in view (Atkinson *et al.*, 1969; Kowler and Steinman, 1979).

For a small number of items visual counting is fast and reliable. When the number of items is four or less, the perception of their number is so immediate, that it gave rise to conjecture regarding special *Gestalt* mechanisms that can somehow respond directly to the number of items in view, provided that this number does not exceed four (Atkinson *et al.*, 1969).

In the following section, we shall see that although such mechanisms are possible in principle, they are unlikely to be incorporated in the human visual system. It will be suggested instead that even the perception of a small number of items involves in fact the execution of visual routines in which marking plays an important role.

3.6.1. Comparing schemes for visual counting

Perception-like counting networks. In their book *Perceptrons*, Minsky and Papert (1969, Ch. 1) describe parallel networks that can count the number of elements in their input (see also Milner, 1974). Counting is based on computing the predicates "the input has exactly M points" and "the input has between M and N points" for different values of M and N. For any given value of M, it is thereby possible to construct a special network that will respond only when the number of items in view is exactly M. Unlike visual routines which are composed of elementary operations, such a network can adequately be described as an elementary mechanism responding directly to the presence of M items in view. Unlike the shifting and marking operations, the computation is performed by these networks uniformly and in parallel over the entire field.

Counting by visual routines. Counting can also be performed by simple visual routines that employ elementary operations such as shifting and marking. For example, the indexing operation described in Section 3.3 can be used to perform the counting task provided that it is extended somewhat to include marking operations. Section 3.3 illustrated how a simple shifting scheme can be used to move the processing focus to an indexable item. In the counting problem, there is more than a single indexable item to be considered. To use the same scheme for counting, the processing focus is required to travel among all of the indexable items, without visiting an item more than once.

A straightforward extension that will allow the shifting scheme in Section 3.3 to travel among different items is to allow it to mark the elements already visited. Simple marking can be obtained in this case by 'switching off' the element at the current location of the processing focus. The shifting scheme described above is always attracted to the location producing the strongest signal. If this signal is turned off, the shift would automatically continue to the new strongest signal. The processing focus can now continue its tour, until all the items have been visited, and their number counted.

A simple example of this counting routine is the 'single point detection' task. In this problem, it is assumed that one or more points can be lit up in the visual field. The task is to say 'yes' if a single point is lit up, and 'no' otherwise. Following the counting procedure outlined above, the first point will soon be reached and masked. If there are no remaining signals, the point was unique and the correct answer is 'yes'; otherwise, it is 'no'.

In the above scheme, counting is achieved by shifting the processing focus among the items of interest without scanning the entire image systematically. Alternatively, shifting and marking can also be used for visual counting by scanning the entire scene in a fixed predetermined pattern. As the number of items increases, programmed scanning may become the more efficient strategy. The two alternative schemes will behave differently for different numbers of items. The fixed scanning scheme is largely independent of the number of items, whereas in the traveling scheme, the computation time will depend on the number of items, as well as on their spatial configuration.

There are two main differences between counting by visual routines of one type or another on the one hand, and by specialized counting networks on the other. First, unlike the perception-like networks, the process of determining the number of items by visual routines can be decomposed into a sequence of elementary operations. This decomposition holds true for the perception of a small number of items and even for the single item detection. Second, in contrast with a counting network that is specially constructed for the task of detecting a prescribed number of items, the same elementary operations employed in the counting routine also participate in other visual routines.

This difference makes counting by visual routines more attractive than the counting networks. It does not seem plausible to assume that visual counting is essential enough to justify specialized networks dedicated to this task alone. In other words, visual counting is simply unlikely to be an elementary operation. It is more plausible in my view that visual counting can be performed efficiently as a result of our general capacity to generate and execute visual routines, and the availability of the appropriate elementary operations that can be harnessed for the task.

3.6.2. Reference frames in marking

The marking of a location for later reference requires a coordinate system, or a frame of reference, with respect to which the location is defined. One general question regarding marking is, therefore, what is the referencing scheme in which locations are defined and remembered for subsequent use by visual routines. One possibility is to maintain an internal 'egocentric' spatial map that can then be used in directing the processing focus. The use of marking would then be analogous to reaching in the dark: the location of one or more objects can be remembered, so that they can be reached (approximately) in the dark without external reference cues. It is also possible to use an internal map in combination with external referencing. For example, the

Figure 18. *The use of an external reference. The position of point* q *can be defined and retained relative to the predominant X nearby.*

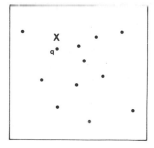

position of point q in Fig. 18 can be defined and remembered using the prominent X figure nearby. In such a scheme it becomes possible to maintain a crude map with which prominent features can be located, and a more detailed local map in which the position of the marked item is defined with respect to the prominent feature.

The referencing problem can be approached empirically, for example by making a point in figures such as Fig. 18 disappear, then reappear (possibly in a slightly displaced location), and testing the accuracy at which the two locations can be compared. (Care must be taken to avoid apparent motion.) One can test the effect of potential reference markers on the accuracy, and test marking accuracy across eye movements.

3.6.3. Marking and the integration of information in a scene

To be useful in the natural analysis of visual scenes, the marking map should be preserved across eye motions. This means that if a certain location in space is marked prior to an eye movement, the marking should point to the same spatial location following the eye movement. Such a marking operation, combined with the incremental representation, can play a valuable role in integrating the information across eye movements and from different regions in the course of viewing a complete scene.[24]

Suppose, for example, that a scene contains several objects, such as a man at one location, and a dog at another, and that following the visual analysis of the man figure we shift our gaze and processing focus to the dog. The visual analysis of the man figure has been summarized in the incremental representation, and this information is still available at least in part as the gaze is shifted to the dog. In addition to this information we keep a spatial map, a set of spatial pointers, which tell us that the dog is at one direction, and the man at another. Although we no longer see the man clearly, we have a clear notion of what exists where. The 'what' is supplied by the incremental representations, and the 'where' by the marking map.

In such a scheme, we do not maintain a full panoramic representation of the scene. After looking at various parts of the scene, our representation of it will have the following structure. There would be a retinotopic representation of the scene in the current viewing direction. To this representation we can apply visual routines to analyze the properties of, and relations among, the items in view. In addition, we would have markers to the spatial locations of items in the scene already analyzed. These markers can point to peripheral

---

[24]The problem considered here is not limited to the integration of views across saccadic eye motions, for which an 'integrative visual buffer' has been proposed by Rayner (1978).

objects, and perhaps even to locations outside the field of view (Attneave and Pierce, 1978). If we are currently looking at the dog, we would see it in detail, and will be able to apply visual routines and extract information regarding the dog's shape. At the same time we know the locations of the other objects in the scene (from the marking map) and what they are (from the incremental representation). We know, for example, the location of the man in the scene. We also know various aspects of his shape, although it may now appear only as a blurred blob, since they are summarized in the incremental representation. To obtain new information, however, we would have to shift our gaze back to the man figure, and apply additional visual routines.

3.6.4. On the spatial resolution of marking and other basic operations

In the visual routines scheme, accuracy in visual counting will depend on the accuracy and spatial resolution of the marking operation. This conclusion is consistent with empirical results obtained in the study of visual counting.[25] Additional perceptual limitations may arise from limitations on the spatial resolution of other basic operations. For example, it is known that spatial relations are difficult to establish in peripheral vision in the presence of distracting figures. An example, due to J. Lettvin (see also Andriessen and Bouma, 1976; Townsend *et al.*, 1971), is shown in Fig. 19. When fixating on the central point from a normal reading distance, the N on the left is recognizable, while the N within the string TNT on the right is not. The flanking letters exert some 'lateral masking' even when their distance from the central letter is well above the two-point resolution at this eccentricity (Riggs, 1965).

Interaction effects of this type may be related to limitations on the spatial resolution of various basic operations, such as indexing, marking, and boundary tracking. The tracking of a line contour, for example, may be distracted by the presence of another contour nearby. As a result, contours may inter-

Figure 19. *Spatial limitations of the elemental operations. When the central mark is fixated, the N on the left is recognizable, while the one on the right is not. This effect may reflect limitations on the spatial resolution of basic operations such as indexing, marking, and boundary tracing.*

N   TNT

*

---

[25]For example, Kowler and Steinman (1979) report a puzzling result regarding counting accuracy. It was found that eye movements increase counting accuracy for large (2°) displays, but were not helpful, and sometimes detrimental, with small displays. This result could be explained under the plausible assumptions that marking accuracy is better near fixation, and that it deteriorates across eye movements. As a result, eye movements will improve marking accuracy for large, but not for small, displays.

fere with the application of visual routines to other contours, and consequently with the establishment of spatial relations. Experiments involving the establishment of spatial relations in the presence of distractors would be useful in investigating the spatial resolution of the basic operations, and its dependence on eccentricity.

The hidden complexities in perceiving spatial relationships. We have examined above a number of plausible elemental operations including shift, indexing, bounded activation, boundary tracing and activation, and marking. These operations would be valuable in establishing abstract shape properties and spatial relations, and some of them are partially supported by empirical data. (They certainly do not constitute, however, a comprehensive set.)

The examination of the basic operations and their use reveals that in perceiving spatial relations the visual system accomplishes with intriguing efficiency highly complicated tasks. There are two main sources for these complexities. First, as was illustrated above, from a computational standpoint, the efficient and reliable implementation of each of the elemental operations poses challenging problems. It is evident, for instance, that a sophisticated specialized processor would be required for an efficient and flexible bounded activation operation, or for the tracing of contours and collinear arrangements of tokens.

In addition to the complications involved in the realization of the different elemental operations, new complications are introduced when the elemental operations are assembled into meaningful visual routines. As illustrated by the inside/outside example, in perceiving a given spatial relation different strategies may be employed, depending on various parameters of the stimuli (such as the complexity of the boundary, or the distance of the X from the bounding contour). The immediate perception of seemingly simple relations often requires, therefore, selection among possible routines, followed by the coordinated application of the elemental operations comprising the visual routines. Some of the problems involved in the assembly of the elemental operations into visual routines are discussed briefly in the next section.

4. The assembly, compilation, and storage of visual routines

The use of visual routines allows a variety of properties and relations to be established using a fixed set of basic operations. According to this view, the establishment of relations requires the application of a coordinated sequence of basic operations. We have discussed above a number of plausible basic operations. In this section I shall raise some of the general problems associated with the construction of useful routines from combinations of basic operations.

The appropriate routine to be applied in a given situation depends on the goal of the computation, and on various parameters of the configuration to be analyzed. We have seen, for example, that the routine for establishing inside/outside relations may depend on various properties of the configuration: in some cases it would be efficient to start at the location of the X figure, in other situations it may be more efficient to start at some distant locations.

Similarly, in Treisman's (1977, 1980) experiments on indexing by two properties (e.g., a vertical red item in a field of vertical green and horizontal red distractors) there are at least two alternative strategies for detecting the target. Since direct indexing by two properties is impossible, one may either scan the red items, testing for orientation, or scan the vertical items, testing for color.[26] The distribution of distractors in the field determines the relative efficiency of these alternative strategies. In such cases it may prove useful, therefore, to precede the application of a particular routine with a stage where certain relevant properties of the configuration to be analyzed are sampled and inspected. It would be of interest to examine whether in the double indexing task, for example, the human visual system tends to employ the more efficient search strategy.

The above discussion introduces what may be called the 'assembly problem'; that is, the problem of how routines are constructed in response to specific goals, and how this generation is controlled by aspects of the configuration to be analyzed. In the above examples, a goal for the computation is set up externally, and an appropriate routine is applied in response. In the course of recognizing and manipulating objects, routines are usually invoked in response to internally generated queries. Some of these routines may be stored in memory rather than assembled anew each time they are needed.

The recognition of a specific object may then use pre-assembled routines for inspecting relevant features and relations among them. Since routines can also be generated efficiently by the assembly mechanism in response to specific goals, it would probably be sufficient to store routines in memory in a skeletonized form only. The assembly mechanism will then fill in details and generate intermediate routines when necessary. In such a scheme, the perceptual activity during recognition will be guided by setting pre-stored goals that the assembly process will then expand into detailed visual routines.

---

[26]There is also a possibility that all the items must be scanned one by one without any selection by color or orientation. This question is relevent for the shift operation discussed in Section 3.2. Recent results by J. Rubin and N. Kanwisher at M.I.T. suggest that it is possible to scan only the items of relevant color and ignore the others.

The application of pre-stored routines rather then assembling them again each time they are required can lead to improvements in performance and the speed-up of performing familiar perceptual tasks. These improvements can come from two different sources. First, assembly time will be saved if the routine is already 'compiled' in memory. The time saving can increase if stored routines for familiar tasks, which may be skeletonized at first, become more detailed, thereby requiring less assembly time. Second, stored routines may be improved with practice, for example, as a result of either external instruction, or by modifying routines when they fail to accomplish their tasks efficiently.

Summary

1. Visual perception requires the capacity to extract abstract shape properties and spatial relations. This requirement divides the overall processing of visual information into two distinct stages. The first is the creation of the base representations (such as the primal sketch and the 2½-D sketch). The second is the application of visual routines to the base representations.

2. The creation of the base representations is a bottom-up and spatially uniform process. The representations it produces are unarticulated and viewer-centered.

3. The application of visual routines is no longer bottom-up, spatially uniform, and viewer-centered. It is at this stage that objects and parts are defined, and their shape properties and spatial relations are established.

4. The perception of abstract shape properties and spatial relations raises two major difficulties. First, the perception of even seemingly simple, immediate properties and relations requires in fact complex computation. Second, visual perception requires the capacity to establish a large variety of different properties and relations.

5. It is suggested that the perception of spatial relation is achieved by the application to the base representations of visual routines that are composed of sequences of elemental operations. Routines for different properties and relations share elemental operations. Using a fixed set of basic operations, the visual system can assemble different routines to extract an unbounded variety of shape properties and spatial relations.

6. Unlike the construction of the base representation, the application of visual routines is not determined by the visual input alone. They are selected or created to meet specific computational goals.

7. Results obtained by the application of visual routines are retained in the incremental representation and can be used by subsequent processes.

8. Some of the elemental operations employed by visual routines are applied to restricted locations in the visual field, rather than to the entire field in parallel. It is suggested that this apparent limitation on spatial parallelism reflects in part essential limitations, inherent to the nature of the computation, rather than non-essential capacity limitations.

9. At a more detailed level, a number of plausible basic operations were suggested, based primarily on their potential usefulness, and supported in part by empirical evidence. These operations include:

9.1. *Shift of the processing focus*. This is a family of operations that allow the application of the same basic operation to different locations across the base representations.

9.2. *Indexing*. This is a shift operation towards special odd-man-out locations. A location can be indexed if it is sufficiently different from its surroundings in an indexable property. Indexable properties, which are computed in parallel by the early visual processes, include contrast, orientation, color, motion, and perhaps also size, binocular disparity, curvature, and the existence of terminators, corners, and intersections.

9.3. *Bounded activation*. This operation consists of the spread of activation over a surface in the base representation, emanating from a given location or contour, and stopping at discontinuity boundaries. This is not a simple operation, since it must cope with difficult problems that arise from the existence of internal contours and fragmented boundaries. A discussion of the mechanisms that may be implicated in this operation suggests that specialized networks may exist within the visual system, for executing and controlling the application of visual routines.

9.4. *Boundary tracing*. This operation consists of either the tracing of a single contour, or the simultaneous activation of a number of contours. This operation must be able to cope with the difficulties raised by the tracing of incomplete boundaries, tracing across intersections and branching points, and tracing contours defined at different resolution scales.

9.5. *Marking*. The operation of marking a location means that this location is remembered, and processing can return to it whenever necessary. Such an operation would be useful in the integration of information in the processing of different parts of a complete scene.

10. It is suggested that the seemingly simple and immediate perception of spatial relations conceals in fact a complex array of processes involved in the selection, assembly, and execution of visual routines.

References

Andriessen, J.J. and Bouma, H. (1976) Eccentric vision: adverse interactions between line segments. *Vis. Res., 16*, 71–78.

Atkinson, J., Campbell, F.W. and Francis, M.R. (1969) The magic number 4 ± 0: A new look at visual numerosity judgments. *Perception, 5*, 327–334.

Attneave, F. and Pierce, C.R. (1978) The accuracy of extrapolating a pointer into perceived and imagined space. *Am. J. Psychol., 91(3)*, 371–387.

Barlow, H.H. (1972) Single units and sensation: A neuron doctrine for perceptual psychology? *Perception, 1*, 371–394.

Barlow, H.B. (1981) Critical limiting factors in the design of the eye and the visual cortex. The Ferrier Lecture 1980. *Proc. Roy. Soc. Lond. B, 212*, 1–34.

Bartlett, F.C. (1932) *Remembering*. Cambridge, Cambridge University Press.

Beck, J. and Ambler, B. (1972) Discriminability of differences in line slope and in line arrangement as a function of mask delay. *Percep. Psychophys. 12(1A)*, 33–38.

Beck, J. and Ambler, B. (1973) The effects of concentrated and distributed attention on peripheral acuity. *Percept. Psychophys., 14(2)*, 225–230.

Beneveneto, L.A. and Davis, B. (1977) Topographical projections of the prestriate cortex to the pulvinar nuclei in the macaque monkey: an autoradiographic study. *Exp. Brain Res., 30*, 405–424.

Biederman, I., Glass, A.L. and Stacy, E.W. (1973) Searching for objects in real–world scenes. *J. exp. Psychol., 97(1)*, 22–27.

Donderi, D.C. and Zelnicker, D. (1969) Parallel processing in visual same–different decisions. *Percep. Psychophys., 5(4)*, 197–200.

Egeth, H., Jonides, J. and Wall, S. (1972) Parallel processing of multi-element displays. *Cog. Psychol., 3*, 674–698.

Engel, F.L. (1971) Visual conspecuity, directed attention and retinal locus. *Vis. Res., 11*, 563–576.

Eriksen, C.W. and Hoffman, J.E. (1972) Temporal and spatial characteristics of selective encoding from visual displays. *Percep. Psychophys., 12(2B)*, 201–204.

Eriksen, C.W. and Schultz, D.W. (1977) Retinal locus and acuity in visual information processing. *Bull. Psychon. Soc., 9(2)*, 81–84.

Estes, W.K. (1972) Interactions of signal and background variables in visual processing. *Percep. Psychophys., 12(3)*, 278–286.

Evans, T.G. (1968) A heuristic program to solve geometric analogy problems. In M. Minsky (ed.), *Semantic Information Processing*. Cambridge, MA, M.I.T. Press.

Fantz, R.L. (1961) The origin of form perception. *Scient. Am., 204(5)*, 66–72.

Fischer, B. and Boch, R. (1981) Enhanced activation of neurons in prelunate cortex before visually guided saccades of trained rhesus monkey. *Exp. Brain Res., 44*, 129–137.

Fuster, J.M. and Jervey, J.P. (1981) Inferotemporal neurons distinguish and retain behaviorally relevant features of visual stimuli. *Science, 212*, 952–955.

Gattas, R., Osealdo Cruz, E. and Sousa, A.P.B. (1979) Visual receptive fields of units in the pulvinar of cebus monkey. *Brain Res., 160*, 413–430.

Glass, L. (1969) Moire effect from random dots. *Nature, 243*, 578–580.

Glass, L. and Perez, R. (1973) Perception of random dot interference patterns. *Nature, 246*, 360–362.

Goldberg, M.E. and Wurtz, R.H. (1972) Activity of superior colliculus in behaving monkey. II. Effect of attention of neural responses. *J. Neurophysiol, 35*, 560–574.

Holtzman, J.D. and Gazzaniga, M.S. (1982) Dual task interactions due exclusively to limits in processing resources. *Science, 218*, 1325–1327.

Humphreys, G.W. (1981) On varying the span of visual attention: evidence for two modes of spatial attention. *Q. J. exp. Psychol., 33A*, 17–31.

Johnston, J.C. and McClelland, J.L. (1973) Visual factors in word perception. *Percep. Psychophys., 14(2)*, 365–370.

Jonides, J. and Gleitman, H. (1972) A conceptual category effect in visual search: O as a letter or as digit. *Percep. Psychophys., 12(6)*, 457–460.

Johnson, R.B. and Kirk, N.S. (1960) The perception of size: An experimental synthesis of the associationist and gestalt accounts of the perception of size. Part III. *Q. J. exp. Psychol., 12*, 221–230.

Julesz, B. (1975) Experiments in the visual perception of texture. *Scient. Am., 232(4)*, April 1975, 34–43.

Julesz, B. (1981) Textons, the elements of texture perception, and their interactions. *Nature, 290*, 91–97.

Kahneman, D. (1973) *Attention and Effort*. Englewood Cliffs, NJ, Prentice-Hall.

Kolmogorov, A.N. (1968) Logical basis for information theory and probability theory. *IEEE Trans. Info. Theory, IT-14(5)*, 662–664.

Kowler, E. and Steinman, R.M. (1979) Miniature saccades: eye movements that do not count. *Vis. Res., 19*, 105–108.

Lappin, J.S. and Fuqua, M.A. (1983) Accurate visual measurement of three-dimensional moving patterns. *Science, 221*, 480–482.

Livingstone, M.L. and Hubel, D.J. (1981) Effects of sleep and arousal on the processing of visual information in the cat. *Nature, 291*, 554–561.

Mackworth, N.H. (1965) Visual noise causes tunnel vision. *Psychon. Sci., 3*, 67–68.

Marr, D. (1976) Early processing of visual information. *Phil. Trans. Roy. Soc. and B, 275*, 483–524.

Marr, D. (1980) Visual information processing: the structure and creation of visual representations. *Phil. Trans. Roy. Soc. Lond. B, 290*, 199–218.

Marr, D. and Nishihara, H.K. (1978) Representation and recognition of the spatial organization of three–dimensional shapes. *Proc. Roy. Soc. B, 200*, 269–291.

Marroquin, J.L. (1976) Human visual perception of structure. MSc. Thesis, Department of Electrical Engineering and Computer Science, Massachusetts Institute of Technology.

Milner, P.M. (1974) A model for visual shape recognitio. *Psychol. Rev. 81(6)*, 521–535.

Minsky, M. and Papert, S. (1969) *Perceptrons*. Cambridge, MA and London: The M.I.T. Press.

Minsky, M. (1975) A framework for representing knowledge. In P.H. Winston (ed.), *The Psychology of Computer Vision*. New York, Prentice Hall.

Mountcastle, V.B. (1976) The world around us: neural command functions for selective attention. The F.O. Schmitt Lecture in Neuroscience 1975. *Neurosci. Res. Prog. Bull., 14*, Supplement 1–37.

Mountcastle, V.B., Lynch, J.C., Georgopoulos, A., Sakata, H. and Acuna, A. (1975) Posterior parietal association cortex of the monkey: command functions for operations within extrapersonal space. *J. Neurophys., 38*, 871–908.

Navon, D. (1977) Forest before trees: the precedence of global features in visual perception. *Cog. Psychol., 9*, 353–383.

Neisser, U., Novick, R. and Lazar, R. (1963) Searching for ten targets simultaneously. *Percep. Mot. Skills, 17*, 955–961.

Neisser, U. (1967) *Cognitive Psychology*. New York, Prentice-Hall.

Newsome, W.T. and Wurtz, R.H. (1982) Identification of architectonic zones containing visual tracking cells in the superior temporal sulcus of macaque monkeys. *Invest. Ophthal. Vis. Sci., Suppl. 3*, 22, 238.

Nickerson, R.S. (1966) Response times with memory–dependent decision task. *J. exp. Psychol., 72(5)*, 761–769.

Noton, D. and Stark, L. (1971) Eye movements and visual perception. *Scient. Am., 224(6)*, 34–43.

Pomerantz, J.R., Sager, L.C. and Stoever, R.J. (1977) Perception of wholes and of their component parts: some configural superiority effects. *J. exp. Psychol., Hum. Percep. Perf., 3(3)*, 422–435.

Posner, M.I. (1980) Orienting of attention. *Q. J. exp. Psychol., 32*, 3–25.

Posner, M.I., Nissen, M.J. and Ogden, W.C. (1978) Attended and unattended processing modes: the role of set for spatial location. In Saltzman, I.J. and H.L. Pick (eds.), *Modes of Perceiving and Processing Information*. Hillsdale, NJ, Lawrence Erlbaum.

Potter, M.C. (1975) Meaning in visual search. *Science, 187*, 965–966.

Rayner, K. (1948) Eye movements in reading and information processing. *Psychol. Bull., 85(3)*, 618–660.

Regan, D. and Beverley, K.I. (1978) Looming detectors in the human visual pathway. *Vis. Res., 18*, 209–212.

Rezak, M. and Beneveneto, A. (1979) A comparison of the organization of the projections of the dorsal lateral geniculate nucleus, the inferior pulvinar and adjacent lateral pulvinar to primary visual area (area 17) in the macaque monkey. *Brain Res., 167*, 19–40.

Richards, W. (1982) How to play twenty questions with nature and win. *M.I.T.A.I. Laboratory Memo 660*.

Richmond, B.J. and Sato, T. (1982) Visual responses of inferior temporal neurons are modified by attention to different stimuli dimensions. *Soc. Neurosci. Abst., 8*, 812.

Riggs, L.A. (1965) Visual acuity. In C.H. Grahan (ed.), *Vision and Visual Perception*. New York, John Wiley.

Riley, M.D. (1981) The representation of image texture. M.Sc. Thesis, Department of Electrical Engineering and Computer Science, Massachusetts Institute of Technology.

Robinson, D.L., Goldberg, M.G. and Staton, G.B. (1978) Parietal association cortex in the primate: sensory mechanisms and behavioral modulations. *J. Neurophysiol., 41(4)*, 910–932.

Rock, I., Halper, F. and Clayton, T. (1972) The perception and recognition of complex figures. *Cog. Psychol., 3*, 655–673.

Rock, I. and Gutman, D. (1981) The effect of inattention of form perception. *J. exp. Psychol.: Hum. Percep. Perf., 7(2)*, 275–285.

Rumelhart, D.E. (1970) A multicomponent theory of the perception of briefly exposed visual displays. *J. Math. Psychol., 7*, 191–218.

Schein, S.J., Marrocco, R.T. and De Monasterio, F.M. (1982) Is there a high concentration of color–selective cells in area V4 of monkey visual cortex? *J. Neurophysiol., 47(2)*, 193–213.

Shiffrin, R.M., McKay, D.P. and Shaffer, W.O. (1976) Attending to forty-nine spatial positions at once. *J. exp. Psychol.: Human Percep. Perf., 2(1)*, 14–22.

Shulman, G.L., Remington, R.W. and McLean, I.P. (1979) Moving attention through visual space. *J. exp. Psychol.: Huma. Percep. Perf., 5*, 522–526.

Sperling, G. (1960) The information available in brief visual presentations. *Psychol. Mono., 74*, (11, Whole No. 498).

Stevens, K.A. (1978) Computation of locally parallel structure. *Biol. Cybernet., 29*, 19–28.

Sutherland, N.S. (1968) Outline of a theory of the visual pattern recognition in animal and man. *Proc. Roy. Soc. Lond. B, 171*, 297–317.

Townsend, J.T., Taylor, S.G. and Brown, D.R. (1971) Latest masking for letters with unlimited viewing time. *Percep. Psycholphys., 10(5)*, 375–378.

Treisman, A. (1977) Focused attention in the perception and retrieval of multidimensional stimuli. *Percep. Psychophys., 22*, 1–11.

Treisman, A. and Celade, G. (1980) A feature integration theory of attention. *Cog. Psychol., 12*, 97–136.

Tsal, Y. (1983) Movements of attention across the visual field. *J. exp. Psychol.: Hum. Percep. Perf.* (In Press).

Ullman, S. (1979) *The Interpretation of Visual Motion*. Cambridge, MA, and London: The M.I.T. Press.

Varanese, J. (1983) Abstracting spatial relations from the visual world B.Sc. thesis in Neurobiology and Psychology. Harvard University.

van Voorhis, S. and Hillyard, S.A. (1977) Visual evoked potentials and selective attention to points in space. *Percep. Psychophys., 22(1)*, 54–62.

Winston, P.H. (1977) *Artificial Intelligence*. Reading, MA., Addison-Wesley.

Wurtz, R.H. and Mohler, C.W. (1976a) Organization of monkey superior colliculus: enhanced visual response of superficial layer cells. *J. Neurophysiol., 39(4)*, 745–765.

Wurtz, R.H. and Mohler, C.W. (1976b) Enhancement of visual response in monkey striate cortex and frontal eye fields. *J. Neurophysiol., 39*, 766–772.

Wurtz, R.H., Goldberg, M.E. and Robinson D.L. (1982) Brain mechanisms of visual attention. *Scient. Am.,* *246(6)*, 124–135.
Zeki, S.M. (1978a) Functional specialization in the visual cortex of the rhesus monkey. *Nature, 274*, 423–428.
Zeki, S.M. (1978b) Uniformity and diversity of structure and function in rhesus monkey prestriate visual cortex. *J. Physiol., 277*, 273–290.

Reference Note

1. Joliceur, P., Ullman, S. and Mackay, M. (1984) Boundary Tracing: a possible elementary operation in the perception of spatial relations. Submitted for publication.

4

Upward direction, mental rotation, and discrimination of left and right turns in maps*

ROGER N. SHEPARD

SHELLEY HURWITZ

Stanford University

Abstract

Whereas, the only direction of which we have always had immediate knowledge is the gravitationally defined vertical, the directions that have beeen most important for finding our way about are largely orthogonal directions along the generally horizontal ground. The first half of the paper argues that the concept of an upward direction has consequently been extended to represent horizontal directions that are (1) uphill, however slightly, (2) upward in the metaphorical sense of toward a salient or important reference object or location, (3) northward in the global environmental frame, or (4) straight ahead in the viewer's egocentric frame. The second half empirically explores this last coupling, between upwards and straight ahead, by two chronometric experiments on the interpretation of bends in a line, as right or left turns on a map. Interpretation time increased markedly with angular departure from upright of the line going into the turn, suggesting that such interpretation requires a mental rotation.

The most pervasive and enduring constraints in the world in which we have evolved are likely to have become most thoroughly internalized in the nervous system (Shepard, 1981). As a consequence, such internal constraints may be both so abstract and so much a part of ourselves that we ordinarily are quite unaware of the extent to which they now determine, as Kant (1781/ 1881) surmised, the very conditions for our experience of the world.

Fundamental among such constraints, for present purposes, are the follow-

*Supported by National Science Foundation research grants BNS 75-02806 and BNS 80-05517 to the first author. Primary responsibility rests with the first author for the theoretical introduction, the initial conception of the two experiments, and the final form of the written report; and rests with the second author for the implementation, conduct, and statistical analyses of the two experiments. The paper has greatly benefited from helpful comments on an earlier draft that were provided by Ronald Finke, Lawrence Parsons, Steven Pinker, and Barbara Tversky. Reprint requests should be sent to: Roger N. Shepard, Department of Psychology, Uris Hall, Cornell University, Ithaca, NY 14853, U.S.A. (during the year 1984–85).

ing (Shepard, 1981, 1982, 1984; also see Clark, 1973): (a) Space is three-dimensional and locally Euclidean and, hence, there are exactly six degrees of freedom of rigid motion of an object relative to the observer or of the observer relative to a surrounding spatial layout (three of translation and three of rotation). (b) Although space itself is otherwise isotropic, the earth's gravitational field determines a locally unique upright direction and, also, a prevailing solid surface that (on a suitable scale) is approximately flat, orthogonal to the local upright direction, and hence bounds the local space of free mobility from 'below'. (c) We ourselves are self-moving solid bodies constrained by gravity to this generally horizontal two-dimensional surface and possessed of a unique top (head) and bottom (feet) defined by our canonical (standing) orientation in the prevailing gravitational field, a unique front and back defined by the orientation of our primary distance receptors and our canonical direction of 'forward' locomotion on this surface, and an approximate bilateral symmetry between our two (left and right) sides.

There is also another, more subtle constraint that will be relevant here and that may also be internalized, though probably not genetically in our species. On the two-dimensional, generally horizontal surface of free mobility, there is a cycle of local directions—including the 90°-separated cardinal points of the compass: north, east, south, west—with a unique orientation that is determined by the continuing regular rotation of the earth (and that may also be determined, for some species, by the prevailing magnetic field induced by this regular rotation—Gould, 1980).

Egocentric, object centered, and environmental frames of reference
With regard to orientation and locomotion on the two-dimensional terrain, one can distinguish three different frames of reference: (a) one's own egocentric frame defined by the directions of up-down, front-back, and left-right with respect to one's own body (disregarding, for present purposes, further distinctions that could be made between frames defined with respect to one's body as a whole, one's head only, or even just one's eyes); (b) an object-centered frame similarly defined with respect to some other person, animal, or object (e.g., vehicle) on the basis of its own intrinsic top and bottom, front and back, and left and right sides; and (c) an environmental frame defined by the directions up-down, north-south, and east-west conferred on a particular location of the surface of the earth by its uniform rotation (with respect to the celestial sphere of 'fixed' stars). Moreover, although all of these three frames, and also the separate opposing directions that are a part of each, can be of critical importance for an individual, they differ widely with respect to their perceptual availability.

The up-down directions are readily accessible for all three frames of reference because these directions ultimately derive from the uniform gravitational field, which directly affects the proprioceptive and, particularly, the vestibular systems; and because the objects of greatest interest have perceptually distinct tops and bottoms (e.g., heads and feet) and are usually oriented in the standard way with respect to gravitationally defined upright. The front-back direction is generally quite salient, too, corresponding as it does, in the egocentric frame, to what can and what cannot be immediately seen and/or approached by natural locomotion, and, in the frames of other bodies, to visually distinct fronts and backs of those objects. Even so, the situation for front and back is more complicated than that for up and down. Because there is no horizontally oriented force field as powerful and invariant as the vertically oriented gravitational field, objects, though usually aligned with each other vertically (with tops above bottoms), are generally not aligned with each other horizontally. Whereas what is up for body A will usually also be up for a neighboring body B, what is in front for body A may just as likely be behind or to the side for body B.

Considerably less accessible is the left-right distinction for which, like the front-back distinction, there is no external field and hence no uniform alignment but for which, unlike the front-back distinction, there is also no salient perceptual difference between the two sides of those many significant objects, including our own bodies, that closely approximate bilateral symmetry. Also relatively inaccessible are the points of the compass. While these may be learned in relation to fixed local landmarks such as bodies of water, mountains, etc., or may be roughly inferred (if proper account is also taken of time of day and of season) from the direction of the sun or shadows, during the day, or of constellations, during the night, the points of the compass are not available to humans in the absence of familiar landmarks, clear sky, and knowledge of time of day and year.

Cognitive primacy of the up-down dimension

These fundamental spatial facts about our world are reflected in the way we perceive and cognitively structure the world and, as linguists (e.g., Fillmore, 1982) and psycholinguists (e.g., Clark, 1973) have pointed out, in the way we talk about the world. Thus, because the up–down dimension is so ubiquitous and salient, we tend to make extensive use of this dimension in structuring our perceptions, our cognitive maps, and our verbal descriptions.

With regard to perception, for example, Rock (1973) has shown that our recognition of what an object is can depend on what we first take to be the top (or bottom) of the object. Moreover, even when the structure of the object strongly determines what is interpreted as its own intrinsic top and bottom, as in the case of the human face (which has a particularly well learned canonical orientation), discrimination may be degraded in perception or memory when the object is presented upside down (Carey, 1981; Hochberg and Galper, 1967; Yin, 1969). Moreover, although people successfully discriminate between enantiomorphic versions of simpler objects (e.g., normal *versus* backward alphanumeric characters) or between subtle perturbations of learned shapes (random polygons), if such an object is presented in an unexpected orientation, people evidently make the discrimination only after either imagining the presented object rotated back into its canonical upright orientation or imagining the canonical upright representation rotated into the orientation of the presented object (Cooper, 1975; Cooper and Podgorny, 1976; Cooper and Shepard, 1973a). Similarly, although one immediately recognizes whether a presented picture is of a human hand and whether it is portrayed with fingers up or down and with back or palm out, if it is not portrayed in its canonical orientation, the discrimination of whether it is a right or a left hand generally requires a mental transformation (Cooper and Shepard, 1975).

Correspondingly, with regard to language, children successfully use terms pertaining to up and down and to front and back long before they master terms pertaining to right and left or to north, south, east, and west. Many otherwise highly intelligent adults continue to confuse the uses of these latter terms. Moreover, terms that ostensibly pertain to differences in vertical position (such as 'up' and 'down') are universally used, as well, to refer to differences in largely horizontal position on the surrounding terrain or on the surface of the earth generally. In some languages, the very grammar requires one to specify, through 'classifiers' or other devices, whether a named object is uphill or downhill from the speaker (e.g., Casad and Langacker, 1982, Reference Note 1; Dixon, 1972).

In English, too, we use 'up' and 'down' not only to specify directions that are almost vertically up or down. We also use the terms when the vertical change in elevation is extremely slight relative to the horizontal distance yielding that change. We also use these same terms when there is no change in literal elevation, as when we use 'up' to refer to a northerly and 'down' to refer to a southerly direction; or, indeed when there is no difference in either elevation or latitude, as when we say "She walked right *up* to me", or "Look who's coming *down* the street". We now consider the possible bases of these extended uses.

Taking the direction of a significant reference object as 'up'

As Clark (1973) has noted, because things that are above the ground plane are more accessible to us than things that are below, the upward direction cognitively dominates the downward direction and, correspondingly, is the linguistically unmarked direction, with many linguistic consequences. For example, the questions "How tall is John?" or "How high is the airplane?" are neutral in the sense that they can be asked without implying that we think that John is tall or that the airplane is high; whereas we would not ask the corresponding questions "How short is John?" or "How low is the airplane?" unless we already had reason to believe that John was unusually short or the airplane especially low.

Similarly, because things that are close to us in space and time are more accessible than things that are remote, 'far' is marked relative to 'near', 'there' is marked relative to 'here', 'then' is marked relative to 'now', and so on. There is, further, a general tendency to treat the marked poles of all such dimensions in one way and the unmarked poles in another. Indeed, this has been taken to account, in part, for the extension of spatial terms into temporal and other domains (e.g., see Jackendoff, 1983; Lakoff and Johnson, 1980; Talmy, 1983).

In this way, the unmarked direction *up* would tend to be metaphorically applied to any direction toward the here, the now, and, also, toward any other significant person, object, or location taken as the focus of our attention. Thus we speak of something "lasting *up* to now", and then "going *down* in history". Likewise, when we say "She walked right *up* to me", or "... *up* to the professor", we choose the unmarked 'up' because it corresponds to the unmarked 'near' in relation to the significant reference point (the speaker or the professor)—not because we wish to convey that the floor or ground literally sloped upward toward that person.

Taking the direction north as 'up'
Somewhat related considerations may explain why 'up' has also come to mean 'north' and, equivalently, why maps are now conventionally oriented with north at the top. Early maps were not consistently oriented in this way. Nevertheless, in agreement with the already noted tendency to regard the direction toward the most significant reference object as up, they were generally oriented so that the upward direction in the map pointed toward some culturally significant or perceptually salient location (e.g., Mecca, Jerusalem, or the eastward point at which the sun was seen to rise). Later, with the growing importance of global navigation, the invention of the magnetic compass, and the realization that the earth was spherical, the unique poles conferred by the earth's rotation became more appropriate, accessible, and invariant reference points. Moreover, to the extent that global navigators and map makers were predominantly from the northern hemisphere, the association between spatial proximity and absence of linguistic marking would favor

the north pole over the south pole as the reference point for 'up'. (For residents of the northern hemisphere, the equatorial line might even play a conceptual role that is analogous to the ground plane in ordinary three-dimensional space.)

Taking the direction ahead as 'up'

We have noted that 'here' and 'up' are both unmarked and, correspondingly, that the direction toward a significant referent object is generally taken as up. From these facts we might expect that on level terrain and in the local egocentric frame, the direction towards oneself (taken as the principal reference point) would also be regarded as 'up'—as it evidently is when we say "She walked right up to me". Yet in indicating someone who is approaching, we also say "Look who's coming *down* the street". We now outline an explanation that one of us (R.N.S.) has proposed for this apparent anomaly.

Because our standard viewpoint is somewhat elevated above the generally horizontal surface of the ground, two points (A and B) on a path leading away in front of us project onto an intervening vertical plane with the farther point, B, *above* the nearer point, A, as illustrated in Fig. 1 by the projections (A' and B'). Correspondingly, in visually fixating and/or pointing first to A and then to B on the horizontal path ahead, we must move our eyes and/or arm upward, as indicated by the dashed lines of sight and of pointing. Thus there is, from a viewer's perspective, a natural correspondence between the forward direction in the horizontal plane, which is orthogonal to gravitationally defined upright, and the upward direction aligned with that upright.

We suggest that it is this correspondence, which is ultimately determined by gravitation and by geometrical optics, that explains why we tend to say "Look who's coming *down* the street", and to do so even when the street appears perfectly level and we have, at the moment, no idea which direction is north. Because, if we were to direct our eyes or finger toward the moving point where the approaching figure is at each moment in contact with the ground, we would in fact successively move our gaze or our finger further and further down. And gravity, once again, determines that the point of contact with the ground provides the best indicator of an object's location—with consequences that are both perceptual (Gibson, 1950, 1979; Sedgwick, 1980) and linguistic (Herskovits, 1983, Reference Note 2). The same consideration undoubtedly explains why in American Sign Language (ASL), an interlocutor points higher (and/or looks higher) to indicate a more distant location and even, by metaphorical extension, a more distant time or a more remote goal (Richard Meier, Elissa Newport and Ted Supalla, personal communications, March 1984).

The natural correspondence illustrated in Fig. 1 makes clear why people,

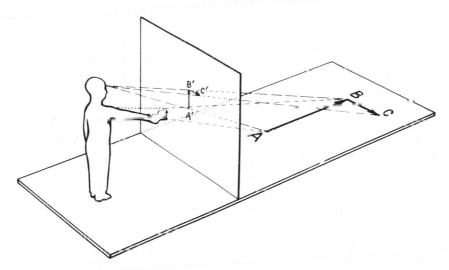

Figure 1.   *A schematic illustration that a point* B *that is further ahead of another point*
A on the horizontal ground is also 'higher' than that point A *from the*
perspective of the canonically above-the-ground viewer. Also illustrated is
the related fact that a right turn (toward a point C) *projects to the right from*
the 'top' of the line leading into that turn within the viewer's egocentric
frame of reference.

in reading vertically held maps, often prefer to rotate the map so that the
upward direction in the map, instead of corresponding to the northward
direction, corresponds to their own forward direction in the environment;
and why, as Tversky (1981, p. 422) has shown, they also tend to draw maps
in this way. For example, and of relevance to the experiments to be described
in a later section, there is then a direct agreement between a turn to the right,
e.g., from *B* to *C*, and the representation of such a turn on the frontal plane,
e.g., from *B'* to *C'*. The high cognitive cost of departure from this preferred
alignment has been strikingly documented by Levine and his co-workers in
their field studies of the use of "you-are-here" maps in shopping malls, university campuses, hospitals, and the like (Levine, 1981; Levine *et al.*, 1982).
They found that when the you-are-here map had the preferred alignment
(indicated in Fig. 1), people who consulted the map were usually successful
in finding their way directly to their destination; but when the you-are-here
map was inverted (as such maps are, with surprising frequency, according to
Levine's (1981) survey), people who consulted the map went off in directions
that were wrong by at least 90° more than 25% of the time.

One can also understand why arrows placed along roads and highways point upward (in the U.S., anyway) to indicate straight ahead. (Less sensible, are markings painted on the road, which are usually placed in the order in which one would pass over them in a vehicle—with the consequence that when, in accordance with Fig. 1, they are read by an approaching driver in the standard top-to-bottom order, they have to be processed in the anomalous reversed order, e.g., "TURN/RIGHT/NO".) Indeed, Fig. 1 may even explain why the canonical portrayal of the human hand is, according to Cooper and Shepard (1975), with the fingers pointing up. Although one may not usually hold one's hand in this vertical position, when one looks at one's hand the fingers will generally be pointing away and, hence, will correspond to a projection on the vertical plane in which the fingers point up.

Summary of what's up in spatial cognition
We seem to have something of a hierarchy of increasingly extended uses of the concept of an upward direction (and of its corresponding term 'up') to apply to essentially horizontal directions. First, the concept was originally based, we presume, on the unique, gravitationally conferred upright direction that has prevailed over the entire surface of the earth throughout biological evolution. Second, because we are, however, constrained by gravity to move on that two-dimensional, roughly orthogonal surface and because even a very slight upward inclination of the local terrain is perceptually more accessible to us than the points of the compass, the concept 'up' was naturally extended to refer to any uphill direction of this terrain. Thus, when the ground possesses a just-perceptible upward slope, the term 'up' in this secondary sense could be consistently used to refer to a direction that is almost orthogonal to the direction specified by 'up' in the original, primary sense. Third, the notion of an uphill direction was metaphorically extended to refer to the direction towards a significant reference object or location, even when there was no literal slope to the terrain. Fourth, as a globally defined reference frame became important (for more wide ranging navigation), 'up' was further extended to refer to the direction toward the closest invariant point conferred by the earth's rotation, namely, the north pole, quite independently of the local pitch of the terrain. And fifth, by the argument given in connection with Fig. 1, 'up' had probably long before been extended, also, to refer to the direction ahead with respect to one's momentary egocentric frame, without regard to the points of the compass and even when the terrain had no perceptible slope.[1]

---

[1]These last two extensions are also subject to conflation. In an early study of cognitive maps, Trowbridge (1913, p. 822) found that it is not uncommon for people to "imagine north as directly in front of them."

Except for the third and most metaphorical use of 'up', all of these uses help us to find our way or to communicate about the physical environment. However, they do this by expressing directions determined by features of that environment and our relation to it that differ in availability or importance to us in different circumstances. The first expresses a direction in three-dimensional space that is ultimately determined only by the local gravitational field. The second expresses a direction on the two-dimensional terrain that is determined by the local slope of that terrain (relative to that field). The fourth expresses a direction that is determined by the global frame conferred by the earth's rotation. And the fifth expresses a direction that is determined by the individual's momentary egocentric frame. In any one case, these four senses of 'up', though all ultimately deriving from the first and most literal sense, could all specify entirely different directions.

Incidentally, these 'cognitive' extensions of the concept of the vertical direction to refer to horizontal directions are not confined to humans, or even to vertebrates. According to von Frisch's celebrated discovery, the returned honey bee communicates the horizontal direction of a source of nectar to its hivemates by a 'dance' in which angular deviation from gravitationally determined upright, on a vertical sheet of comb within the hive, represents angular deviation from the sun's azimuth, on the horizontal terrain outside (see Dyer and Gould, 1983; von Frisch, 1967).

Mental rotations with respect to different frames of reference

In a simpler universe with only one natural frame of reference (e.g., one's own egocentric frame), one might have no need to imagine rotations in space. Our world, however, is greatly complicated by the existence of the many different natural frames of reference that, moreover, are subject to continuous spatial transformations with respect to each other. Thus, as two individuals *A* and *B* independently move about on their common terrain, *C*, the relations between the principal directions of each frame constantly change. Although the direction *up* in its primary sense, typically remains in alignment between all three frames, what is *right* for *A* may become *left* for *B* and may assume any angular relation to the *north* that is fixed by *C*. Mental rotation may well facilitate our anticipation, planning, and communication of events in such a world.

Indeed, the 'canonical encounter' between two persons (Clark, 1973) is face to face, for which left and right directions and forward and backward directions are both relatively reversed. Consequently, If *A* attempts, for example, to inform *B* as to which side *B*'s face has egg on it, *A* can mentally perform the 180° transformation that carries *A*'s egocentric frame into *B*'s and, from this modified perspective, cast the news in a form that is directly interpretable by *B*, in terms of *B*'s own egocentric frame. Alternatively, if *A* takes the easier course of formulating the disclosure in terms of *A*'s frame only, *B* must then perform the required 180° mental transformation in order to achieve a correct interpretation of the communication.

Related considerations provide an answer to the otherwise puzzling question of why mirrors seem to reverse left and right but not up and down (see Gardner, 1959, pp. 162–173). In fact, mirrors reverse neither left and right nor up and down: they reverse front and back. Relative to one's own egocentric frame, one's image in the mirror still has one's right hand on one's right and one's left hand on one's left, just as it has one's head at the top and feet at the bottom. However, the reflection has reversed the direction of facing so that one and one's image do not face in the same direction but oppositely— that is, toward each other. Because the body is approximately bilaterally symmetric, one tends to reinterpret this reflection through a plane in space—a transformation that is impossible for an actual three-dimensional body[2]—as a different, physically realizable transformation, namely a 180° rotation about a vertical axis. In other words, the image of one's right hand in the mirror is still a right hand; but one reinterprets it as the left hand of the image because one is used to allowing for a 180° rotation in relating one's egocentric frame to the egocentric frame of another with whom one is in the canonical face-to-face encounter. However, if we were not approximately bilaterally symmetric, we could not make this rotational interpretation and hence we would be forced to recognize that the reflected image is indeed a reflection in space and not a rotation.

Imagining the rotation of an object or of a frame of reference

Experimental studies of mental rotation have led to an as yet incompletely resolved theoretical issue concerning the different kinds of mental rotation that might mediate between the frames defined with respect to the self, with respect to an independently movable object, and with respect to the surrounding environment. Most of the early experiments on mental rotation required participants to compare the shape of localized external objects pre-

---

[2]Strictly, we mean "impossible within our local neighborhood of the universe". For our purposes, we can disregard the theoretical possibility that in its large-scale topological structure, the universe may be a non-orientable manifold, in which case a person who 'circumnavigated' the universe could return spatially reflected (just as a 'p' that is slid around a Möbius strip can return as a 'q'). Those of us who remained on earth would be inclined to say that the voyager had changed, say, from a right-handed into a left-handed person, but the voyager, feeling unchanged, would claim, rather, that during the trip everything back on earth must miraculously have undergone a mirror reversal.

sented in different orientations relative to each other (Shepard and Metzler, 1971) or to their own canonical orientation (Cooper, 1975; Cooper and Shepard, 1973b). Since the egocentric frame was aligned with the fixed environmental frame, participants generally imagined a rotation of the localized objects relative to that fixed environmental or, equivalently, egocentric frame. When Cooper and Shepard (1973) then provided advance information as to the orientation of an ensuing test stimulus, they found chronometric evidence for a preparatory mental rotation only if they also provided advance information as to the identity of that ensuing stimulus. Evidently the participants prepared for a specified visual shape in a specified orientation by imagining that shape rotated into that orientation, but found it difficult to prepare for an unknown shape in a specified orientation by mentally rotating an 'abstract frame of reference' with respect to which they might then immediately interpret the test stimulus when it appeared.

This finding that the imagination of a rotation in advance is more successful when it is the rotation of a specific object rather than merely an interpretive frame has been corroborated by several subsequent studies (e.g., Hintzman *et al.*, 1981; Koriat and Norman, In Press; also see Rock, 1973). True, Hinton and Parsons (1981) have devised conditions under which people evidently are able to prepare for the presentation of an incompletely specified object in a specified orientation. However people appear to do this most successfully when they have some advance information about the shape of that object and, hence, may be able to imagine the rotation of an at least partial or schematic shape. Although one may be able to imagine the rotation of an abstract frame of reference, one may not be able to preserve the intrinsic 'handedness' of the frame needed to discriminate enantiomorphic (i.e., mirror-image) objects (see Hinton and Parsons, 1981).

In any case, there are now many studies that agree in indicating that the different frames of reference— egocentric, object-centered, and environmental—are not equivalent with respect to mental rotation (e.g., Hintzman *et al.*, 1981; Huttenlocher and Presson, 1973; Presson, 1982; also see Corballis, 1982; Corballis *et al.*, 1978; Corballis *et al.*, 1976). Although the change in relation between an observer and a localized external object will be the same whether the object rotates with respect to the observer or the observer moves around the object, the two transformations differ with respect to the environmental frame. In the former case, only, the observer's egocentric frame remains fixed with respect to the environmental frame.

There is considerable evidence that animals, generally, tend to orient with respect to the environmental frame (e.g., Dyer and Gould, 1983; Emlen, 1975; Gallistel, 1980; Hölldobler, 1980; Maier, 1929; Sauer, 1958; Tolman, 1948; Tolman *et al.*, 1946; von Frisch, 1967; and, in the case of humans,

Lynch, 1960) and there is a clear adaptive utility of such a strategy. It is not surprising, therefore, that there is also evidence that we more readily imagine the change that would result from the rotation of a localized external object while we remain fixed with respect to the environment than we imagine the more radical change in our total experience that would result from our own motion about that object, which also changes the orientational relation between us and the surrounding world (Huttenlocher and Presson, 1973; Presson, 1982). Similar considerations may explain why advance mental rotation may be more successful in preparing for a holistic visual match than in orienting with respect to a cognitive map or a spatial surround (Hintzman et al., 1981).

We now turn to a report of some experiments that we have carried out in an attempt to explore, more specifically, the relation between mental rotation of the sort originally investigated, particularly, by Cooper and Shepard (1973a) and the interpretation of maps, which, as Hochberg and Gellman (1977) have noted, may also require mental rotation. These experiments provide evidence concerning the (a) close cognitive connection posited (on the basis of the relations illustrated in Fig. 1) between the directions upward and straight ahead, (b) general theoretical problem of how we compensate for changes between the different frames of reference we have been discussing here, and (c) practical problems of interpreting maps including, specifically, the you-are-here maps investigated by Levine et al. (1982).

Two experiments on mental rotation in the interpretation of left and right turns in maps[3]

In accordance with expectations based on the relations illustrated in Fig. 1 and with the empirical results of Levine et al. (1982), people generally report that it is easier to interpret a turn as a right or a left turn when the road that leads into that turn has been heading upward on the map (i.e., northward, if the map is itself oriented in the conventional way). Under this condition a turn that goes to the right on the map is a right turn and a turn that goes to the left is a left turn. When a road is being traced in a downward direction on the map, these relations are reversed. Many people then find it easier to turn the map upside down in order to restore the simpler relations (even though this entails an inversion of words and numbers printed on the map).

―――――――
[3]These experiments, completed during the year 1979-80 while S.H. was a research assistant with the first author, were supported by NSF grant BNS 75-02806. We thank Peter Smith for his help in implementing the computer-controlled graphical display.

People who, instead, prefer to leave the map in its conventional upright orientation must use mental operations to compensate for large departures from the canonical upward approach to each turn. If the direction is nearly 180° from the canonical (i.e., if it is nearly straight downward) or if the direction is more or less downward and, in addition, the turn is close to 90°, then a simple strategy of reversal of interpretation will suffice: if the turn goes to the right, it is a left turn; if it goes to the left, it is a right turn. (Such a strategy has a precedent in the already-noted reversal of interpretation that we use in communicating about left and right with someone with whom we are in the canonical encounter.) For arbitrary directions of approach to the turn and for arbitrary angles of the turn itself, however, this strategy of reversal of interpretation often yields incorrect results.

Strategies using mental rotation could yield more reliable results. To imagine the entire map rotated at each turn to keep the path leading into each new turn upright in the mental representation would generally exceed the capabilities of visual memory. However, there are several other, more reasonable possibilities: (a) Map readers might imagine each successive turn (i.e., visually presented pattern of two lines meeting at a certain angle) separately rotated from its given orientation into the preferred canonical orientation, in which the line going into the turn is upright, and determine whether the line going out is then properly to the right or left. (b) They might imagine a schematic representation of a canonical right turn (say), that is either visual (e.g., a shape resembling a capital Greek gamma) or kinesthetic (e.g., a representation of themselves, with attention focused on their right hand) rotated, for each new turn, from upright into the orientation of that visually presented turn; and they might then test for a match or mismatch. (c) Or, in order to test for this match or a mismatch, they might imagine such a schema (whether visual or kinesthetic) rotated into the orientation of each new turn, but starting each time from the orientation of the last turn rather from canonical upright.

In the first two strategies (a and b), the time to classify each turn as right or left should increase monotonically with the angular departure from upright of the line leading into that turn—just as the time to classify an alphanumeric character as normal or reversed was found to increase monotonically with its angular departure from upright (Cooper and Shepard, 1973a, 1973b, 1978; Shepard and Cooper, 1982). Indeed, in the visual variant of this strategy, the discrimination between a left and a right turn would be essentially the discrimination between a normal and backward 'L' (when the letter is presented upside down). Either of these first two strategies should permit a correct classification of all possible turns. However, these strategies would be relatively inefficient for interpreting the successive turns in a generally downward (i.e., southerly) route because the rotations, all being relative to upright, would mostly be large (e.g., greater than 90°). For generally downward paths, the second strategy, if it tended to be used in preference to the first, would therefore presumably tend to go over into the third.

In the third strategy (c), in which the reorientation at each turn is from the previous orientation rather than from upright, the time to classify each turn should depend on the angular size of the preceding turn and not on the absolute orientation of the line leading into the new turn. If adopted, such a strategy should be more efficient in following a downward path because most of the rotations would be smaller (e.g., less than 90°). However, the previous results by Cooper and Shepard (1973a), Hintzman *et al.* (1981), Huttenlocher and Presson (1973), Koriat and Norman (In press), and Presson (1982) raise the question of how readily people will adopt this third type of rotational strategy. Accordingly, we carried out two experiments designed to provide further information concerning the strategies actually adopted by people who attempt to interpret a turn (on a vertically oriented display) as a right or left turn, when the line leading into the turn has an arbitrary orientation.

Experiment 1 (separated-trials task)

The three conditions in the experiment now to be described are alike in that a directed line was presented in some orientation, a shorter line segment was then added to the end of that line at some angular deviation from it and at some delay after its onset, and the time was recorded that the participant took to classify the bend formed by the addition of the shorter line as a right or a left turn from the path represented by the longer line. By presenting the longer line in advance on some trials, we provided an opportunity for participants to carry out preparatory rotation of whatever frame of reference they might use before they saw the particular turn to be classified as right or left. The instructions and other details were varied between conditions, however, so that the first condition was most like mentally orienting with respect to a map, the third was most like preparing for a rotated visual object (in the case of a 90° turn, like preparing for a rotated standard or reflected letter 'L'), and the second was intermediate. We hoped in this way to obtain some clarification of the relation between mental rotation of the sort studied by Cooper and Shepard (1973a, b) and the mental operations carried out in the interpretation of turns in disoriented maps and, in particular, to learn more about which of the alternative rotational strategies tends to be adopted in the two types of tasks.

Method

Participants
Each of 39 college students participated in a 50-minute session in one of the three successively devised experiments—referred to hereafter as 'conditions'. In Condition 1 there were 15 participants (4 female and 11 male, 13 right- and one left-handed). In Condition 2 there were 13 participants (7 female and 6 male, 9 right- and 4 left-handed). And in Condition 3 there were 12 participants (8 female and 4 male, all right-handed).

Stimuli
Each stimulus consisted of an angular bend formed by the junction, in the center of a CRT display screen, of a short straight line segment added to the end of a long straight line segment already positioned in some orientation on the screen. The added short segment was to be interpreted, as in reading a map, as a right or left turn for a traveler regarded as moving along the long segment toward the junction with the short segment. Although the turn was always positioned at the center of the screen, a small circle was attached at the other, more peripheral end of the long segment as a visible indication of the traveler's supposed point of origin. This long line could appear in any of 12 orientations coming from points of origin spaced in equal 30° steps in a circle around the perimeter of the screen.

The short line was constructed to form a turn (i.e., an angular deviation from a straight continuation) of 30, 60, 90, 120, or 150° in either direction, in Conditions 1 and 2, or of just 90° in either direction, in Condition 3. (Cases of 0° and 180°, which would be indeterminate as to left or right, were excluded in all conditions.) The presentation of the short line was delayed following the presentation of the long line by either 0, 100, 400, 700 or 1000 msec, which are the delays used by Cooper and Shepard (1973a) in their study of the effects of advance orientation information on the time to discriminate normal from reversed alphanumeric characters in various orientations. In addition, Condition 3 also included an even longer, 1600 msec delay.

In the dimly lit experimental room, the segments appeared as luminous green lines on the face of a 13 by 10 cm Tektronix 604 CRT display with P31 phosphor, under the real-time control of a Data General Corporation Nova 820 computer. The long and short lines were 3.8 and 1.9 cm in length, respectively, and, at the viewing distance of about 45 cm, subtended visual angles of approximately 4.8 and 2.4°.

Procedure
Following a two-second warning dot in the center of the display screen and

an ensuing half-second blank screen at the beginning of each trial, the two-line stimulus for that trial appeared in some orientation and, usually, with some delay of the shorter segment. The two-line pattern remained on until the participant responded by operating a right-hand or left-hand switch to indicate whether the short segment corresponded, respectively, to a right or a left turn from the path represented by the long segment. The reaction time was measured from the onset of the added short segment.

All experimental sessions began with instructions and practice until the participant felt fully ready to proceed with the task, as defined for that condition. The instructions were successively modified in the three conditions in order to provide increasing encouragement to form an appropriately oriented mental image in advance of the onset of the short line and, hence, to be able to respond as efficiently as possible to stimuli that were not in the canonical 'upright' orientation (the orientation in which a short line to the right is sufficient to signify a right turn). Feedback was not provided as to the correctness of individual responses.

Condition 1.   The participants in the first condition were merely told (a) to look at the dot when it appeared in the center of the screen, (b) to consider the long line, when it appeared, as representing a path of travel from the point of origin (represented by the small circle on the periphery) toward the center of the screen, and (c) to operate the right or left switch as quickly and accurately as possible, when the short line appeared, to indicate whether the turn from the long line onto that short line represented a right or left turn. The participants were not given advance information about which of the orientations, angular deviations, or delays would be presented on any given trial. Nor were any suggestions made as to strategies or imagery that might be used to prepare for each upcoming test stimulus. Each session consisted of five blocks of 100 trials within which the orientation of the long line, the angle of the turn, and the delay of the short line were chosen at random (with replacement).

Condition 2.   In order to encourage the participants to prepare, during the delay, for the classification of the upcoming turn in the indicated orientation, the trials in the second condition were blocked by delay. The prevailing length of delay was announced at the beginning of each block and participants were urged to take maximum advantage of the advance information provided by the long line before the short line appeared. Otherwise, the instructions were as in Condition 1. In particular, there was again no explicit suggestion to use visual imagery. This time there were 25 blocks of 20 trials each. Within each block, the orientation of the long line and the angular deviation of the short line from it were randomly chosen; but the delay of the short line, announced to the participant at the beginning of the block, remained constant throughout that block.

Condition 3.   In order to encourage the use of concrete visual imagery in preparing for the appearance of the short line, several further modifications were made in the third condition: (a) The angle of the bend was confined to 90° (right or left turn), so that the task became very much like one of discriminating a normal from a backward 'L'—much as in the experiments by Cooper and Shepard (1973a, b). (b) Right turns were presented twice as often as left turns, so that as soon as the long segment appeared, participants would be motivated to anticipate and hence to form a concrete visual image of the visual shape corresponding specifically to a right turn (*viz.*, a backward L-shape in the appropriately rotated orientation). (c) The instructions given in Condition 2 were supplemented with the specific suggestion that participants first imagine a canonical right turn (with the long line vertical and the short segment going off at 90° to the right from the top, as in the capital Greek gamma) rotated into the orientation indicated by the presented long line, and that they then check for a match of this rotated image against the pattern formed by the onset of the short line. (d) A longer, 1600 msec delay was added to make sure that participants would have sufficient time to prepare in this way. There were 24 blocks of 20 trials with, again, the delay of the short line constant throughout each block.

Results

Of principal interest here is the way in which the time to classify a visually presented turn as a right or a left turn depended, jointly, on the orientation of the line leading into the turn (the longer line) and the delay of presentation of the line leading out of the turn (the shorter line). As in the earlier experiments by Cooper and Shepard (1973a, b) on discrimination of normal and reversed alphanumeric characters, orientation was important only with respect to its absolute magnitude (not its direction) of departure from vertical; reaction times for clockwise and counterclockwise departures of the same angular magnitude (up to 180°) were not reliably different and so are averaged together in the analyses and summary plots presented here. Further, since the effect of the absolute magnitude of the angular deviation of the short from the long line (a magnitude that varied between 30° and 150° in Conditions 1 and 2) was negligible and not of theoretical interest here, reaction times for all angles of turn are also averaged together. Finally, the plots and analyses presented here are for reaction times for correct responses only. (Error rates for individual participants in the three conditions were comparable to those reported for individuals by Cooper and Shepard (1973a)—*viz.*, between 4% and 8%.)

Panels A, B, and C of Fig. 2 present the principal chronometric results for Conditions 1, 2, and 3, respectively; while, for purposes of comparison, Panel D summarizes the corresponding results from the earlier experiment by Cooper and Shepard (1973a). Each of the plotted curves shows how reaction time increased with angular departure of the principal axis (or longer line) of the test pattern in either direction from upright, for a particular delay between the presentation of the orientation cue and the presentation of the rest of the pattern (or shorter line). Right and left responses are averaged together in these curves. However, in agreement with the results of Cooper and Shepard (1973a, b), when participants were specifically instructed to prepare for the appearance of a right turn and when right turns were in fact presented twice as often as left turns (Condition 3), reaction times averaged approximately 100 msec shorter for right than for left turns, though the reaction-time curves appeared indistinguishable in shape for the two types of turns. (The averages plotted for Condition 3 include twice as many responses to right, as opposed to left, turns.)

As in the experiment by Cooper and Shepard (1973a), in all three of the present conditions reaction time increased with departure from upright and decreased with the delay of the completion of the pattern following the advance information as to orientation (provided, here, by the longer line). Also as in that earlier experiment, statistical analysis revealed a significant curvilinearity of the dependence on angle of departure. As can be seen in Fig. 2, reaction times generally increased more sharply as departure from upright approached 180°. (For discussions of some possible interpretations of this kind of departure from linearity, see Cooper and Shepard, 1973a; Hock and Tromley, 1978; Shepard and Cooper, 1982.)

In addition, an interaction between the effects of orientation and delay becomes increasingly evident as we move through the three successive conditions, 1, 2, and 3. For Condition 1, the separate curves, though differing in height, are roughly parallel. For Condition 3, the reaction-time curves become flatter (as well as lower) as the onset of the shorter line segment is increasingly delayed. And for the intermediate Condition 2, the curves are lower than for Condition 1, and the curve for the longest delay of the shorter line (1000 msec) appears somewhat flatter than the other curves (and was clearly flatter for some individual participants) though it still exhibits an appreciable upswing near 180°. Only when the participants were explicitly instructed to use the delay to prepare for the ensuing short segment by forming a properly oriented visual image (Condition 3) did the reaction-time curves clearly exhibited the kind of flattening with delay that is so evident in the results of Cooper and Shepard (1973a, b) on discrimination of rotated alphanumeric characters (cf., Panel D in Fig. 2).

Separate analyses of variance of the reaction times for the three conditions provided quantitative support for these qualitative characterizations of the results. The main effects of orientation and delay were highly significant in all three conditions ($p < 0.0001$ in all six cases), while the interaction between these two factors (manifested in the flattening of the dependence on orientation for longer delays) was nonsignificant for Condition 1 ($p = 0.5$), marginally significant for Condition 2 ($p < 0.03$), and highly significant for Condition 3 ($p < 0.0001$). Examination of the curves corresponding to the average curves displayed in Fig. 2, plotted separately for the individual participants (but too numerous to reproduce here), further corroborated these conclusions. Most pertinently, for every one of the 12 participants in Condition 3 the fitted linear slope of the reaction-time curves was less for the long delays (e.g., 1000 and 1600 msec) than for the short delays (e.g., 0 and 100 msec). Indeed, for half of the participants the long-delay curves appeared nearly flat (slopes less than 0.40 msec/degree)—though not quite as flat as in the earlier experiment by Cooper and Shepard. (For comparison, the corresponding linear slope coefficient estimated for the 1000 msec, bottom curve in Panel D of Fig. 2 is 0.23 msec/degree).

Discussion

In discriminating right and left turns in the simplified map-like displays used here, reaction time consistently increased with the departure of the display from the canonical one in which the line interpreted as leading into the turn is upright. This finding, in all three conditions, indicates that people are initially set to interpret turns only when they appear in this unique, canonical orientation and that they have to carry out an additional mental operation to compensate for appreciable departures from that preferred orientation. As Cooper and Shepard (1973a, 1973b) argued on the basis of their similar findings concerning the discrimination of disoriented alphanumeric characters, this additional mental operation seems to be one of 'mental rotation' (also see Metzler and Shepard, 1974, pp. 190–192).[4]

---

[4]The rates of mental rotation, estimated from the reciprocal of the slopes of the reaction-time functions obtained here, fall roughly between 600 and 700 deg/sec. These are comparable but somewhat higher than the 480 deg/sec average rates implied by Cooper and Shepard's (1973a) data for the mental rotation of alphanumeric characters and the 400–700 deg/sec rates implied by Cooper's (1975) data for the mental rotation of two-dimensional shapes by highly practiced participants.

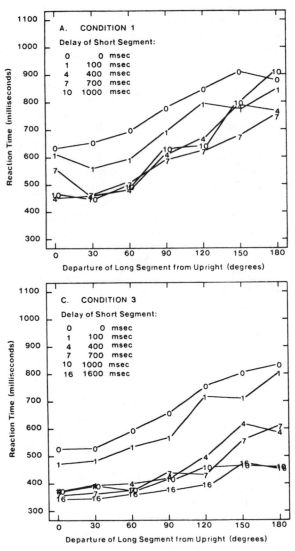

Figure 2.   *Chronometric results of Experiment 1. Reaction time to classify a two-line pattern as a right or a left turn is plotted as a function of the angular departure from upright (in either direction) of the line leading into the turn. The separate curves are for different delays of the addition of the second line. Panels A, B, and C present the results for Conditions 1, 2, and 3,*

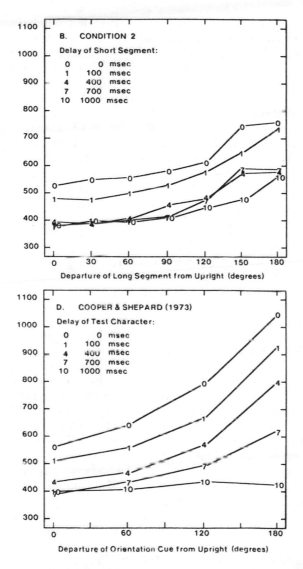

respectively. Panel D presents, for comparison, the earlier results of Cooper and Shepard (1973a) on discrimination of normal and reversed alphanumeric characters presented in various angular departures from upright and after various delays following advance information as to orientation.

What, however, happens when readers of a disoriented map have advance information as to the angle of its disorientation? Can such readers imagine themselves, and hence their egocentric frame, rotated in advance of the visual presentation of the test map and, thus, be able to respond to that ensuing map about as quickly as if both they and the map were in the canonical upright orientation? Cooper and Shepard (1973) found that advance information as to the orientation of a to-be-presented alphanumeric test character flattened the function relating reaction time to angle of disorientation only when advance information was also provided as to the specific identity of that ensuing character. Whereas the participants in Cooper and Shepard's experiment readily imagined a prespecified character rotated into any designated orientation, they were not successful in mentally reorienting their egocentric frame of reference in order to prepare for an unspecified character.

The present results lend themselves to a similar interpretation. When the participants were specifically instructed to form a visual image of a 90° right turn in the appropriately rotated orientation in advance (Condition 3) and were given enough time to carry out the required mental rotation (1000 msec or more), reaction time to the rotated test stimulus became short (about 400 msec) for all such predesignated orientations—much as in the experiment by Cooper and Shepard. True, the overall level of the reaction times was decreased at all orientations by advance orientation information in all three conditions. However, as Cooper and Shepard (1973a) argued, the lack of dependence of this roughly 150 msec decrease on orientation implies that this decrease is the time to interpret the advance orientation information and not the time to carry out the mental rotation called for by that orientation information. So, although people evidently can prepare for the dicriminative interpretation of right and left turns in a disoriented map by carrying out a mental rotation in advance, unless the conditions of presentation and motivation strongly favor such advance preparation, people evidently tend to wait until the map is visually before them to carry out any necessary mental operations—including mental rotations. As in the experiments reported by Cooper and Shepard (1973a), Hintzman et al. (1981), Huttenlocher and Presson (1973), Koriat and Norman (In press), and Presson (1982), the present results suggest that people do not find it easy to prepare for a rotated visual pattern by imagining their own egocentric frame of reference rotated into that orientation.

Incidentally, relative to the curves obtained by Cooper and Shepard (Fig. 1D), the curves obtained here show some tendency to decrease in slope in the immediate vicinity of 180°. Possibly, in the particular case of the L-shaped test patterns participants were able to take more advantage of the different strategy (mentioned before) in which, for completely inverted test patterns, they would simply give the response opposite to the absolute right-left direction of the short segment. Hintzman *et al.* (1981, p. 157) proposed a similar explanation for an even more extreme reduction in reaction times that they obtained near 180° (cf. also, Metzler and Shepard, 1974, pp. 162–163).

Experiment 2 (continuous map-reading task)

A continuous, steady-state task was devised for Experiment 2 that provided for a more direct test of the relative importance of departure from upright and departure from the orientation of the preceding turn. Although more complex than the separated-trials task used in Experiment 1, the continuous task of Experiment 2 is also more like actual map reading. On a CRT screen, new straight segments of a randomly bending path were added, one by one, and participants indicated, as quickly as possible, whether each new segment turned left or right from the preceding segment. As each new segment was added, all previous segments were reduced in brightness in such a way that only the last three segments were visible at any one time.

Two variables are of particular interest: the absolute orientation of the segment that leads into the newly added turn; and the angular size of the previous turn (see Fig. 3). The results of Experiment 1 suggest that the time to classify the new turn should increase markedly as the segment leading into that turn departs from upright. Suppose, however, that the participants were

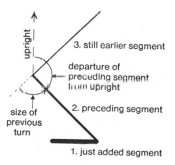

Figure 3.   *An illustrative example, from Experiment 2, of a CRT-displayed path of three successive line segments (the solid straight lines, 1, 2, 3), each of which has decreased in intensity as the next was added. Marked on this example are the two important orientational parameters of the middle segment: its absolute departure from upright, and the size of its turn from the still earlier segment.*

to prepare in advance for the interpretation of each new turn by imagining themselves reoriented along the preceding segment. Reaction times should then depend more on the angular difference between the orientation of the preceding segment and the orientation of the still earlier segment (i.e., on the size of the turn by which they must reorient themselves) than on the absolute orientation of the preceding segment (i.e., on its angular departure from upright). Although the results obtained in our Experiment 1 and in the earlier experiment by Cooper and Shepard (1973a) suggest that people do not tend to carry out advance mental reorientations of this kind, the possibility remains that they might do so in the present route-following task.

Method

Participants
Fourteen of the 15 participants in Condition 1 of Experiment 1, also participated in what we here refer to as Experiment 2. Each of the two possible orders of these two experiments was administered to each of two random halves of this set of 14 participants.

Stimuli
In the continuous map-reading task, the discriminative response to each newly added line segment as a right or left turn brought on the next segment or 'turn' in the same computer-driven CRT display used in Experiment 1. The successively added segments were chosen at random with angles of deviation from a straight continuation, called 'turn angles', of 45°, 90°, or 135° in either direction and with lengths of 2.2 or 1.1 cm (corresponding to visual angles of about 2.8 and 1.4°, respectively). All combinations of angle and length were equiprobable (with, again, 0° and 180° turns omitted).

In order to prevent the display from becoming too cluttered, only the last three segments were retained at any one time. Indeed, each segment was decreased in brightness (in the ratios 10:5:1) as its status changed from newest to middle and, again, from middle to oldest, and then faded away completely with the next addition (as illustrated in Fig. 3, for a particular sequence of three segments). And in order to ensure that the randomly added segments would not wander off the display screen, the entire three-line display was subjected to a continuous slow rigid drift in the direction that would bring the free end of the most recently added segment back towards the center of the screen. The rate of rigid drift of the whole configuration was proportional to the momentary distance of the free end from that center.

Procedure

We instructed participants to imagine travelling along the growing path in the direction from the dimmest and oldest to the brightest and most recently added line segment. As each new segment was added, they were to operate a right or left switch as soon as they could accurately classify the turn into that newest segment as a right or a left turn, respectively. Each successive reaction time was measured from the onset of the most recently added segment, and each response triggered the immediate presentation of the next segment. Each participant went through five series of 100 continuous trials of this type. The entire session of five series was generally completed in about 15 minutes.

Results

The individual reaction times in this steady-state map reading task could be related to a large number of independent variables—including, for each response, the length and direction of each of the three visible segments, the magnitude of each of the two turning angles between these, and the response actually made (right or left). However, on the basis of previous work on mental rotation and Experiment 1 reported here, the two variables of greatest interest to us were the absolute departure from upright of the preceding segment and the magnitude of the preceding turn (i.e.,the middle segment's deviations from upright, and its angular deviation from the orientation of the still earlier segment, as shown in Fig. 3). The finding of a marked increase in reaction time with absolute departure of the preceding segment from upright would indicate that the results obtained in the separated-trials task of Experiment 1 (Fig. 2) carry over to a continuous route-following task. The finding of an increase in reaction time with relative departure from the still earlier segment would suggest that participants sometimes imagine reorienting from the preceding segment, rather than from upright, in order to prepare for the next.

We used stepwise linear regressions to estimate the influences of various independent variables on the reaction times. Both the orientation of the segment leading into the turn and the magnitude of the preceding turn had coefficients that significantly differed from zero in jointly affecting reaction time ($p < 0.005$, in each case). The dependence of reaction time on these two variables is summarized in Fig. 4, where mean reaction time (for correct responses only) is plotted against departure of the preceding segment from upright, for each of the three magnitudes of preceding turn (45, 90, and 135°). (The points plotted at 0° and 180°, for which there are not both

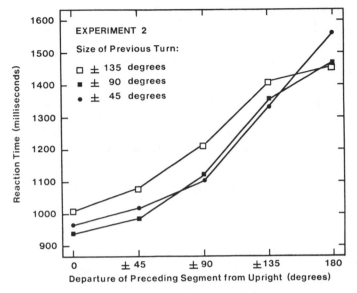

Figure 4.   *Chronometric results of Experiment 2. Reaction time to classify, as a right or left turn, a straight segment newly added to the end of a continuously growing path of such segments is plotted as a function of the angular departure from upright (in either direction) of the preceding segment. A separate curve is plotted for each of the three different absolute magnitudes of the preceding turn.*

clockwise and counterclockwise deviations, are based on half as many observations.)

Over all, the reaction times in Experiment 2 were some 600 msec longer than those in Experiment 1. Presumably, this is a consequence of the greater information processing load and, hence, the less complete readiness during the continuously on-going task of Experiment 2. Apart from this mean difference, the curves are very similar in shape to those of Experiment 1. Clearly there is, again, a strong and consistent increase in reaction time with departure from upright of the line leading into the critical turn (an increase from about 1000 msec at 0° to over 1400 msec at 180°). And again, this increase seems to have a nonlinear tendency to grow more rapidly at the larger angular departures (and possibly to level off again close to 180°). The effect of the magnitude of the preceding turn, represented by the differences between the three plotted curves, is relatively small. Nevertheless reaction times were generally longer following preceding turns of the largest magnitude (135°).

(The only exception to this relative elevation of the 135° curve occurs at 180° departures from upright for which, however, there were half as many observations.) This difference suggests that participants may sometimes have carried out a mental reorientation in order to compensate for the departure of the preceding segment from upright.[5] However, the reaction times following preceding turns of small angles (e.g., 45°) do not exhibit the significant decrease in dependence on absolute departure from upright that would be expected if participants had consistently imagined rotations from the preceding orientation rather than from upright.

When the two variables just considered were not included in the regression analysis, the two other variables that had statistically reliable influences on individual reaction times were: the departure from upright of the most recently added segment, and the (binary-valued) agreement or nonagreement between the absolute direction of the last added segment (more to the left or more to the right) and the participant's classification of the turn into that segment as left or right. Responses tended to be faster when the newest segment pointed upwards, suggesting that the participants may have been speeding up in anticipation of an easier decision at the next turn; and responses tended to be faster when there was agreement between absolute direction and response, suggesting the operation of an overall stimulus-response compatibility effect or, perhaps, a linguistically mediated 'congruence' effect (cf. Clark and Chase, 1972; Trabasso *et al.*, 1971).

Of course, unlike the independently manipulated variables of orientation and delay in Experiment 1, the 'independent' variables explored in the regression analyses of Experiment 2 were subject to selection *post hoc* and to intercorrelation. In particular, for the included correct responses, the variable of principal interest—departure from upright of the line leading into the turn—had correlations of about −0.24 both with the magnitude of the preceding turn and with the left-right agreement between the absolute direction of the last segment and the response. (The remaining correlations, however, were all close to zero.) The negative sign of the correlations mentioned and the fact that a second variable was found to be significant after the first had been partialled out in a regression analysis appear to preclude the possibility that the effects mentioned could be attributed to a single variable. However, we do not claim that our statistical analyses are conclusive concerning the relative importance of the different variables in Experiment 2.

---

[5] If so, that the difference between a 90° and a 135° reorientation is greater than the (indeterminate) difference between a 45° and a 90° reorientation may be another manifestation of the nonlinearity of the dependence of time on angle of rotation evident in Fig. 4, where the rise for all three curves is greater from 90° to 135° than it is from 45° to 90° (a nonlinearity first reported by Cooper and Shepard (1973a, 1973b) and replicated in many subsequent experiments including Experiment 1, here).

Discussion

Experiment 2, though lacking the close control and analysis achievable with the separated trials and orthogonal design used in Experiment 1, represents a closer approximation to real life situations of reading a map during an ongoing journey. We are encouraged, therefore, by the apparent coherence of the results arising from the two experiments. In both cases, the time to classify a bend in a portrayed path as a right or left turn increased markedly with the departure from upright of the path leading into that turn. And in both cases, the classification time increased with the extent of what appears to be a compensatory mental rotation—when that compensatory rotation was necessarily included in the measured reaction time (Experiment 2) or when insufficient time and motivation was provided for the completion of such a compensatory rotation in advance (Experiment 1). Experiment 2 also agrees with Experiment 1 in suggesting, once more, that people find it difficult to reorient their own egocentric frame of reference in order to prepare for a pattern that is rotated on the vertical plane. As shown in Fig. 4, classification times depended much more strongly on the absolute orientation of the segment leading into a turn than on the angular departure of that segment from the still earlier segment; and there was no noticeable flattening of the dependence of reaction time on departure from upright when the orientation of the segment leading into the new turn was closer to the orientation of the preceding segment.

General discussion of the experiments

The single most clear-cut and consistent of our findings is that the identification of a map-like representation of a turn, as a right or a left turn, takes increasingly longer as the direction of the line going into the turn departs further from upright. We have thus provided strong and explicit confirmation of what most map readers implicitly know and what has also been implied by some of the experimental results of Hintzman et al. (1981, see their Fig. 3). The extreme case of a 180° departure, as in reading a completely inverted map, was consistently the most difficult in our task. In this respect, our results, obtained before we knew of the work on you-are-here maps by Levine and his co-workers (Levine, 1981; Levine et al., 1982), are in full agreement with theirs.

We believe that our experiments on the interpretation of right and left turns, though carried out in the idealized and artificial conditions of the laboratory, complement the more naturalistic experiment of Levine and his coworkers in some significant respects: First, by simplifying a map-reading task to its bare essential (the interpretation of a single turn in a path) and by recording reaction times, we have been able to demonstrate that people can successfully interpret a misaligned map but that to do so requires more time and hence, presumably, an additional cognitive operation. Second, by including test cases departing from the optimum, upright alignment to various intermediate degrees (e.g., 30, 60, 90, 120, or 150 degrees) and by providing information as to the angle of misalignment at different times in advance of the test, we have been able to furnish evidence that the additional cognitive operation needed to compensate for the misalignment is specifically one of 'mental rotation' in the sense of Shepard and Metzler (1971) and, particularly, Cooper and Shepard (1973a; Shepard and Cooper, 1982). We suggest that when the people observed by Levine *et al.* were successful in interpreting a you-are-here map despite its 180° misalignment, those people too were doing so by means of a mental rotation. We further suggest that their frequent failures stemmed from the difficulty of preserving, under mental rotation, the structure of relatively complex and unfamiliar layouts.

By varying the conditions favoring advance preparation for a rotated test pattern (in Experiment 1), we have also obtained further evidence that imagining the reorientation of a schematic representation of a concrete visual pattern is more effective than an attempt to reorient one's egocentric frame of reference. Nevertheless, the considerable cognitive load entailed even by the former, concrete operation—particularly when the structure or layout that must be mentally manipulated is complex and/or unfamiliar—may account for the less frequent, incomplete, or faulty use of that operation under demanding conditions (including, perhaps, some of those studied by Hintzman *et al.*, 1981; Huttenlocher and Presson, 1973; Levine *et al.*, 1982; Presson, 1982).

Map-like representations of right and left turns, when displayed in arbitrary orientations, are not distinguishable by any local feature (such as a line projecting to the viewer's right or left). Under these circumstances, the easiest way to identify whether such a turn is right or left may be to transform an internal representation or schema of a canonical right turn, say, into a representation of the appropriately rotated configuration and to check for a match or mismatch. The identification of right and left turns may thus be carried out in essentially the same way as the identification of right and left hands—which Cooper and Shepard (1975) have already shown to require something like mental rotation. One can also prepare to identify a turn before it is actually presented; but to do so one apparently needs both foreknowledge of the appropriate orientation and the ability, motivation, and time to carry out the required concrete mental transformation in advance.

Conclusion

A variety of earlier results on the interpretation of disoriented objects (e.g., Carey, 1981; Hochberg and Galper, 1967; Rock, 1973; Yin, 1969) and on the role of mental rotation in comparing differently oriented objects (e.g., Cooper, 1975; Cooper and Shepard, 1973a, b, 1975; Corballis *et al.*, 1976; Shepard and Cooper, 1982), have confirmed that the upright orientation provides the primary reference direction with respect to which such objects are interpreted or mentally reoriented. The results we have reported here, along with the results obtained by Levine *et al.* (1982), indicate that the upright orientation also plays a preeminent role in the way we represent the surrounding environment, and in the way we orient and find our way about in it.

That the up–down dimension should be so important in this latter connection can seem remarkable. The terrain on which we have mostly had to find our way about is to a rough approximation horizontal; its ups and downs are usually quite small compared with the horizontal distances we must traverse to get from one significant location to another. However, as a consequence of its gravitational basis, the upright direction has always been the most salient, constant, and unique direction in our world. Hence, we have come to use the concepts *up* and *down* to refer to mostly horizontal directions when there is only a just perceptible correlation between a horizontal direction and change in elevation, or when there is no more than a metaphorical connection (as when we use 'up' to mean 'north'), or, perhaps merely by linguistic habit, when there is no basis at all.

Thus while it is not obligatory in English, as it is in some languages, to specify whether a named object is uphill or downhill from the speaker, an optional specification of this sort is frequently used in English even when the speaker has little or no basis for choosing between 'up' and 'down'. We may say, with equal probability, "Come up to see us" or "Come down to see us" when we have no idea of a difference in elevation, when we may be uncertain as to whether we are north or south, and when, even if we believe ourselves to be north, we would not be likely to say "Come north to see us".

The horizontal direction with which the environmentally defined upward direction appears to have the strongest and most immediate cognitive connection is the egocentric direction of straight ahead. The strength of this connection is demonstrated by the experimental results reported here, and in the study of Levine *et al.* (1982). When the upward direction on a vertical map corresponds to straight ahead for someone facing the map, interpretation of the map and of a turn that lies ahead is fast and accurate. But when the map departs significantly from this alignment, or when a turn that must be made lies behind rather than ahead, the map reader evidently must imagine a rotation, which takes a time that increases markedly with the angle of the rotation, and can lead to large errors. Finally, in a paper on describing spatial layouts, which came to our attention as the present paper was going to press, Levelt (1982) reports highly relevant evidence both for the cognitive connection between ahead and up, and for individual differences in use of a fixed egocentric frame *versus* mental rotation.

References

Carey, S. (1981) The development of face recognition. In G. Davies, H. Ellis and J. Shepherd (eds.), *Perceiving and Remembering Faces*. New York, Academic Press.

Clark, H.H. (1973) Space, time, semantics, and the child. In T.E. More, (ed.), *Cognitive Development and the Acquisition of Language*. New York, Academic Press.

Clark, H.H. and Chase, W.G. (1972) On the process of comparing sentences against pictures. *Cog. Psychol., 3*, 472–517.

Cooper, L.A. (1975) Mental rotation of random two-dimensional shapes. *Cog. Psychol., 7*, 20–43.

Cooper, L.A. and Podgorny, P. (1976) Mental transformations and visual comparison processes: Effects of complexity and similarity. *J. exp. Psychol.: Hum. Percep. Perf., 2*, 503–514.

Cooper, L.A. and Shepard, R.N. (1973a) Chronometric studies of the rotation of mental images. In W.G. Chase (ed.), *Visual Information Processing*. New York, Academic Press.

Cooper, L.A. and Shepard, R.N. (1973b) The time required to prepare for a rotated stimulus. *Mem. Cog., 1*, 246–250.

Cooper, L.A. and Shepard, R.N. (1975) Mental transformations in the identification of left and right hands. *J. exp. Psychol.: Hum. Percep. Perf., 104*, 48–56.

Cooper, L.A. and Shepard, R.N. (1978) Transformations of representations of objects in space. In E.C. Carterette and M.P. Friedman (eds.), *Handbook of Perception*, (*Vol. VIII, Perceptual Coding*). New York, Academic Press.

Corballis, M.C. (1982) Mental rotation: Anatomy of a paradigm. In M. Potegal (ed.), *Spatial Abilities: Development and Physiological Foundations*. New York, Academic Press.

Corballis, M.C., Nagourney, B., Shetzer, L.I. and Stefanatos, G. (1978) Mental rotation under head tilt: Factors influencing the location of the subjective frame of reference. *Percep. Psychophys., 24*, 263–272.

Corballis, M.C., Zbrodoff, N.J. and Roldan, C.E. (1976) What's up in mental rotation? *Percep. Psychophys., 19*, 525–530.

Dixon, R.M.W. (1972) *The Dyirbal Language of North Queensland*. London, Cambridge University Press.

Dyer, F.C. and Gould, J.L. (1983) Honey bee navigation. *Am. Sci., 71*, 587–597.

Emlen, S.T. (1975) Migration: Orientation and navigation. In D.S. Farner and J.R. King (eds.), *Avian Biology*. Vol. 5. New York, Academic Press.

Fillmore, C. (1982) Towards a descriptive framework for deixis. In R. Jarvella and W. Klein (eds.), *Speech, Place and Action: Studies in Deixis and Related Topics*. New York, John Wiley & Sons.

von Frisch, K. (1967) *The Dance Language and Orientation of Bees*. Cambridge, MA, Harvard University Press.

Gallistel, C.R. (1980) *The Organization of Action: A New Synthesis*. Hillsdale, NJ, Erlbaum.

Gardner, M. (1959) *Mathematical Puzzles and Diversions*. New York, Simon & Schuster.

Gibson, J.J. (1950) *The Perception of the Visual World*. Boston, Houghton-Mifflin.

Gibson, J.J. (1979) *The Ecological Approach to Visual Perception*. Boston, Houghton-Mifflin.

Gould, J.L. (1980) The case of magnetic sensitivity in birds and bees (such as it is). *Am. Sci., 68*, 256–267.

Hinton, G.E. and Parsons, L.M. (1981) Frames of reference and mental imagery. In J. Long and A. Baddeley (eds.), *Attention and Performance IX*. Hillsdale, NJ, Erlbaum.

Hintzman, D.L., O'Dell, C.S. and Arndt, D.R. (1981) Orientation in cognitive maps. *Cog. Psychol., 13,* 149–206.

Hochberg, J. and Galper, R.E. (1967) Recognition of faces: I. An exploratory study. *Psychon. Sci., 9,* 619–620.

Hochberg, J. and Gellman, L. (1977) The effect of landmark features on mental rotation times. *Mem. Cogn., 5,* 23–26.

Hock, H.S. and Tromley, C.L. (1978) Mental rotation and perceptual uprightness. *Percep. Psychophys., 24,* 529–533.

Hölldobler, B. (1980) Canopy orientation: A new kind of orientation in ants. *Science, 210,* 86–88.

Huttenlocher, J. and Presson, C.C. (1973) Mental rotation and the prespective problem. *Cog. Psychol., 4,* 277–299.

Jackendoff, R. (1983) *Semantics and Cognition*. Cambridge, MA, The MIT Press.

Kant, I. (1881) *Critique of Pure Reason*. (F.M. Muller, Trans.). New York, Macmillan. (Original work published in German, 1781)

Koriat, A. and Norman, J. (In Press) What is rotated in mental rotation? *J. exp. Psychol: Learn., Mem. Cog.*

Lakoff, G. and Johnson, M. (1980) *Metaphors We Live By*. Chicago, IL, University of Chicago Press.

Levelt, W. (1982) Cognitive styles in the use of spatial direction terms. In R. Jarvella and W. Klein (eds.), *Speech, Place and Action*. New York, John Wiley & Sons.

Levine, M. (1981, August) Cognitive maps and you-are-here maps. Invited address presented at the annual meeting of the American Psychological Association, Los Angeles, CA.

Levine, M., Jankovic, I.N. and Palij, M. (1982) Principles of spatial problem solving. *J. exp. Psychol.: Gen., 111,* 157–175.

Lynch, K. (1960) *The Image of the City*. Cambridge, MA, MIT Press.

Maier, N.R.F. (1929) Reasoning in white rats. *Comp. Psychol. Mono., 6* (Serial No. 29).

Metzler, J. and Shepard, R.N. (1974) Transformational studies of the internal representation of three-dimensional objects. In R. Solso (ed.), *Theories in Cognitive Psychology: The Loyola Symposium*. Potomac, MD, Erlbaum.

Presson, C.C. (1982) Strategies in spatial reasoning. *J. exp. Psychol.: Learn., Mem. Cog., 8,* 243–251.

Rock, I. (1973) *Orientation and Form*. New York, Academic Press.

Sauer, E.G.F. (1958) Celestial navigation by birds. *Scient. Am., 199,* (2), 42–47.

Sedgwick, H. (1980) The geometry of spatial layout in pictorial representation. In M. Hagen (ed.), *The Perception of Pictures: Vol. 1*. New York, Academic Press.

Shepard, R.N. (1981) Psychophysical complementarity. In M. Kubovy and J. Pomerantz, (eds.), *Perceptual Organization*. Hillsdale, NJ, Erlbaum.

Shepard, R.N. (1982) Perceptual and analogical bases of cognition. In J. Mehler, M. Garret and E. Walker (eds.), *Perspectives on Mental Representation*. Hillsdale, NJ, Erlbaum. pp. 49–67.

Shepard, R.N. (1984) Ecological constraints on internal representation: Resonant kinematics of perceiving, imagining, thinking, and dreaming. *Psychol. Rev. 91,* 417–447.

Shepard, R.N. and Cooper, L.A. (1982) *Mental Images and Their Transformations*. Cambridge, MA, The MIT Press/Bradford Books.

Shepard, R.N. and Metzler, J. (1971) Mental rotation of three-dimensional objects. *Science, 171,* 701–703.

Talmy, L. (1983) How language structures space. In H. Pick and L. Acredolo (eds.), *Spatial Orientation: Theory, Research, and Application*. New York, Plenum.

Tolman, E.C. (1948) Cognitive maps in rats and men. *Psychol. Rev., 55,* 189–208.

Tolman, E.C., Ritchie, B.F. and Kalish, D. (1946) Studies in spatial learning. II. Place learning versus response learning. *J. exp. Psychol., 36,* 221–229.

Trabasso, T., Rollins, H. and Shaughnessy, E. (1971) Storage and verification stages in processing concepts. *Cog. Psych.*, *2*, 239–289.

Trowbridge, C.C. (1913) On fundamental methods of orientation and 'imaginary maps'. *Science*, *38*, 888–891.

Tversky, B. (1981) Distortions in memory for maps. *Cog. Psychol.*, *13*, 407–433.

Yin, R.K. (1969) Looking at upside-down faces. *J. exp. Psychol.*, *81*, 141–145.

Reference Notes

1. Casad, E.H. and Langacker, R.W. (1982) "Inside" and "outside" in Cora grammar. Unpublished manuscript, University of California, San Diego.
2. Herskovits, A. (1983) Space and the prepositions in English: Regularities and irregularities in a complex domain. Unpublished manuscript, University of California, Berkeley.

5

Individual differences in mental imagery ability: A computational analysis

STEPHEN M. KOSSLYN*

JENNIFER BRUNN

Harvard University

KYLE R. CAVE

Massachusetts Institute of Technology

ROGER W. WALLACH

Bolt, Beranek, and Newman Inc.

Abstract

This study addressed two questions: is mental imagery ability an undifferentiated general skill, or is it composed of a number of relatively distinct subabilities? Further, if imagery is not an undifferentiated general ability, can its structure be understood in terms of the processing components posited by the Kosslyn and Shwartz theory of imagery representation? A set of tasks was devised, and a model was specified for each task. These models invoked different combinations of the processing components posited in the general theory. Fifty people were tested on the tasks, and their scores on each measure were then correlated. A very wide range of correlation coefficients was found—which suggests that the subjects were not simply good or poor at imagery in general. In addition, the similarity of each pair of processing models was computed by considering the number of shared processing components. The correlations among scores were then compared to the predicted similarities in processing, and were found to be highly related to these measures. A common sense theory was also considered, based on the idea that people differ on variables such as 'image vividness' and 'image control'. The Kosslyn and Shwartz theory proved a better predictor of the results than the common sense theory. Thus, imagery ability is not an undifferentiated general skill, and the underlying components bear a strong correspondence to those posited by the theory. Various additional analyses supported these conclusions.

*Requests for reprints should be sent to Stephen M. Kosslyn, 1236 William James Hall, 33 Kirkland St., Cambridge, MA 02138, U.S.A. This work was supported by ONR contracts N00014-79-C-0982 and N00014-82-C-0166. The authors wish to thank Earl B. Hunt, Edward E. Smith, Saul Sternberg, and Robert, J. Weber for valuable criticisms and comments, and Gail Pendleton for editorial and secretarial assistance.

Introduction

It has long been believed that people differ in their abilities to use mental imagery. In fact, the earliest scientific investigations of imagery, reported by Fechner (1860) and Galton (1883), provide support for this notion. More recent work by MacLeod et al. (1978), Mathews et al. (1980), Egan and Grimes-Farrow (1982) and others has shown that some people will adopt imagery strategies in solving problems whereas others will not. The long history of the field notwithstanding, however, little progress has been made in characterizing differences in imagery ability. In this paper, we consider one of the most basic issues in the field, the possible differentiation of 'imagery ability' into distinct subabilities.

The attempts to study distinct aspects of imagery ability to date have focused on introspectively apparent properties of imagery. For example, Betts (1909) and Marks (1973) have devised questionnaires to study individual differences in image vividness, and Gordon (1949) devised a questionnaire to study individual differences in imagery control. However, these instruments have had only mixed success in predicting performance (see Ernest, 1977; Marks, 1977; White et al., 1977, for reviews). One potential problem was revealed in diVesta et al.'s (1971) factor analysis of the items on the Gordon test, which indicated that four distinct factors were tapped by the test. Thus, the same overall score could be produced by a wide range of combinations of loadings on the underlying factors, and it may be that the loading on any given factor is more or less important for performing a given task. It was not obvious how best to characterize the factors apparently tapped by this test.

Perhaps the major impediment to studying individual differences in imagery has been the constructs used, which have focused on common sense characterizations of introspectively-evident properties of the experience (such as vividness and control). But comparing aspects of the phenomenological experience is rather like comparing the observable properties of rocks, ice, and water: commonalities in color, shape, rigidity, and so on may be misleading, and only by having a theory of the underlying structure can one penetrate beneath the surface phenomena themselves. Kosslyn and Shwartz (see Kosslyn, 1980, 1981) provide an analysis of some of the processing mechanisms used in imagery, and the present study examines the usefulness of this analysis as a characterization of individual differences in imagery ability.

The present study, then, has two foci: first, we want to know whether imagery ability is a relatively general, undifferentiated capacity, or whether 'imagery ability' is in fact a collection of abilities that can vary relatively independently. Second, we want to know whether the components specified by the Kosslyn and Shwartz imagery theory have psychological validity. Insofar as underlying imagery abilities (should they exist) are easily understood as reflecting variations in the efficacy of the components posited by the theory, the theory itself attains additional credibility.

The logic underlying this investigation is straightforward: if imagery ability is general and undifferentiated, then we expect that people who do relatively well on one imagery task should do relatively well on other imagery tasks, and people who do poorly on one task should do poorly on the others. Thus, in this study we tested a group of people on a set of tasks. If imagery ability is general and undifferentiated, then we expect the scores from the various tasks we administered to be highly correlated across the board. At the other extreme, if each of our imagery tasks taps a distinct independent 'skill', then we expect essentially zero correlation among the scores. In contrast, if tasks are accomplished by using some combination of a small number of available processing components, then the correlation between any two tasks will depend on the number of shared processing components—with higher numbers shared being reflected by higher correlations. In this last case, then, we expect a wide range of correlations (not just high ones or zero ones), and we expect that the pattern of correlations will reflect the similarity of underlying processing.

Thus, we will first describe the general imagery theory, from which we will derive models for each of our tasks. We next will consider each task in turn, along with the specific model for that task. Following this, we will compare our predictions with the observed correlations among task performance. In this section we will also compare our theory with a plausible alternative. Finally, we will perform a cluster analysis and factor analysis of the data, and examine the extent to which the models can account for the structure thereby revealed in the data.

1. Overview of the theory of imagery

The theory of visual mental image representation and processing is being developed with the aim of specifying the representations and media (buffers) used in imagery, as well as the distinct 'component' processing modules and algorithms used to perform specific tasks. The theory has been embodied in a computer simulation model, which provides accounts for most of the data on image processing (see Kosslyn, 1980).

Abilities to be explained

Kosslyn (1980) presents a detailed review of the literature on imagery phenomena. These phenomena seem to reflect two general classes of abilities: (1) Our ability to use images to retrieve information from memory about visible properties of objects (e.g., as occurs when one is asked whether a donkey has pointed ears). (2) Our ability to use imagery in the course of visual thinking (e.g., as when one decides how furniture will look when rearranged in various ways). These abilities require mental operations that not only generate and 'inspect' images, but that perform various image transformations. The theory posits a relatively small set of structures and processing modules that are used to carry out these abilities, as is briefly described below.

Structures

Our theory distinguishes between media and representations. A medium does not convey any information inherently; rather, it is a structure that can support representations. The representations actually store the information being conveyed. A blackboard or wax tablet are media, which support representations composed of chalk marks and etchings, respectively. The imagery theory posits distinct short-term memory and long-term memory structures, as noted below.

Short-term memory structure

The 'visual buffer' is a special visual short-term memory medium. This structure mimics a coordinate space in the way that an array in a computer can mimic such a space. In a computer, cells in an array correspond to 'words' in memory, but the physical arrangement of the words is not like an array. Indeed, the 'words' that correspond to the cells in the array need not even be stored in memory banks in the same room, let alone in the appropriate physical juxtaposition. Rather, the array-like properties emerge from how the words are accessed. That is, the order in which words are accessed reflects their functional organization into an array, with 'adjacent' words being accessed in succession, with more words falling 'between' words corresponding to cells further apart, and so on. The way the stored words are retrieved, then, imparts a functional organization into a spatial array, such that it makes sense to talk about some cells being 'adjacent' to or 'diagonal' from each other. Similarly, there need be no physical array in the brain in order to have a functional coordinate space; all that is necessary is that representations be organized spatially in the process of accessing them (see Kosslyn (1983) for a more detailed discussion of the idea of a 'functional space').

The visual buffer supports representations that depict information. That is, portions of the medium are filled, and each filled location corresponds to a portion of the depicted object such that the 'distances' among the portions in the medium are monotonically related to the actual distances among the corresponding portions on the planar projection of the object. When one has the experience of 'seeing with the mind's eye', we take this to be indicative of a depictive representation being processed in the medium. (The representation, and not the experience, is what is referred to as "the image" in this paper.) We theorize that the visual buffer is used to support images derived from memory and from the eyes during perception proper.

Properties of the medium are especially important because they affect all representations that occur within it. As on a TV screen (which is a type of medium), mental images begin to fade as soon as they are placed in the mental visual medium; the grain of the medium constrains how small an object can be in an image while still remaining 'visible'; and the size of the medium constrains how large an object can be imaged (i.e., the visual angle it seems to subtend) while still all remaining 'visible' at once.

Long-term memory structures

According to our theory, there are (at least) two distinct media in long-term memory, which store different information. One stores lists of facts about objects, including descriptions about how parts are put together, their size, the names of superordinate categories, and so on. (For example, for 'car', the list includes the facts that it has front and rear wheels, a steering wheel, and bumpers.) The other stores encodings of the 'literal' appearance of the object (not a description). In our computer simulation model, the literal appearance is stored as a list of coordinates, which indicates where points should be placed in the visual buffer to depict the stored pattern. The theory of the properties of the long-term memory structures emerges directly from the theory of the various processes that use this information as input, as is discussed below.

Processing modules

The various structures posited by the theory are used by *processing modules* that accomplish various ends. A processing module is a 'black box' that produces some well-specified output from an input. Each module has a specific purpose within the processing system, and is treated as a distinct processing unit.

Processing modules using the image as input

Once an image is formed in the visual buffer, it can be used in three kinds of processing. First, the object or pattern in the image can be 'inspected'. This kind of processing is required whenever imagery is used, whether for remembering information or as a vehicle for reasoning. Our theory posits a FIND processing module that performs specific tests on the pattern in the visual buffer (e.g., traces lines, locates intersections, etc.) to check whether the pattern depicts a specific object or part. Our theory also posits a RESOLUTION processing module, which takes as input a pattern in the visual buffer and produces as output a measure of the relative clarity of the pattern; this processing module was required in order to decide whether to zoom in or pan back when 'looking' for a part of an imaged object. The details of how this module actually operates in our computer simulation model are not important here; the important claims in our theory of processing are about what is accomplished by the modules and what are the contexts in which various modules are used.

Second, images can be maintained over time. We claim that images begin to 'fade' as soon as they are generated and are retained only with effort. To maintain images, a REGENERATE processing module is used. This module purportedly refreshes units one at a time. (A unit is a part of an image that was generated from information stored as a single 'packet' in long-term memory.) Because this module takes time to operate, if too many units are present not all of them can be refreshed before any one of them has faded away. This property puts a 'capacity limit' on how much material can be represented in an image at one time. According to our theory, images are always regenerated immediately prior to 'inspecting' the object or pattern depicted in them, in order to ensure that the image is as clear as possible when trying to access information represented in it.

Third, images can be altered in various ways, such as by reorganizing the depicted patterns (as will be described shortly) or 'rotating' them (i.e., transforming the representation in such a way that the represented orientation of the object is altered). These transformations are critical in most visual thinking, where one 'observes' the consequences of manipulating objects in images in various ways. According to our theory, all image transformations are carried out by the operation of a module that alters the shape representation working in conjunction with another module that 'monitors' the transformation (i.e., one of the 'inspection' processing modules discussed above), providing information about when the image has been correctly adjusted.[1]

---

[1] See Shwartz (1979) for evidence that at least one image transformation, mental rotation, is performed on the image itself (as opposed to the underlying representation in long-term memory).

We posit a set of specific transformation modules (which are stored as separate routines in our computer simulation model), such as ZOOM, PAN (the inverse of ZOOM), TRANSLATE (move), ROTATE, and SCAN.[2] The final type of transformation we posit allows one to reorganize the internal structure of an image, such as would occur when an imaged Star of David is changed from two overlapping triangles to a central hexagon with six small triangles flanking it; this reorganizing is accomplished by a PARSE processing module, which will be discussed in more detail below.

Processing modules using the long-term memory representations as input
One of the most obvious facts about mental images is that they are not always present. Rather, images are created on the basis of information stored in long-term memory. That is, a pattern in the visual buffer (i.e., the image proper) is formed on the basis of information stored in long-term memory. We claim that this ability is carried out by three processing modules:

(1) The PICTURE processing module activates the stored encodings of appearance, creating a pattern in the visual buffer. For example, in the simulation model an image of a car's body is created by activating the points whose coordinates are stored in the literal encoding of its appearance.

(2) The PUT processing module coordinates separate encodings such that they form a single, composite image. That is, in long-term memory, parts' positions are defined with respect to other parts in a hierarchy; we claim that images are generated by working down the hierarchy part by part. The PUT module operates by using a description of the location of a new part to set the PICTURE module so that parts are imaged in the correct relative positions. For example, a car's wheels may be described as belonging "in the wheel wells"; the PUT module would use this information so that the images of a car's wheels could be properly integrated into the image of the body. In addition, the PUT processing module is necessary to account for the fact that imagery is a creative activity which can produce new combinations of previously viewed objects, including those evoked by verbal descriptions of novel scenes (such as an image of an elephant flying over the moon).

---

[2]The SCAN module performs a kind of transformation, with patterns being shifted across the visual buffer so that different parts are in the center, most resolved region. This procedure was desirable to explain why we do not seem to 'bump into an edge' when scanning 360° around us, in addition to explaining why the rate of scanning between two locations in an image is the same as the rate of scanning the same distance to a location initially 'off screen', as is discussed in Kosslyn (1980, ch. 8). However, in addition to this sort of scanning, one can also shift attention within a stable image (just as one can scan across an icon without using eye movements), and in our theory this is accomplished within the FIND module. The distinction between the two kinds of scanning parallels the distinction between scrolling text across a CRT and moving the cursor within the text on the screen (cf. Pinker, 1980).

(3) The FIND processing module is also used in image generation. This module, as was mentioned above, is used when one 'inspects' an imaged object for a given characteristic. In image generation, the FIND processing module is always invoked by the PUT module, being used to 'see' where a to-be-imaged part belongs in relation to what is already in the image. The place where a new part belongs is called a 'foundation part'. This procedure is necessary here because images can be formed at different sizes and locations, and hence parts must be described relative to other parts—not an absolute location in the buffer. And if a part's location is defined relative to another part, then one must first find the other part before imaging the new one. Thus, the PUT module uses both the description of the relationship between two parts and the location of the 'foundation part' (provided by the FIND module) to calibrate the PICTURE module correctly.

In summary, images can be generated from separately-stored parts. The first part imaged is usually the central part or overall shape (e.g., a car's body). This part is imaged using only the PICTURE processing module. As an image of each subsequent part is formed (e.g., the rear wheel), the FIND processing module 'looks' for the location where it belongs, and the PUT processing module uses this information in conjunction with the description of the relation between parts (stored in long-term memory or provided in a verbal instruction) to calibrate the PICTURE processing module so that the new part is imaged in the correct location in the composite object or scene. According to our theory of the generation algorithm, parts are imaged sequentially, and in fact an image composed of increasingly more parts requires increasingly more time to generate (see Kosslyn, 1980, chs. 4 and 6). In earlier work we provided evidence that the FIND processing module was in fact used in both image inspection and generation by showing that discriminability factors affected both activities in the same way (see Farah and Kosslyn, 1981; Kosslyn, 1980, chs. 6 and 7; Kosslyn et al., 1983b). More recent work provides further evidence for the separability of the three modules (Kosslyn et al., In press; this paper also includes a more detailed development and justification of the theory of image generation).

An important consequence of our theory of image generation is the preservation of stored units in the image itself. That is, parts are stored as individual 'packets' in long-term memory (i.e., in separate literal encodings) that are activated individually. The images of parts begin to fade as soon as they are formed. Thus, each part will be at a different level of activation, which results in the parts being maintained as separate units in the image because each portion of the unit—each point used to depict it in the computer simulation model—will group together according to the Gestalt law of similarity (i.e., points at the same level of activation will be grouped together).

Finally, there is one last processing module that is related to the PICTURE module, but which operates on input from the eyes rather than long-term memory. According to the theory, the eyes automatically and always feed the visual buffer. The LOAD processing module retains perceptual input from the eyes by temporarily squelching subsequent visual input (which normally supplants the contents of the buffer). Thus, this process is analogous to the PICTURE process, except that it loads the visual buffer with input from the eyes rather than from information stored in long-term memory.[3]

In summary, the theory posits a set of processing modules that operate on a set of representations (images, stored literal memories, and stored descriptions) which are stored in different media. One question we will ask here, then, is whether these component structures and processing modules vary separately in their efficiency from person to person. Table 1 summarizes the processing modules posited by the theory.

Formulating specific models

Specific models for each of the tasks used in this study were formulated within the constraints imposed by our general theory of imagery representations and processing. These constraints were:

(1) All tasks must be performed using some combination of the processing modules posited by the theory, which operate on the structures posited by the theory.

(2) There are rules about the specific circumstances and combinations in which modules must be used. In particular, whenever an image is formed, the PICTURE processing module (if the image is formed from memory) or the LOAD processing module (if it is formed from the eyes) must be used; the FIND or RESOLUTION processing module must be used to 'inspect' the image, which is required before any decision can be made on the basis of imagery; the REGENERATE processing module must be used immediately prior to using the FIND or RESOLUTION processing module to reach a decision prior to producing a response; the FIND or RESOLUTION

---

[3]In Kosslyn (1980) two executive processing modules, IMAGE and LOOKFOR, are also discussed. It now seems that much of the control they assumed can be achieved locally (by specifying the input/output characteristics of the individual processing modules more precisely) or by a more general executive (not specific to imagery). Given these possibilities, we decided that it made the most sense to take seriously only the specific processing modules described above.

Table 1.   Summary of processing modules.* Parentheses indicate optional input.

Name	Input	Operation	Output
PICTURE	Name of a literal encoding stored in long-term memory (size, location, orientation)	Produces a pattern in the visual buffer; may vary the size, location and orientation	A visual image of the named perceptual unit (a part or general shape of an object)
FIND	Name of a sought part, image in the visual buffer	Looks up a description of part; looks up tests for that pattern; executes tests on image, looking for pattern corresponding to named part	Locate/Not Locate decision; if finds, indicates the location of part in the image
PUT	Name of to-be-placed part	Looks for image encoding of part; if locates, then looks up description of the relation and foundation part; then invokes FIND to locate the foundation part in the image; computes size and location values for new part, provides PICTURE with these values and name of literal encoding of to-be-imaged part	Part integrated into the image at correct size and location
LOAD	Input to the eyes	Temporarily suppresses additional input, 'fixing' a perceptual image in the visual buffer	Image of material just viewed
RESOLUTION	Image in the visual buffer	Computes sharpness of the image	A measure of image resolution
REGENERATE	Image in the visual buffer	Refreshes image, working a unit at a time; recycles over and over	Image retained over time
PARSE	Image in the visual buffer; names of units in new reorganization	Refreshes selected segments of the image, creating new units; uses FIND to select new segments	Pattern, part, or object organized into new units
ROTATE	Image in the visual buffer, (angle, direction rate)	Shifts image around a pivot point; uses FIND to monitor progress. May be set to rotate in specified direction, angle, rate.	Reorients imaged pattern, part, or object
SCAN	Image in the visual buffer, direction of scan (rate)	Shifts image through visual buffer; fills in new material along leading edge, uses FIND to guide path	Imaged material is shifted so that new portion is in central, most acute part of the buffer

Table 1 contd.

Name	Input	Operation	Output
ZOOM	Image in the visual buffer, target resolution (rate)	Dilates image, uses RESO-LUTION to monitor progress uses PUT to add parts as resolution permits	Scale change in the image; higher resolution; added parts
PAN	Image in the visual buffer, target resolution (rate)	Contracts image, uses RESOLUTION to monitor progress	Scale change in the image; lower resolution
TRANSLATE	Image of a pattern, part, or object in the visual buffer; direction of movement (rate)	Moves part of image relative to other parts (unlike SCAN, which moves entire contents in a uniform way); uses either FIND or RESOLUTION to monitor progress	Spatial relationships changed among parts of the imaged pattern, part, object or scene

*For a more detailed summary of a slightly earlier version of the theory, see Kosslyn (1980, pp. 150–151).

processing module must be utilized to monitor the progress of any image transformation; the FIND and PICTURE processing modules always must be used when the PUT module is used.

(3) The tasks were designed in such a way that specific processing modules were logically necessary for specific tasks (e.g., using the ROTATE module to rotate an image; using the REGENERATE module to maintain an image over time).

(4) Finally, we had a parsimony assumption: if more than one strategy could be devised, we selected (for better or worse) the one utilizing the fewest processing modules.

The foregoing considerations allowed us to specify which processing modules should be used in a given task; however, they were not sufficient to determine uniquely the flow among modules. There often are options about the order in which one can use various operations (e.g., when one regenerates the image), and it seemed impossible to design tasks in such a way as to preclude such options. Thus, in all analyses in this paper we take seriously only the claims about which components of the system (structures and processing modules) are recruited in performing a given task, and ignore the details of the order of execution. Furthermore, because the processing modules must make use of specific structures (indeed, they are defined in part by which kinds of representations they operate on), we considered the contribution of variations in structures only in the context of variations in the efficacy of the modules.

Weighting modules

All else being equal, the sheer number of shared components should predict the similarity in performance among tasks. Unfortunately, the situation is not so simple because not all processing modules are of equal importance in performing a task. This fact is unavoidable because different measures of performance are sensitive to the efficacy of different processing modules. That is, measures of the time, speed, correlations across conditions, accuracy, and various ratings data could be collected for each of the tasks we examined, and most of these dependent measures are sensitive to different aspects of processing. Thus, we needed to identify which processing modules contributed most highly to the performance measure used in each of our tasks. These processing modules were then 'weighted' in subsequent analyses because we expected that individual differences in their efficiency would be central in affecting task performance.

Our method of determining which modules should be weighted for a given task was as follows. For each task, we 'hand simulated' how the model would operate (the tasks are sufficiently simple that the computer is not necessary to see how the models work). We then considered how variations in the efficacy of each processing module used in the model would affect our measure of task performance. We assumed that if a person can perform the task at all, then all of the relevant processing modules must be operating at some minimal level of efficacy. The question was, for which modules will increased efficacy improve the score on the dependent measure? For some modules there is nothing gained—on a specific dependent measure—by performance above the bare minimum. For other modules, increased speed, capacity, sensitivity, or accuracy will directly affect the performance measure. It was these processing modules that were weighted.

After determining the weights this way, we attempted to validate them in the following manner. We reasoned that the processing modules that are increasingly taxed when stimulus factors are varied—and the task becomes more difficult, according to the dependent measure—would have disproportionate influence in the converse situation, when the task difficulty was constant but the component could vary in efficacy. Thus, we considered which stimulus factors had been already shown to affect the dependent measure in group data (the tasks were similar to those already studied, so we usually had this information), and then considered which processing modules were taxed by variations in these stimulus factors. For example, in one of our tasks subjects hear a series of directions one at a time (e.g., "North, West, North"), and have to add a new segment in the described direction to a 'mental pathway'. The number of line segments to be maintained in the image is varied. When we measure memory for the pathway, group performance is poorer when more segments have to be maintained in the image. The PICTURE, PUT, and FIND modules, which integrate each segment into the composite, do no more work for each new segment no matter how many segments are in the image. In contrast, the REGENERATE module must work increasingly harder with each additional segment, because more previous ones must be carried along. We felt justified in weighting a processing module if it was one that should be increasingly taxed when stimulus factors were varied and performance on our dependent measure decreased. If this procedure is amiss, this should become obvious in our later analyses using the individual models.

In describing the models for each of the tasks, we will note which modules have been weighted; we will attempt to justify our decisions by reference to previous results showing that particular factors—which should selectively affect the weighted modules—affect task difficulty. In some cases, group data collected in the tasks themselves will provide justification for our weightings, serving to underline the importance of specific modules.

2. The task battery

General method and procedure

The tasks we used all either had been shown previously to tap imagery or were similar to such tasks. Performance on these tasks typically demonstrates some distinctive hallmark of imagery processing, such as increasing amounts of time with increasing amounts of image rotation or scanning, decreased resolution when imaged patterns subtend smaller 'visual angles', increased time to 'see' parts of more complex patterns, and so on (the specific hallmarks will be discussed when they become relevant). By replicating previous results, when group data are considered, we have *prima facie* evidence that imagery was used in performing the task. The group results, then, are used to confer construct validity on the tasks used to study individual differences in imagery abilities. This approach is an improvement over previous studies of individual differences in imagery abilities, which typically provide no evidence that the tests or questionnaires are measuring some aspect of imagery *per se*. Further, such group results will also provide support for our weighting of specific processing modules. Thus, all of the results sections contain two kinds of information, that pertaining to the group data—to establish construct validity and to justify the weightings—and that pertaining to the individual differences measure.

Each subject was tested individually, for a total of approximately 6 hours. Testing required three sessions, the third being completed within three weeks of the first. Testing was conducted individually by two experimenters, one male and one female; half of the subjects were randomly assigned to a given experimenter, with the constraint that each experimenter tested approximately equal numbers of males and females. The experimenters were blind to the specific model for each task. The subjects were told only the general purpose of the study and were ignorant of all hypotheses, specific (i.e., pertaining to group results in a given task) and general. The specific method and procedure for each of the experimental tasks are summarized below, along with the most relevant group results. Space limitation preclude a detailed discussion of both the methods and results; for additional details, see Kosslyn *et al.* (1983a).

The tasks were presented to all subjects in the same order, with the same written instructions being used for all subjects. The Mental Rotation, Acuity, and Extent tasks were administered during the first session; the Image Capacity and Imaging Described Scenes tasks during the second; and the Image Generation, Image Reorganization, and Image Inspection tasks during the third. In addition, at the end of the third session the subjects were given an imagery questionnaire and paper-and-pencil test, plus four tests of other kinds of abilities, as described below.[4]

Subjects

A total of 50 subjects were tested. The male experimenter tested 25 subjects, 12 women and 13 men. These women ranged in age from 17 to 48 years, with a mean age of 29.6 years; the men ranged in age from 18 to 46 years, with a mean age of 29.2 years. The female experimenter tested the other 25 subjects, 13 women and 12 men. These women ranged in age from 19 to 47, with a mean age of 30.7; the men ranged in age from 18 to 36, with a mean age of 26.8. All subjects were volunteers, most having answered a classified advertisement placed in the *Boston Sunday Globe*. The subjects had quite varied backgrounds, as assessed by questions included in an informed consent form administered at the beginning of the first day of testing.[5] Subjects were

---

[4]The question of how to order the tasks left us on the horns of a dilemma. On the one hand, the order could be counterbalanced over subjects. Unfortunately, this procedure would make it difficult to disentangle individual differences *per se* and order effects. On the other hand, giving the tasks in the same order to all subjects leaves open the possibility that tasks administered on the same day will appear related, but only because of the consistent presentation order. This possibility could be ruled out easily after the data were collected, and hence this procedure seemed the lesser of the two evils.

[5]The ethnic backgrounds of the subjects included Anglo, Black, Irish, Italian, Hispanic, Jewish, and Portugese, the predominant groups in the Boston/Cambridge area. Their educational levels ranged from one man who completed only the 11th grade to a Ph.D. candidate in Art History. The majority of subjects had completed a bachelor's degree, and several had Master's degrees (in fields other than Psychology or related disciplines). According to the subjects, their occupations included cook, story-teller, English tutor, clerk, TV station owner, dancer, mother, geriatrician, artist. EEG technician, writer, engineer, stockboy, secretary and student (only 12 full-time students were tested, 5 of whom attended Harvard/Radcliffe).

paid a total of $20 over the three sessions, $4 after the first session, $4 after the second session, and $12 after the third session. This payment schedule encouraged the subjects to complete the entire series, and in fact all but six of the subjects who initially began the study completed all the sessions.

Summaries of tasks and group results

Acuity task

In this task subjects studied a striped grating, closed their eyes and then imaged it as if it were moving away from them. The subjects were told to stop the imaged grating at the point when the stripes seemed to blur together and then to indicate the apparent distance at which the grating seemed to blur.

The subjects first were shown a practice grating projected so that the stripes just began to blur, and learned to adjust the projector to produce this amount of blurring. This 'blur criterion' was to be used in determining when to stop the image. Subjects also received training at estimating distances, and practiced until they became adept at this task. Gratings were presented on a rear-projection screen. Three gratings were used, which differed in terms of how wide the stripes were and how many stripes were present. The subjects imaged a stimulus as if it were moving away from them, and estimated the apparent 'distance' at which the imaged pattern matched the blur criterion. This task was very similar to one used by Pennington and Kosslyn (1981), who found that the distance at the point of blur increased when the stripes were broader, and who found similar results in imagery and in a perceptual condition, when the gratings were physically present during the task.

The model. The model for this task is as follows. Subjects first use the LOAD processing module to form an image in the visual buffer, encoding and retaining the appearance of the grating. They then use the REGENER-ATE processing module, which is always invoked when an image must be maintained over time. Only a clear image of segments of two stripes needs to be maintained to perform the task (in fact, pairs of dots are often used as stimuli in this sort of task; see Finke and Kosslyn (1980)). Thus, the different numbers of stripes need not affect our measure of performance and the RE-GENERATE processing module is not weighted. Next, the PAN processing module is used, and the image is (effectively) contracted. The RESOLU-TION processing module is used to monitor the image as it is being trans-formed, waiting until the edges of two or more stripes blur. When this hap-pens, the PAN processing module is stopped and the distance is estimated on the basis of how much panning was required to reach the blur criterion. We assume that the amount of panning allows the system to estimate the 'size' of the image (i.e., angle subtended by the imaged pattern), and that subjects learn the rule relating the angle subtended by the image and distance during the distance-estimation training prior to the experiment.

Our measure of performance for this task is the average distance at which the gratings seemed to blur. According to the model, provided that the subject can do the task at all (and hence can see the distinct stripes when encoding the image and can remember at least two of the stripes), any improvement in the dependent measure will stem from increased sensitivity of the RESOLUTION processing module. That is, we expect that the sensitivity of this processing module will determine the greatest 'distance' (i.e., smallest visual angle) at which the bars are distinct.[6] Furthermore, this module is the only one that will be increasingly taxed as the visual angle between stripes becomes smaller. If this is so, then wider bars, should seem to blur at further distance, as was found by Pennington and Kosslyn (1981, Reference note 1). Because the sensitivity of the RESOLUTION processing module purportedly contributes disproportionately to our measure, this module will be weighted in later analyses. This decision receives further justification from the fact that stripe width of a grating affected distance estimates in similar ways in the imagery task and in the perceptual analogue, where the gratings are actually viewed as they move further away (Pennington and Kosslyn, *op. cit.*). When subjects actually viewed the gratings, they did not use any of the processing modules used in the imagery task except the RESOLUTION processing module, and hence the similarity of performance in the two tasks implicates this module as being of paramount importance.

The processing modules purportedly used in this and each succeeding task are summarized in Fig. 1. With the addition of each task in the figure the pattern of shared processing modules emerges; heavy lines indicate weighted modules, and light lines indicate unweighted modules.

---

[6]The functional vividness or resolution of an image will in fact reflect two factors: the grain of the visual buffer and the sensitivity of the RESOLUTION processing module. When speaking of properties of the processing module we are in fact speaking of its properties in the context of properties of the visual buffer.

Figure 1.   *Processing modules used in the different tasks.*

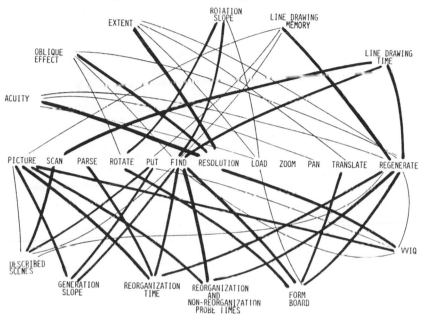

Results. As expected, when group results were examined, distance estimates increased for wider stripes, $F(2,62) = 13.38$, $p < 0.001$, which is evidence that the RESOLUTION processing module was a primary contributor
to the measure.[7] These results confer construct validity on our measure,
given the similarity to those found earlier in imagery and perception. For
additional details of the group results in this and all other tasks described in
this paper, see Kosslyn *et al.* (1983a). For purposes of the individual differences analyses, a mean distance estimate over all trials was computed for
each subject; larger means were taken as evidence of better performance.[8]

---

[7]Although data from all subjects were considered in the individual differences analyses for each of the
tasks, in this and all other tasks reported in this paper only data from subjects who could perform the task
were analyzed in the group results. These analyses were intended to discover whether imagery was in fact
used to perform the task and whether our decisions about weighting specific components received support;
hence, we could sensibly consider only data that did in fact reflect task performance. Fortunately, as is evident
in Table 2, the vast majority of subjects were able to perform the tasks.

[8]For purposes of later analyses subjects were assigned *z* scores for each of the task measures. Subjects who
could not perform the task were given scores 0.01 below the lowest *z*, in this and all the other tasks. The
conversion to *z* scores is superfluous for all of the analyses reported in this paper, which use correlations as
measures of the similarity in task performance (correlation is a dimensionless statistic, which involves a
standard score in its computation).

Table 2.   *Summary statistics for individual differences measures*

Task	Mean	Standard error	Range	n	Units
Acuity	51.00	5.20	8.0–190.0	45*	cm distance at blur
Oblique	0.32	0.05	0–1.0	45	proportion reporting
Extent	35.20	3.10	6.2–71.9	41	cm separation at blur
Rot. Slope	11.00	1.60	0.06–52.3	47**	msec/degree
Line Dr. Mem.	53.60	2.30	14.3–82.7	50	percent correct
Line Dr. Time	2262	225	843–9733	50	msec
Des. Scenes	0.02	0.06	−0.68–+0.95	50	r time and distance
Gen. Slope	191	40	2–1715	50	msec/unit
Reorg. Time	2946	225	1017–9025	50	msec
Reorg. Probe	2622	178	830–6968	50	msec
Nonreorg. Probe	2403	134	1062–5482	50	msec
Form Board	34.5[†]	2.74	−3.0–80.0	50	number correct
VVIQ	70.4[§]	3.40	34–147	50	vividness rating (1–5 scale; 1 = most vivid)

*The n indicates how many subjects could perform the task. Subjects who could not perform a task were assigned a z score 0.01 below the lowest score for the remaining subjects.
**Three subjects produced negative slopes. The most sharply negative slope was −1.0 msec/deg.
[†]Out of a maximum of 120 possible.
[§]Out of a maximum of 160 (eyes-closed only).

Table 2 presents the mean, standard error of the mean, and range of the scores from this and all of the other tasks used in this study.

Oblique Effect task

After making a distance estimate in the acuity task, the subjects were then asked to image the grating rotating 45° clockwise, so it now consisted of oblique stripes. The subjects were then asked to tell the experimenter if the image still matched the blur criterion. If a subject said that it did not, he or she was asked whether the image would have to be moved closer in or further away to match the blur criterion. The reported direction of distance adjustment was recorded. This task was included because Pennington and Kosslyn (1981, Reference note 1) found that subjects in this situation evince an "oblique effect" (see Appelle, 1972), in which oblique gratings are less acute (i.e., seem closer when they blur) than vertical ones; thus, this seemed a potentially strong measure of how well subjects could 'see' patterns in images.

The model. The task began with the grating being imaged at the point of blur, and hence the image must be maintained using the REGENERATE processing module. The image is then rotated 45°, with the FIND processing module monitoring the operation of the ROTATION processing module, stopping it when the image has been rotated the correct amount. Once the image is correctly aligned, the RESOLUTION processing module determines whether the blur is the same as, less than, or more than the blur criterion. All subjects who could perform the acuity task could rotate the image and make a judgment. Given this fact, greater efficiency in the ROTATION, FIND and REGENERATE modules will not affect the judgment, leaving us with the RESOLUTION module as the presumed locus of the effect (in conjunction with properties of the visual buffer). We do not have a theory of the oblique effect per se, but merely assume that it is a consequence of the neural underpinnings of the RESOLUTION processing module and/or the visual buffer. Thus, we assume that the oblique effect should occur in everyone and a failure to notice it reflects low sensitivity of the RESOLU-TION processing module (and/or a coarse-grained visual buffer which it operates on). Thus, the RESOLUTION processing module is weighted here. The fact that the effect also occurs in vision, where only this module is shared, provides further justification for this weighting.

Results. Of the 45 subjects who could perform the acuity task, only 10 reported on at least two-thirds of the trials that the oblique gratings would be closer at the point of blur than the vertical ones. For purposes of later analyses, we computed for each of the 45 subjects the proportion of trials on which he or she reported that the grating became more blurred after rotation. More frequent reports of the oblique effect were taken as evidence of better performance; the subjects who could not perform the task were given a score of 0.01 below the lowest score from the other subjects.

Extent task

Subjects studied two identical gratings which were positioned side by side, and then imaged them moving apart at the same rate (one moving to the left, the other to the right). The subjects stopped the movement when the stripes blurred, again using the 'blur criterion' taught at the beginning of the acuity task. Subjects were taught to move their index fingers apart to indicate the positions of the gratings, and the distance between the two fingers was used as a measure of the horizontal extent of a person's 'imagery field' at the point of blur. The gratings were small circles the size of a quarter, with vertical black and white stripes within; the stripes were at the same three widths used in the acuity task. This task is a variation of one used by Finke and Kosslyn (1980).

The model. As in the Acuity task, the LOAD and REGENERATE processing modules are used initially. Now, instead of being panned away from, the TRANSLATE processing module is used to move the imaged disks away from each other, with the RESOLUTION processing module monitoring the level of blur. The subject moves his or her fingers along where the image would be, and stops both the movement of the image and the fingers when the gratings blur.

Our measure for later analyses is the mean distance between the gratings at the point of blur. The same reasoning that led us to weight the RESOLUTION processing module in the Acuity task led us to weight it here. Furthermore, this weighting is justified by Finke and Kosslyn's (1980) finding that the farther apart two dots were, the farther subjects could image the pair of them moving toward the periphery before they became indistinguishable; the distance between the dots or stripes in theory affects only the RESOLUTION processing module. Thus, we have evidence that the efficiency of this module can affect the dependent measure. (Note that the sensitivity of this module in part also reflects differences in the coarseness of the grain of the visual buffer at different locations.)

Results. As expected, the wider the grating, the farther it was moved into the periphery before the subject reported that it matched the blur criterion, $F(2, 50/ = 33.33, p < 0.0001$. This result supports the inference that the data do in fact reflect properties of the visual buffer and the sensitivity of the RESOLUTION processing module. In addition, the mean estimate of 35.2 degrees of visual arc is in the range of that reported by Kosslyn (1970) and in Experiment 2 of Finke and Kosslyn (1980), which was taken to reflect the range of simultaneous attention over an image. This finding confers construct validity to our individual differences measure. For purposes of later analysis, larger separations at the point of blur were taken as evidence of better performance.

Mental Rotation

In this task subjects were shown alphanumeric characters at different tilts. The characters R, G, 2, 5 and 7 were used, and each was presented at six different orientations about the circle (spaced at 60° increments). Half the time the characters faced normally and half the time they were mirror-reversed. Subjects were asked to image the character revolving in a clockwise direction until it was upright, and then were to classify the direction in which it faced. Earlier work revealed that subjects spontaneously mentally rotate figures to the upright in this task even without being instructed to do so, but usually go the 'shortest way around'—not in a single direction (see Shepard and Cooper, 1983). Cooper (1975) demonstrated that subjects could rotate images in a single direction, and we used her instructions in an effort to obtain more stable estimates of an individual's speed of mental rotation.

The model. The LOAD processing module is used to encode the stimulus, and then the ROTATE processing module is used to rotate the image clockwise. As the image is rotated it is monitored by the FIND processing module, which stops the rotation when the figure is upright. After the image is correctly oriented the REGENERATE processing module is used prior to using the FIND processing module to classify the direction in which the character faces (which in part involves first identifying the character).

The speed of rotation is our measure, and hence the only two processing modules that are relevant are ROTATE and FIND. Differences in the speed of both modules will affect the speed of rotation, assuming that the ROTATE processing module will not operate faster than the FIND processing module can monitor its progress. Thus, both processing modules were weighted. This decision is justified by the fact that times are slowed down when stimuli are presented at more extreme angular disparities from the standard upright; differences in orientation in theory selectively tax only the ROTATE and FIND processing modules (the LOAD module operates the same regardless of the orientation of the stimulus). Thus, variations in the efficacy of these modules should affect our dependent measure, and we felt justified in weighting these two processing modules in later analyses.[9]

Results. Increasingly more time was required to classify figures that were rotated increasing amounts, $F(5, 170) = 20.76$, $p < 0.0001$, replicating Cooper (1975) and being consistent with our weightings. This result is good evidence that subjects generally followed the instructions and confers construct validity on our measure. (Errors did not tend to increase as times decreased, belying a speed–accuracy tradeoff). For purposes of later analyses, we computed the speed with which each subject rotated the image. (In computing these slopes, however, we omitted the times from stimuli rotated 300°

---

[9]The dependent measure used in the rotation task was the speed of rotation, which is completely independent of the efficiency of the REGENERATE processing module used to refresh the image after it is rotated, prior to being classified (the speed of this processing module would contribute to the intercept of the function, not the slope). Thus, in all analyses reported here we have deleted this component from this one model, which clearly could not have contributed to the performance measure we used.

because there was evidence that at least some subjects rotated these stimuli the 'short way around'.) We reasoned that if the slope was not positive (as it was not for three subjects) we could not take it to reflect the speed of rotation. Faster rates of rotation were taken as evidence of better performance. The three subjects producing negative slopes were scored lower than the steepest slope (we reasoned that if rotation had been easy for these subjects, they would not have been motivated to use an alternative strategy).

Line drawings memory
The performance measures in this task were designed to be especially sensitive to how much material a given person could maintain in an image at once. Subjects imaged configurations of different numbers of one-inch lines (from 2 to 10) connected end to end, hearing a sequence of instructions (e.g., North, Northwest, East ...) and constructing each imaged short segment attached to the end of the previous one. After all directions were presented, the subject made a speeded judgment about whether the end was above or below the starting point (this task encouraged use of imagery, in addition to providing a measure of how well the image was maintained—as will be discussed in the following section). Finally, the subjects drew the configuration. Subjects received training in drawing configurations prior to the experiment and no subject had difficulty in drawing *per se*. This task was modeled after one by Bower (1972), who found that the inclusion of more segments impaired memory for the configuration.

The model. The PICTURE processing module is used to image the first line at the center of the visual buffer. The REGENERATE processing module is used to maintain the image until the next command is heard. If this command specifies the location of a new item, the PUT processing module uses the FIND processing module to locate where the new segment should be placed, and then uses this information to set the PICTURE processing module so that a new segment is imaged in the correct location. Once this is done, the image is again regenerated until a new command is received. When the command is not a new direction, but is the word "endpoint", a second task (described below) is performed and then the imaged pattern is drawn.

The dependent measure used in this task was the mean number of segments correctly drawn. As was discussed earlier (in the section describing the weighting procedure), only the REGENERATE processing module was weighted in subsequent analyses.

Results. Subjects were generally less accurate in reproducing the line drawings that contained more segments, as witnessed by decreased drawing scores (percent of lines drawn correctly), $F(8, 272) = 51.36$, $p < 0.0001$. This result is as expected if the REGENERATE processing module is taxed increasingly more when increasing numbers of segments must be maintained in the image. For purposes of later analyses our measure was the mean percent correct across trials. Drawings were scored by considering each pair of lines in turn. If two lines were correctly positioned relative to each other, they were considered correct—even if previous lines were incorrect. Two judges scored the drawings independently and the few disagreements were resolved easily. Higher drawing scores were taken as evidence of better performance.

Line drawings probe times

As noted above, immediately before drawing the imaged pattern of line segments, subjects judged whether the endpoint was above or below the starting point.

The model. The REGENERATE processing module is first used to make the image as clear as possible. Next, the FIND processing module is used to 'glance' in the rough direction of the start point (in the simulation model it would execute tests in the relevant region of the visual buffer). If the start point is not immediately 'visible' (because it is not in the region of highest acuity in the visual buffer), the SCAN processing module is used to 'see' the start point clearly. We assume that the subject can quickly compute the rough direction in which to scan on the basis of at least partial memories of the directions *per se* (which were used by the PUT processing module to position the line segments correctly; see Kosslyn, 1981). Finally, the actual spatial judgment is carried out by the FIND processing module.

Our dependent measure here is the time to make the above/below judgment. Variations in the efficacy of the REGENERATE, FIND and SCAN processing modules all can affect the speed of response, and hence all three processing modules were weighted. This decision is supported by an analysis of how stimulus factors can affect the dependent measure; variations in the number of segments will tax the REGENERATE processing module to greater or lesser degrees, with more time being required to regenerate the image on each cycle (see Kosslyn, 1980, ch. 7 for a discussion of relevant data). In addition, the distance between the endpoints will affect both the time required to scan (with more time being required to scan further distances, as was found by Kosslyn *et al.* (1978)), and the decision time (with closer points being more difficult to judge, as was found by Kosslyn *et al.* (1977)). The effects of distance on scanning time in theory reflect the speed of operation of both the SCAN and FIND modules (with the FIND module monitoring the SCAN one). In addition, the effects of distance on judgment time in theory affect the speed of the FIND module in reaching a decision. Thus, we were justified in weighting all three processing modules used in performing this task.

Results. The primary determinant of response times was the vertical distance between the starting and endpoints (presuming that the configuration was imaged correctly), with times increasing with closer—and hence less discriminable—points, $F(8, 368) = 7.76$, $p < 0.0001$. This result confers construct validity on the Line Drawings task, as it would not be expected if a visual image were not being processed. Thus, we have confidence that both measures from this task reflect imagery processing ability. There was no effect of the number of segments *per se* on the response times, $p < 0.25$ in a regression analysis. This finding may indicate that subjects gave the first and last segments a high priority in their efforts to maintain the image— perhaps in part because they knew that they would need to remember these segments to do this judgment task. Finally, there was a mean of 10.8% errors, which is a higher degree of accuracy than would be expected if people did not in fact visualize the configurations (and instead used verbal rehearsal or the like). Our measure for later analyses was the overall mean time subjects took to decide whether the endpoint was above or below the start point. Faster times were taken as evidence of better performance.

Imaging Described Scenes
This task was designed to be sensitive primarily to a person's ability to image scenes on the basis of verbal descriptions. Subjects heard the names of four objects and their relative locations, and were asked to form an image of the described scene (e.g., "Briefcase; 4 inches up place a Horse; 1 inch left place a Beaver; 1 inch down place an Onion"). After imaging the described scene, subjects mentally focused on one object and scanned to another, indicating whether they had scanned left or right by pressing one of two buttons as soon as they were focused on the second, 'target' object in the image. Pairs were arranged such that eight different distances occurred. Scan time was used as an index of distance, with the aim of assessing how accurately the scene was constructed. This paradigm is a variation of one used by Kosslyn *et al.* (1978, Experiment 4). Subjects received practice drawing displays and answering on the basis of the drawings prior to the task, and all subjects clearly understood the instructions and could draw correctly arranged displays of labeled dots.

The model. The PICTURE processing module is used to image the first object named. For the following three items the direction and distance are input to the PUT processing module, which (using the FIND processing module to locate the previous object in the image, which serves as the 'foundation part' for the new one, and the PICTURE processing module to form the image) places the subsequent images in the correct locations. After each item is arranged, the REGENERATE processing module is used to maintain the image. After the image is completed, subjects focus on the first object of the to-be-scanned pair, which is located via the FIND processing module. They then hear the name of the second object, and scan to it. Scanning is accomplished using the SCAN processing module, with the FIND processing module monitoring it so that scanning stops when the target is in focus. Finally, when the FIND processing module discovers that the target item is in focus, a response is made. The response is determined by the direction, left or right, of the trajectory of the scan path (computed by the FIND module).

Our dependent measure in this task is the correlation between the assumed distance and scan time. This measure is especially sensitive to deviations from the correct distances among objects—which would be produced by the PUT processing module—and the regularity and direction of the SCAN processing module. Thus, the PUT and SCAN processing modules were weighted for later analyses. (Because we are not assessing the speed of scanning, the FIND processing module is not weighted.) Previous results have shown that the time to scan depends on where points are placed in an image and the directness of the scan path (see Kosslyn *et al.*, 1978), which underline the importance of the PUT and SCAN modules in this task.

Results. Much to our surprise, there was no systematic relationship between scan time and presumed distance, $F(7, 238) = 1.27$, $p < 0.25$. The error rates were quite high for some of the distances (e.g., 20% and 22% for 2.24 and 4.24 inches, respectively), providing further evidence that most subjects did not preserve distances accurately in their images. As is evident in Table 2, some subjects did reveal the familiar relationship between time and distance scanned (see Kosslyn, 1983 for a review), but many did not. Our individual differences measure was the correlation between the distance separating the objects, as implicit in the description, and the time taken to scan between the objects. For purposes of later analysis, higher correlations with distance were taken as evidence of better performance. We felt justified in treating larger negative correlations as worse scores because they are indications of increasingly greater distortions of the presumed distances and/or of increasingly less direct scan paths.

Image Generation

Subjects saw a series of ambiguous geometric figures (those used in Experiment 3 of Kosslyn et al., 1983b). Before seeing a figure, the subject saw a description and was asked to 'see' the figure as being composed according to the description. There were two sets of stimuli: in one, the figures were described as a set of overlapping shapes (e.g., two triangles, for the Star of David); in the other, the figures were described as a set of contiguous shapes (e.g., a hexagon and six triangles for the Star of David). The figure was then removed, and the subject was cued to form an image of it, pressing a button when the image was completed. This task was identical to one reported by Kosslyn et al. (1983b), who found that image generation times increased with the number of units predicated in the descriptions of the figures. (Thus, the same shape took different amounts of time to generate in an image, depending on the way it was described.)

The model. The most central part of a figure is imaged via the PICTURE processing module, and this part then serves as the foundation part for the next part. The PUT processing module then accesses the stored description (which indicates how the parts are arranged), and uses the FIND processing module to locate where each subsequent part belongs and the PICTURE processing module to image the part in the correct location.

Our measure here is the average increase in time to form images as each additional part is added (i.e., the slope of the function relating image formation time to the number of parts). This measure is clearly sensitive to differences in the speed of all three processing modules. Hence, our criterion leads us to weight all three modules. This decision is consistent with findings by Kosslyn et al. (1983b) that demonstrate that the complexity of parts and the difficulty of 'seeing' the foundation part affect generation time, which in theory taxes the PICTURE and FIND modules, respectively. Beech and Allport (1978) showed that differences in the described relation affect image generation time, which presumably tax the PUT processing module to different degrees. Thus, all three modules have been implicated in previous research as affecting generation time in similar tasks, and it makes sense that individual differences in their speed would affect processing here. These results justify our weighting all three processing modules.

Results. More time was required to generate images of figures described using many units (contiguous parts) than using fewer units (overlapping parts), $F(1, 34) = 58.85$, $p < 0.0001$. In addition, times increased with the number of predicated units *per se*, $F(5, 170) = 32.77$, $p < 0.0001$. Thus, we have replicated the results of Kosslyn et al. (1983b), and have reason to believe that subjects performed the task as instructed. For later analyses, we computed for each subject the slope of the increase in image formation time with increasing numbers of units. This measure indexed the speed with which additional parts could be placed on an image. Faster speeds (shallower slopes) were taken as evidence of better performance. Three subjects produced negative slopes, suggesting that they were not doing the task. If the task had been easy for them, we reasoned, they would have been likely to do it. Thus, we assigned these three people scores 0.01 below the lowest obtained from the other subjects.

Reorganization task

On half the trials, the subjects were asked to alter the organization of the imaged figure: if it was organized as contiguous forms, it was to be reorganized into overlapping forms and *vice versa*. The subject simply pressed a button when the reorganization was complete.

The model. The REGENERATE processing module is used first to make the image as sharp as possible. The FIND processing module is then used to locate a new unit (i.e., one included in the new description, for example a hexagon in the Star of David). If it fails to locate one before the image has faded, the PICTURE processing module is used to fill in the missing parts and the FIND processing module tries again.[10] Once a configuration of lines corresponding to a new part has been found, the PARSE processing module is used. This processing module regenerates only selected segments, in this case just those segments that should be organized together. Thus, these segments are now at the same 'fade phase', and become organized together into a single unit in accordance with the Gestalt law of similarity (see the discussion in section 1). Once a new unit is parsed, the image is regenerated and the entire procedure is repeated until the figure is completely reorganized.

Our measure in the reorganization task is the time to reorganize the image. Variations in the speed of all four processing modules will affect response

---

[10]The REGENERATE processing module can only maintain images in the visual buffer; once they have faded, it cannot bring them back from long-term memory. In the computer simulation model the PICTURE processing module is given parameter values for the size and location (in the visual buffer) of the to-be-imaged pattern. These parameter values can be stored temporarily, associated with the long-term memory encoding of the pattern, and thus the PUT and FIND processing modules are not necessarily required to generate an image of a pattern immediately after it has faded. We assume that this is also true of people, who presumably can use the PICTURE processing module to regenerate an image from long-term memory. However, the PICTURE processing module can be used to regenerate an image only if the requisite parameter values are being stored. In the Line Drawings task subjects presumably did not have time to store the sets of parameter values for each segment, and hence had to rely on the REGENERATE processing module.

time, and hence all four were weighted. This decision is consistent with previous research demonstrating that variations in the complexity of an imaged object, pattern, or scene affect inspection and generation times (see Kosslyn, 1980, chs. 6 and 7). Such variations in stimulus complexity in theory affect the speed of the FIND, REGENERATE, and PICTURE processing modules (as was described earlier), which is consistent with our emphasizing the importance of these modules for affecting this dependent measure. There is no independent evidence supporting our weighting of the PARSE processing module, and thus we will have to look at the group data in this experiment to justify this weighting; generally faster times to switch from an overlapping to a contiguous organization rather than *vice versa* will reflect in part the importance of the PARSE module, for reasons to be described below.

Results. Subjects took less time to reorganize an imaged figure from the overlapping to the contiguous description than *vice versa*, $F(1, 34) = 36.48$, $p < 0.0001$. This finding is evidence that subjects were in fact reorganizing their images, given that it confirms a prediction of the theory: it should be difficult to form a single overlapping unit from segments belonging to different contiguous units because they are at different 'fade phases', and hence are difficult to 'see' at the same time; in contrast, most of the segments of a to-be-created contiguous unit are contained in a single overlapping unit in the initial image. This finding also justified our weighting of the PARSE module, given that its speed of operation will affect the degree of this difference in organizational ease. In addition, times differed with changes in the number of units between the original and the reorganized description, $F(4, 136) = 16.74$, $p < 0.0001$ (going from overlapping to contiguous, 2026, 2182, and 2326 msec were required for changes of one, three, and five units). These and other, more subtle, results (see Kosslyn *et al.*, 1983a) provide evidence that subjects did indeed reorganize the figures and serve to indicate the importance of all four processing modules. Thus, the group results confer construct validity to our measure of individual differences and credibility to our weightings. For purposes of later analyses, shorter times were taken as evidence of better performance.

Image Inspection

After the geometric figure was imaged in the task just described, the subjects reorganized the figure on half of the trials; on the other half of the trials they were asked instead to 'see' a feature of the figure. If the figure was reorganized, then such a probe was presented after reorganization. On most of the probe trials (whether they followed image generation immediately or followed image reorganization), the subjects were asked whether a given geometric form (e.g., triangle, square) could be 'seen' in the image. On two of the twenty trials of each type (overlapping or contiguous) subjects were not asked to look for a form, but were asked whether the figure was symmetrical along a given axis (horizontal, vertical, or diagonal); these trials were included to encourage subjects to generate and maintain good images. Subjects responded 'true' by pressing one button, and 'false' by pressing another. This task was identical to that used in Experiment 3 of Kosslyn *et al.* (1983b).

The model. For 'true' trials, where a pattern is actually located in the imaged figure, our model is as follows (this model is incomplete for 'false' trials, which will not be considered here). The REGENERATE processing module is used to make the image as clear as possible prior to inspection, and the FIND processing module is used to search for the named feature. If the figure is complex or the part is composed of segments from different units in the image, the image may fade before the part is found. In this case, the PICTURE processing module will be used to fill in the image again, and the inspection procedure will continue until the feature is found.

Our dependent measure here is the time to find a feature of the imaged figure. The speed of all three processing modules will affect this time, and hence all three were weighted. As noted above, response time is affected by stimulus factors (complexity, type of feature) that should affect the speed of each of the three processing modules, which supports our hypothesizing that individual differences in their efficacy are important determinants of image inspection time.

Results. We examined the probes following directly after image generation separately from those following image reorganization (suspecting that the quality of the image might be different in the two cases). For non-reorganized figures, times were generally faster for figures described in terms of relatively few, overlapping shapes instead of relatively many, continuous shapes, $F(1, 46) = 15.08, p < 0.001$. This finding supports the inference that subjects were in fact inspecting imaged patterns, given that more complex objects or patterns tend to be more degraded in an image and more difficult to inspect (see Kosslyn, 1980, ch. 7). In contrast, once a figure was reorganized it took less time to inspect if it was composed of contiguous forms, $F(1,46) = 19.17, p < 0.001$. Apparently, figures reorganized from initial contiguous organizations were imaged poorly and were difficult to inspect. Errors did not tend to increase as times decreased, belying speed-accuracy tradeoffs.

For purposes of later analyses, the mean time to 'see' a part was computed for non-reorganized and reorganized images for each subject. Faster times were taken as evidence of better performance.

Form Board

At the conclusion of the final session each subject was given five written tests and one questionnaire; the Form Board test and VVIQ questionnaire have been taken by previous researchers to assess imagery ability, and thus these scores were analyzed along with the measures collected in our other tasks. The remaining tests have not been taken to reflect imagery ability, and thus these scores were analyzed later with an eye toward discovering whether individual differences in imagery abilities reflect differences in more general cognitive abilities.

The Form Board test (VZ-1) was taken from the "Kit of factor referenced cognitive tests", prepared by Ekstrom *et al.* (1976). This test requires a person to decide how many of a set of five two-dimensional shapes could be fitted together into a pattern that matched a standard form. Because of time constraints we used only Part 1 of the test, containing 24 trials.

The model. Unlike the tasks we created, which were designed to be relatively simple, there were multiple possible models for performance of this task—each representing a different possible strategy. We chose the one utilizing the fewest number of processing modules for purposes of analysis, which is as follows. The LOAD processing module first forms an image of a part, and then this image is compared to the shape of the standard form. If there is no possible way it could fit (e.g., it is too tall), a 'no' response is made for that part and a new one is encoded. When there is a possibility that the part could fit into the standard, the TRANSLATE and ROTATE processing modules are used to explore possible fits, until the FIND processing module determines whether or not it will fit. When a part fits, a 'yes' response is made, and then an image of it is maintained in the proper location in the standard form. The image must be maintained because the composite of the parts imaginally inserted into the form constrains the 'space' available to fit other parts. Thus, the REGENERATE processing module is used to maintain the image prior to using the LOAD module to encode a new part. This entire procedure is repeated until the standard is filled with imaged parts.

Our method for determining weights depends on which processing modules can improve performance (on a specific dependent measure) if they operate more efficiently. Given that the task is timed, the speed of each module is important; this consideration led us to weight all of the processing modules. However, when we attempted to justify these weightings, we considered which stimulus factors affect performance, and tried to identify these effects with specific modules. These factors are the similarity of forms to the standard, the amount of rotation and translation necessary, and the number and complexity of the forms that must be maintained in the image over time. We had evidence that these stimulus factors affect performance in similar tasks, and our theory localized these effects to all but the LOAD processing module (we have no evidence that the differences in part shape *per se* made the part more or less difficult to encode into an image). Thus, all but the LOAD processing module was weighted in subsequent analyses.

For purposes of later analysis, each subject's score was the total number of parts marked correctly minus the total number marked incorrectly; this measure allows 'partial credit' for combinations that were nearly correct. Higher scores were taken as evidence of better performance.

Vividness of Visual Imagery Questionnaire

The VVIQ consists of a set of descriptions of scenes or properties of scenes that the subject is to image. For example, "The sun is rising above the horizon into a hazy sky" and "The color and shape of a lake". The subject is to rate the vividness of each image, using a five-point rating scale (ranging from "perfectly clear and as vivid as normal vision" to "no image at all, you only 'know' that you are thinking of the object"). The subject rated each of the 32 items twice, once with eyes open and once with eyes closed.

The model. The PUT, FIND, and PICTURE processing modules are used to form a composite image as described. Once formed, the REGENERATE processing module is used to sharpen the image prior to using the RESOLU-TION processing module to assess its vividness.

Determining which components should be weighted in this task was extremely difficult, given the number of possible factors that can affect a subjective rating. Considering the model, however, it seemed clear that differences in the RESOLUTION processing module would affect differences in apparent vividness, as would differences in the efficiency of the PICTURE processing module which produces an image in the visual buffer. Thus, it seemed most conservative to weight only these two processing modules. Previous results reviewed by Finke (1980) and Marks (1977) showed that people who report less vivid images perform more poorly on a variety of imagery tasks than do people who report more vivid imagery. These findings impart some construct validity to this measure, and the RESOLUTION and PICTURE processing modules would be primarily responsible for variations in vividness.

For purposes of later analysis, each subject's score was the sum of the ratings for all the items.

Non-imagery Tests

Four additional tests were administered from the Ekstrom *et al.* kit, none of which involved imagery. The Auditory Number Span Test (MS-1) assessed how many digits a person could hold in short-term memory; the Extended Range Vocabulary Test (V-3) assessed how well subjects could identify synonyms; the Different Uses Test (XU-4) assessed how many uses subjects could associate quickly in common objects (soap, barrel, sock and snap); and the Nonsense Syllogisms Test (RL-1) assessed how well subjects could determine whether specific conclusions were implied by nonsensical premises in simple syllogisms (e.g., "All trees are fish; All fish are horses; Therefore, all trees are horses").

3. Processing analysis

We now are in a position to address the questions that motivated us to do this study, namely, is imagery ability general and undifferentiated or is it a consequence of a set of relatively independent subabilities? And if the latter, do these subabilities correspond to those posited in the Kosslyn and Shwartz theory? We began to address these questions by correlating the scores assigned to each person across the different tasks, producing the matrix presented in Table 3.

If imagery ability were general and undifferentiated (i.e., people were either 'good' or 'bad' at imagery in general), then these correlations should have been uniformly high. This clearly was not the case. Further, as is evident in Table 4, the split-half reliabilities of the individual tasks are reasonably high (with a mean of $r = 0.78$), and are much higher than most of the correlations. Thus, the low correlations evident in Table 3 are not due to

Table 3.   *Correlations among scores for performance measures for the different tasks*

	1	2	3	4	5	6	7	8	9	10	11	12	13
1. Acuity	X												
2. Oblique	0.43	X											
3. Extent	0.55	0.59	X										
4. Rot. Slope	−0.09	0.06	−0.12	X									
5. Line Dr. Mem.	−0.19	−0.10	0.13	−0.09	X								
6. Line Dr. Time	0.11	−0.22	0.16	−0.23	0.39	X							
7. Des. Scenes	−0.08	−0.13	−0.17	−0.02	0.05	−0.25	X						
8. Gen. Slope	0.02	0.26	0.04	0.02	0.05	0.21	−0.10	X					
9. Reorg. Time	0.02	0.10	−0.04	0.11	0.00	−0.04	−0.18	0.26	X				
10. Reorg. Probe	0.00	0.09	−0.04	0.21	0.28	0.23	−0.27	0.30	0.64	X			
11. Nonreorg. Probe	0.08	0.19	0.10	0.16	0.18	0.01	−0.25	0.28	0.63	0.79	X		
12. Form Board	−0.31	0.01	0.02	−0.01	0.51	0.01	0.06	−0.04	−0.01	0.26	0.32	X	
13. VVIQ	−0.06	−0.44	−0.26	−0.19	0.04	0.08	−0.14	−0.19	0.29	0.07	0.06	0.07	X

Table 4. *Split-half reliabilities for each of the imagery tasks*[†, §]

Task	Mean for first half	Mean for second half	r	t (first half–second half)
Acuity	49.1	52.9	0.87	−1.27
Oblique	0.33	0.30	0.67	0.73
Extent	6.4	7.6	0.91	−3.80**
Rot. slope	10.1	12.4	0.86	−2.30*
Line Dr. mem.	50.6	56.7	0.80	−3.96**
Line Dr. time	2457	2067	0.95	−5.35**
Des. Scenes	0.01	0.05	0.58	−0.79
Gen. Slope	337	181	0.63	2.54*
Reorg. Time	2978	2266	0.65	3.61**
Reorg. Probe	3119	2773	0.86	2.61*
Nonreorg. Probe	2300	2507	0.72	−1.87

[†]Units are described in Table 2.

[§]The reliability used for the Form Board tests was $r = 0.81$, reported in Ekstrom *et al.* (1976, p. 15); the reliability used for the VVIQ was the average of the 0.84 reported by Marks (1977) and the 0.82 obtained with our subjects.

Significant values here in all cases reveal the effects of practice (the sign of the value depends on the units of measurement); $* = p < 0.05$, $** = p < 0.01$.

error of measurement or exceptionally noisy data.[11] In addition, the correlations are not simply uniformly low, as would be expected if each task recruited an entirely independent ability. Rather, there was a range between −0.44 and 0.79 (with an absolute mean of 0.28), as would be expected if the tasks shared greater or lesser numbers of the same underlying component processing modules. Presumably, the more shared processing modules, the higher the correlation. Negative correlations arise when non-shared processing modules are negatively correlated across people (as could occur, for example, between the ROTATE and REGENERATE processing modules, if people who are good at maintaining images over time tend not to develop fast image transformations). In theory, such negative correlations among the efficacies of individual processing modules should be increasingly less likely to show up as negative correlations among measures of task performance when the tasks have more processing modules in common, because the influence of the common processing modules should lead to a positive correlation,

---

[11]The split-half reliabilities were computed by calculating separate scores for the first and second halves of the trials for each task, and then correlating these scores across subjects. In the Mental Rotation and Image Inspection tasks there were slightly more observations in one half than in the other because an odd number of trials was used in each condition.

overshadowing the influence of the remaining non-shared processing modules.

The pattern of correlations in Table 3 is also interesting because it provides some face validity to the dramatic differences we sometimes found between these results and those from the corresponding experiments performed with college student subjects. That is, we were repeatedly surprised at how poorly many of our subjects performed our tasks; indeed, the average rotation slope was about three times steeper than that found by Cooper (1975) with college subjects. One could argue that this poor performance is in part a motivational factor, that these people were not 'good subjects'. But if so, some surely would have been more motivated than others, and we would have expected results indicating simply that some people are generally better than others. This was not the case. One could also argue that subjects were motivated to perform only some of the tasks, with different subjects being motivated more or less for different tasks. But why would motivation differ systematically across tasks, if there is indeed an underlying structure to the pattern of correlations? If the subject neglected those tasks that were especially difficult for him or her, then the fact that subjects did poorly on a task still serves to provide a measure of underlying ability.

If our tasks were in fact performed using a relatively small set of distinct processing modules, and these modules are specific to image representation and use, then we would not expect correlations between our measures and scores on non-imagery tests. As is evident in Table 5, this was by and large true. First, the mean absolute correlation between imagery and non-imagery tasks was $r = 0.15$, which is not significant. However, 15% of these correlations were significant, which is greater than we would expect by chance alone. A closer look at Table 5 reveals that for nine of the thirteen imagery tasks there were no significant correlations between scores on our performance measures and scores on the non-imagery tests, and for two more of our tasks there was a relatively low correlation with one of the non-imagery tests. For these eleven tasks, then, there were about as many significant correlations as would be expected due to chance alone. In contrast, the line drawing scores were clearly related to the non-imagery test scores, with all four of these scores being significantly correlated with performance in the Line Drawing task. Similarly, the Form Board scores were significantly correlated with two of the non-imagery test scores. Both the Line Drawing task and the Form Board test purportedly critically require using the REGENERATE processing module to maintain information over time. This processing module may be enhanced if one is good at figuring out the optimal way to 'chunk' the image, to organize it into fewer units. This chunking skill may reflect a more general 'intelligence' factor that is also tapped by the non-imagery tests (but not, apparently, the other imagery tasks). This notion is consistent with the fact that there were significant correlations between 83% of the non-imagery test scores (every possible pair but one). These results converge nicely with those of Kosslyn *et al.* (1984), who found that a Broca's and a Wernicke's aphasic—both of whom exhibited severe impairments in verbal ability—performed relatively well on imagery tasks. In any event, it is clear that in general our imagery tasks are not simply tapping a general undifferentiated imagery ability or general cognitive skill.[12]

Given the evidence that the imagery tasks recruited distinct processing components, it makes sense to ask whether the Kosslyn and Shwartz theory adequately characterizes the underlying processing. We began by estimating the similarity in the processing of each pair of tasks using a simple procedure: For each pair, we counted how many different processing modules were used; this number was treated as a denominator. We then counted how many processing modules were purportedly shared in the two tasks; this number became the numerator. Further, if a processing module was shared and was weighted in *both* tasks, we added two more points to the numerator; this number was chosen because on the average the tasks had about two non-weighted processing modules, and we considered one weighted processing module to be at least as important as the non-weighted processing modules in a task. In addition, if a processing module was weighted and used in only one task, we added two points to the denominator, producing the values presented in Table 6. This measure of similarity can vary from 0 to 3.0, given the tasks used here; thus, we are not predicting correlations *per se*, but merely the similarities among the different pairs of measures.

The first measure of adequacy of the Kosslyn and Shwartz theory was the simple correlation between the predicted and observed similarities (i.e., Tables 3 and 6). This correlation was $r = 0.56$, $p < 0.0001$. This correlation is highly significant and must be evaluated in light of the average split-half reliability of $r = 0.78$, which provides one measure of the systematic variance in the data. (If performance on a task correlates with itself only this amount,

---

[12]It is tempting to compare the mean absolute correlation between the imagery tasks (0.28) with the absolute correlation between the imagery and non-imagery tasks (0.15), looking for an overall difference. However, if the correlations reflect the proportion of shared processing modules, then the magnitudes of the correlations will be determined by the particular tasks and tests used. The low mean correlations suggest that few weighted processing modules are shared, on average, by the imagery tasks—as per our intentions—or by the imagery and non-imagery tasks. Perhaps the best estimate of how similar the two types of processing can be is the highest correlation, 0.47 for imagery/non-imagery correlations, compared to 0.79 for imagery/imagery correlations. Clearly, the imagery tasks can share more common processing with each other than they can with the non-imagery tests examined here.

Table 5.   *Correlations between scores from four non-imagery tests and the imagery performance measures*

	Mem. span	Vocab.	Diff. uses	Syllogism
Acuity	0.03	−0.15	−0.17	0.06
Oblique	−0.02	−0.01	−0.08	0.15
Extent	0.14	−0.04	−0.09	0.18
Rot. Slopes	−0.06	0.10	−0.08	0.20
Line Dr. Mem	0.45**	0.37**	0.29*	0.35*
Line Dr. Time	0.24	0.23	−0.04	0.35*
Des. Scenes	−0.07	−0.09	−0.03	−0.18
Gen. Slopes	−0.02	0.01	−0.13	0.16
Reorg. Time	0.18	0.03	−0.10	−0.03
Reorg. Probe	0.35*	0.11	−0.01	0.15
Nonreorg. Probe	0.17	0.15	0.06	0.21
Form Board	0.19	0.32*	0.47**	0.20
VVIQ	0.02	0.01	0.25	−0.03
Mem. Span	X	0.29*	−0.05	0.35*
Vocab.		X	0.41**	0.39**
Diff. Uses			X	0.28*
Syllogism				X

Table 6.   *Predicted similarities among task performance, using the Kosslyn and Shwartz theory*

	1	2	3	4	5	6	7	8	9	10	11	12	13
1. Acuity	X												
2. Oblique	0.67	X											
3. Extent	1.00	0.67	X										
4. Rot. Slope	0.08	0.29	0.08	X									
5. Line Dr. Mem	0.11	0.25	0.11	0.10	X								
6. Line Dr. Time	0.08	0.22	0.08	0.27	0.57	X							
7. Des. Scenes	0.07	0.15	0.07	0.08	0.57	0.71	X						
8. Gen. Slope	0.00	0.08	0.00	0.27	0.50	0.23	0.71	X					
9. Reorg. Time	0.07	0.17	0.07	0.21	0.71	0.55	0.25	0.55	X				
10. Reorg. Probe	0.08	0.22	0.08	0.27	1.25	0.75	0.33	0.75	1.50	X			
11. Nonreorg. Probe	0.08	0.22	0.08	0.27	1.25	0.75	0.33	0.75	1.30	3.00	X		
12. Form Board	0.13	0.30	0.25	0.78	0.36	0.50	0.13	0.18	0.40	0.50	0.50	X	
13. VVIQ	0.44	0.63	0.44	0.08	0.57	0.17	0.40	0.71	0.50	0.71	0.71	0.13	X

we cannot expect much more than this when performance on different tasks is correlated.) In a second analysis, we simply eliminated the Form Board and VVIQ measures. The Form Board test is quite complex and clearly can be performed using numerous different strategies, only one of which (the simplest, in our judgment) was considered here. For example, one could encode each part into long-term memory and then use the PUT, PICTURE, and FIND processing module to try to fit the parts into the standard figure, instead of using the LOAD processing module, followed by various transformations, as we have assumed. And, there is no reason to assume that different people perform the tasks in the same way. The VVIQ requires a judgment rating that is difficult to relate to the putative underlying processing modules, which kept us particularly uncertain about our weighting assignments. Thus, we decided to examine only those tasks for which we had confidence in our models. The correlation between the predicted and observed similarities was now $r = 0.67$, $p < 0.0001$.[13]

We next examined our claim that the efficiency of the weighted processing modules was more important for determining performance than was the efficiency of the non-weighted processing modules. Now we simply compared the weighted processing modules in each task, adding 1 to the denominator for each additional weighted processing module used in the two tasks (i.e., used in either model) and adding 1 to the numerator for each additional shared weighted processing module (i.e., one used in both models). The correlation between this measure of similarity and the observed correlations among performance scores was $r = 0.61$ when all tasks were considered and $r = 0.78$ when the Form Board and VVIQ were excluded. Ignoring the weights resulted in correlations between predicted and observed of 0.26 and 0.37 for the two analyses. Clearly, variation in the weighted processing modules is primarily at the root of the observed individual differences in task performance. Although not perfect, the Kosslyn and Shwartz theory characterizes the underlying processing at least reasonably well.

Probably the best way to evaluate our theory is to contrast it with a plausible alternative theory. Unfortunately, there is no alternative theory for imagery processing, and thus we had to make up our own. We began by considering image *vividness* and *control*, two factors often assumed to underlie indi-

---

[13]We used Pearson r correlations because they are sensitive to the actual differences in the scores, not simply the rank ordering. However, one could question the underlying assumptions of linear relations among scores, even though no striking deviations from linearity were visible in the data. Thus, we re-computed the correlations in Table 3 using Spearman's *rho*, correlating the rank performances rather than the scores. This correlation matrix was then correlated with the predicted similarity matrix (Table 6), producing a correlation of 0.596, compared to 0.564 before. Clearly, our use of the Pearson's r has not led us astray.

Table 7.   *Performance factors in the common sense theory*

Task	Factors			
	Vividness	Control	Memory	Speed
Acuity	X	X		
Oblique	X	X	X	
Extent	X	X		
Rot. Slope		X		X
Line Dr. Mem			X	
Line Dr. Time		X	X	X
Des. Scenes		X	X	
Gen. Slope				X
Reorg. Time	X	X		X
Reorg. Probe	X		X	X
Nonreorg. Probe	X		X	X
Form Board	X	X	X	X
VVIQ	X			

vidual differences in imagery ability (see Marks, 1977; Richardson, 1969; White *et al.*, 1977). In addition, a person's overall *speed* of processing and *memory* ability seemed intuitively plausible as factors that affect results in our tasks. Two of us familiar with the tasks categorized each task in terms of whether or not each factor was relevant, as is presented in Table 7; this categorization was done before the actual correlation matrix was obtained. These categorizations did not rest on any of the assumptions of our theory, such as those concerning the role of the FIND processing module in image generation, but rather were based on 'common sense'.

The alternative 'common sense theory' was used to generate a new set of predicted similarities among all pairs of tasks. First, we simply computed a measure of similarity for each pair of tasks as we did with our models. The numerator was the number of shared positive values on each factor, and the denominator was the total number of different factors that purportedly contributed to processing in either task (with a maximum of 4). This measure of processing similarity correlated with the observed correlations among the performance scores only $r = 0.30$. This result is comparable to the analysis using our models without weights, and seemed hardly fair, given that the common sense theory was so much simpler than ours; thus, we proceeded to make more subtle comparisons using regression analysis (cf. Sternberg, 1977).

In our first regression analysis we created four independent variables. For each pair of tasks, the vividness, control, speed, and memory requirement scores presented in Table 7 were compared. If the values were the same (both + or both blank), a 2 was assigned to that factor; if they were different, a 1 was assigned. The observed correlations were regressed onto these values. The simple correlations between each factor and the observed correlations were: vividness, $r = 0.18$; control, $r = -0.04$; speed, $r = 0.21$; memory, $r = 0.01$. The multiple correlation was $R = 0.29$.

The comparable analysis was done using our models. Now a 4 was assigned if a processing module was weighted and used in the two tasks being compared, a 3 if it was either present or not present in both (but not weighted in both), a 2 if it was in one but not the other, and a 1 if it was in one and weighted but not in the other. The multiple R was now 0.55. The similarity of the multiple correlation and the correlations observed in our initial analysis (comparing predicted task similarity and observed correlations among performance scores) is, of course, exactly as one would expect and gives us confidence in this regression procedure.

There are two problems with comparing the regression analyses evaluating the two theories. First, our theory has many more parameters. However, this theory was not invented just to explain the present data; rather, these processing modules were necessary to provide accounts for a wide range of data having nothing to do with individual differences (see Kosslyn, 1980). Nevertheless, it was of interest to concoct a slimmed-down version of our theory, considering only the four processing modules that were weighted most often, the FIND, PICTURE, REGENERATE, and RESOLUTION processing modules, which reflected all but the transformation abilities. The second problem in comparing the regression analyses testing the two theories lies in the fact that only binary values were used for the common sense theory whereas a wider range of weights (1, 2, 3, or 4 values) were used for our theory.

We therefore reanalyzed the data, this time considering only the four processing modules noted above and using a narrower range of values; we now assigned a 2 when two tasks shared a module *and* it was weighted in both tasks, and assigned a 1 otherwise. The multiple R between the similarities in shared processing modules and the observed correlations was 0.60. Even this slimmed-down version of our theory was superior to the intuitive common sense one, based on easily-observable surface properties of the tasks (such as whether speed or memory was important).

All of the foregoing correlations are improved if we ignore the Form Board and VVIQ measures. The common sense theory now produces a multiple R of 0.48 with the observed correlations, compared to an R of 0.70 for our theory. Remarkably, the multiple R now reached 0.82 when we consider only the weighted relations among the four most frequently weighted processing modules noted above. (Note, however, that as we slim down the theory we encounter another problem in performing the regression analyses, namely that of a restricted range: with fewer points being correlated, the apparent percentage of variance accounted for, R^2, is inflated.) In any event, performance on these two tasks apparently reflects complex processing that is not being characterized very well by the models, and/or the tasks are measuring substantially different things in different people.

Given the importance of the weighting scheme, we decided to conduct an independent test of how good our weighting procedure was. Table 8 presents a summary of a regression analysis using no weights at all. Here, a 2 was assigned if two tasks both included or excluded a given processing module and a 1 was assigned if only one of the tasks included the processing module. The observed correlations were than regressed on these independent variables. The beta weights in Table 8 represent the relative importance of each processing module in accounting for the correlations among the performance measures, and those differences in relative importance ought to be reflected by the theoretical weightings we have assigned. That is, according to our theory, the reason some processing modules have higher beta weights than others is that these processing modules are more often weighted when they occur, and hence when they occur they account for a greater amount of the similarities among task performance.

To examine this conjecture we performed a simple test. For each processing module, we examined how many times it occurred in the various tasks (see Fig. 1), and how many of those times it was weighted. We then computed

Table 8.   *Regression analysis using no weights*

Variable	Multiple R	Beta	Predicted weight
RESOLUTION	0.270	0.28139	1.0
SCAN	0.388	0.32299	1.0
PUT	0.434	0.18913	0.5
ROTATE	0.457	0.13787	0.67
REGENERATE	0.474	0.14769	0.55
FIND	0.485	0.14379	0.64
PICTURE	0.487	0.08099	0.71
LOAD	0.490	−0.07404	0
PARSE	0.491	−0.01869	−

a proportion, the number of times weighted relative to the number of times it occurred, for each processing module that was used more than once (all but the PAN and PARSE processing modules). These proportions were then simply correlated with the corresponding beta weights. This correlation was $r = 0.90$. When the Form Board and VVIQ were eliminated, this correlation was $r = 0.75$—the drop in correlation in part reflecting the decrease in the number of processing modules (the TRANSLATE processing module now appeared in only one model, and hence was not included) and the relatively higher contribution of the disparity between the predicted and observed contribution of the PICTURE processing module (evident in Table 8). It is not clear, however, whether this result is an artifact due to the FIND module being used whenever the PICTURE module is used in these tasks, or whether the weighting scheme was amiss (i.e., it should have been weighted in additional tasks or was weighted in some tasks where it should not have been). In any event, our weighting rule did a remarkably good job in assigning weights to the different processing modules in the different tasks.

'Bottom-up' analyses

So far we have been considering 'top-down' analyses of the data, examining the extent to which different models can account for the patterns of correlations. One could argue that such an approach forces the data into patterns that may not best characterize it. Thus, in this section we consider 'bottom-up' analyses of the data, considering the patterns of correlations in their own right. If the prior analyses have not done violence to the results, we should find that the patterns inherent in the data are easily explained by the theory.

Cluster analysis

The correlation matrix presented in Table 3 was submitted to a hierarchical cluster analysis (AGCLUS, written by D. Oliver). In this analysis, the most similar (highly correlated, in our case) items are grouped into an initial cluster and other items are added until the cluster consists of maximally-similar items, with the aim of also maximizing the inter-item similarity within the remaining clusters (see Johnson, 1966). The inter-cluster similarities, which are used to group the clusters hierarchically, are computed on the basis of the average similarity among items in a cluster (including the diagonal entries, which has the effect of biasing the solution toward clusters with small numbers of items). Negative signs were retained in this analysis: negative correlations are taken to reflect lower similarity than positive ones, given that we assume that when more processing modules are shared a negative correlation becomes increasingly less likely (see the discussion of Table 3 above).

Figure 2.   *Results of the AGCLUS cluster analysis. Underlining indicates that the processing module was weighted. When abbreviations are used, the first four or five letters of the name have been used.*

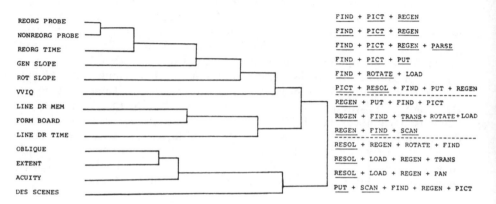

Figure 2 presents the results of performing the hierarchical clustering analysis on the data. The shorter the line connecting two measures into a cluster, the more tightly they are clustered. The first thing to notice about Fig. 2 is that clearly demarcated clusters were produced, as expected if a relatively small set of processing modules are used in imagery processing and tasks differ in the number of common modules recruited. The second thing to notice is that the clusters are easily interpreted in terms of the structures and processing modules posited by the Kosslyn and Shwartz theory:

The top cluster (starting with the reorganization probe times and ending with the VVIQ) contains all tasks in which both the FIND and PICTURE processing modules are weighted. It also includes the rotation slopes and VVIQ scores. This cluster, then, seems to reflect the efficiency of the FIND processing module in conjunction with transformation operations—either ones that produce images in the visual buffer on the basis of stored information or ones that manipulate the image in some way. The fact that the FIND processing module was not weighted in the VVIQ is probably best regarded as additional evidence of our failure to characterize adequately the model for the VVIQ.

The next cluster (starting with line drawing number and ending with line drawing probe times), which is joined with the first under a superordinate node, contains all three of the tasks in which the REGENERATE processing module was weighted and was required to maintain an image over a relatively long period of time. Thus, this cluster seems to indicate that the capacity (not speed) of the REGENERATE processing module was an important factor in task performance. Note also that the FIND processing module is used in each task, explaining why this cluster is joined with the first.

Finally, the third major cluster (starting with the Oblique Effect Task and ending with Described Scenes) seems to reflect structural properties of the visual buffer. The Acuity, Extent, and Oblique Tasks were designed to be especially sensitive to bottlenecks imposed by the efficacy of the RESOLUTION processing module and the grain of the visual buffer. This limitation on vividness has a different source, evidently, from that assessed by the VVIQ Task (which may reflect variations in the RESOLUTION processing module, as opposed to the grain of the buffer). The cluster including these three measures is included in a larger cluster which also contains the Described Scenes measure (the correlation between time and the distance that should have been scanned). At first glance, this organization was a puzzle. One possible reason for this clustering, however, makes perfect sense: Most of the described scenes extended over five inches (at arm's length subtending about 16° of visual angle), which was within the range typically found in studies testing college students (see Kosslyn, 1980, chs. 3 and 7). However, we failed to anticipate just how large the range of individual differences would be; this angle was greater than the 'visible' extent of the visual buffer estimated by many of our subjects (the minimum estimate was 1.2 inches, subtending around 4° at arm's length. Thus, some subjects may have had difficulty in maintaining the correct distances in the described scenes because they overflowed the available extent of the visual buffer. In order to image the scene, then, they may have had to distort the distances among the objects, and hence produced low correlations between scan time and expected distance. In short, all four measures in this last cluster may reflect variations in properties of the visual buffer itself.

One could argue that these clusters— and, for that matter, the patterns detected in our earlier analyses—reflect nothing more than the days on which tasks were tested, with performance being similar for tasks administered on the same day. Examination of the data allows us to reject this conjecture. The mean correlation among scores for tasks that were administered together on the same day was $r = 0.17$ on Day 1, 0.10 on Day 2, and 0.24 on Day 3.

One could also argue that the first cluster merely reflects tasks in which the speed of responding was important. We have three reasons not to accept this argument: First, when we directly tested this idea, in our analysis of the 'common sense' theory, we found that tasks were only weakly related by whether or not speed was important. Second, not all of the tasks clustered here involved speed. Third, the steepness of a slope is a different sort of time estimate than overall speed; the 'units' being compared (e.g., number of parts in the image being generated) are determined by an underlying theory of processing (other theories might not lead one to expect increase in time with increases with those units). Thus, this measure is not simply a reflection of speed of responding.

Alternatively, one could argue that the first cluster reflects primarily the fact that many of the measures were derived from a single experiment (the one involving imaging and processing geometric forms). If this were all that was going on, we would expect the various dependent measures from this experiment to be more or less equally related. This was not true; the range of correlations was from $r = 0.26$ to $r = 0.79$. In addition, we would not expect any systematic ordering among the correlations if this view were correct. Our theory, in contrast, led us to expect four levels of relatedness, as indicated by the predicted similarity values between the pairs of measures in Table 6. The two image inspection times were predicted to be most highly related (the value was 3.00, the maximum possible using our scheme), and they were, $r = 0.79$ (see Table 3). The correlations between reorganization times and the two inspection times were predicted to be the same and next most highly related (1.50 in both cases, using our scheme), and this also was true, $r = 0.64$ and 0.63. The correlations between the image generation slopes and the two inspection times were predicted to be the same and next most highly related 0.75, using our scheme), and this was also true, $r = 0.30$ and 0.28. And finally, the correlation between the reorganization time and generation slopes was predicted to be lowest of all (0.55, using our scheme), which was indeed (barely) true, $r = 0.26$. The pattern of relations clearly is not haphazard, as would be expected if the correlations were due simply to the fact that they were derived from different aspects of the same task, and the pattern of relations is as we expected on the basis of our theory.

Factor analysis

Finally, we performed a factor analysis on the data, specifying that we wanted oblique axes rotated (direct quartimin, using the BMDP package) into the best fit. This seemed to be the most conservative approach because we could not be certain that the efficiency of the various processing modules was in fact independent. The most interesting results of this analysis are evident in the factor pattern matrix, presented in Table 9. The loadings in this matrix reflect the importance of each factor for each of our tasks. The easiest way to interpret this matrix is to consider only values over some absolute magnitude, 0.2500 being a common criterion.

When we consider only values over 0.2500 in Table 9, we see that the two Image Inspection times, Reorganization times, Described Scenes, Generation

Table 9. *Rotated factor loadings (pattern matrix)*

	Factor 1	Factor 2	Factor 3	Factor 4	Factor 5
1. Acuity	0.066	0.754	−0.287	0.098	−0.144
2. Oblique	0.108	0.784	0.018	−0.271	0.284
3. Extent	−0.040	0.091	0.170	0.118	−0.002
4. Rot. Slope	0.222	−0.163	−0.066	−0.476	0.365
5. Line Dr. Mem	0.031	−0.024	0.797	0.366	0.040
5. Line Dr. Time	−0.019	−0.050	0.112	0.913	0.168
7. Des. Scenes	−0.397	−0.150	0.203	−0.343	0.052
8. Gen. Slope	0.250	−0.053	−0.131	0.327	0.713
9. Reorg. Time	0.876	−0.037	−0.116	−0.104	−0.096
10. Reorg. Probe	0.839	−0.045	0.228	0.081	0.155
11. Nonreorg. Probe	0.859	0.140	0.257	−0.120	0.036
12. Form Board	0.155	−0.002	0.875	−0.130	0.116
13. VVIQ	0.359	−0.287	−0.072	0.163	−0.743

slopes and VVIQ all are weighted on the first factor. In every case the PIC-TURE processing module occurs in our model for the task, and this module is weighted in every case but for the Described Scenes— which is the only measure that has a negative factor loading here. Note that this first factor is *not* simply the speed of response. If it were, the Rotation slopes, Line Drawing times, and Form Board measures should have been weighted, but they were not; furthermore, the VVIQ should not have been included, but it was.

Similarly, the four measures that load heavily on the second factor, Acuity, Extent, the Oblique Effect, and the VVIQ, all include a weighted RESOLUTION processing module in their models. The VVIQ loads negatively on this factor, however, which is consistent with our results from the cluster analysis; the VVIQ apparently is not simply a measure of 'image vividness', as has been assumed. (Recall also that in our earlier regression analyses the VVIQ was not as systematically related to the predictions as were most of the other tasks.) This second factor clearly corresponds to the importance of the RESOLUTION processing module (in conjunction with the grain of the visual buffer, of course).

The third factor is more difficult to interpret, although the high loadings for the Line Drawing scores and the Form Board suggest that it reflects the effectiveness of the REGENERATE processing module in maintaining an image over time. The importance of this module for the speed of making a subsequent decision seems to be reflected by the fourth factor, as witnessed by the very high loading of the Line Drawing judgment times. The fifth factor is uninterpretable.

The first factor, then, corresponds roughly to the first cluster of our AGCLUS analysis; note that the three measures that loaded most highly on this factor were the first three factors entered into the cluster; and the last factors entered into the cluster (which were the least tightly clustered) have relatively low weightings on this factor. The second factor corresponds fairly closely to our third major cluster, both apparently reflecting the contribution of the RESOLUTION processing module and the grain of the visual buffer. The VVIQ is clearly a more complex measure than is usually realized. Finally, the third factor corresponds roughly to the second cluster, both apparently reflecting how much information can be maintained in an image over time.

In short, the cluster analysis and factor analysis revealed patterns in the data that are consistent with our theory; our earlier fine-grained analyses did not distort our picture of the inherent structure in the correlation matrix.

4. Conclusions

The results of this study support two broad assertions. First, imagery ability is not general or undifferentiated. Rather, a number of relatively independent subabilities can be drawn upon when one uses visual mental imagery. Second, the Kosslyn and Shwartz theory lends insight into the underlying structure of imagery. This theory predicts the observed correlations among task performance reasonably well, and provides a straightforward way of interpreting the results from our cluster analysis and factor analysis. The present study, then, provides evidence that we are making progress in breaking down into manageable components what once was undifferentiated complexity.

We also found that performance on the imagery tasks was not generally correlated with performance on verbal abilities and reasoning tests. Not only is imagery not a simple, unitary ability, but it is not part of a larger, more general undifferentiated system. We expect that the non-imagery abilities themselves are composed of distinct representations, buffers, and processing modules (plus associated algorithms—see Marr, 1982). Some of these modules may in fact be recruited in imagery tasks, specifically when performance can be improved by organizing the stimulus material more effectively. However, we need a theory of the non-imagery abilites before we can discuss such interactions between systems.

Another result of the study was that practice improved performance on most of the tasks (see Table 4). This result raises two questions. Would these improvements be retained over time? And would they generalize to new stimulus materials? For example, would training on image maintenance improve general performance in the future, and would it improve with new materials?

The highest correlation in the various analyses we performed between the predictions and the observed correlations was 0.82, which is exceptionally high for an individual differences study. The reason we were so successful, even given the various simplifications of the theory, is that we knew what to look for. Explicit, empirically motivated, computational theories specify the mechanisms that allow one to perform a task. Once one has a theory of the way or ways in which a task can be performed, one is in a very good position to ask about ways in which people may differ in their performance. It would be interesting to see if this sort of effort, based on normative computational theories developed originally to account for group data, can also illuminate other kinds of individual differences.

References

Appelle, S. (1972) Perception and discrimination as a function of stimulus orientation: the "oblique effect" in man and animals. *Psychol. Bull., 89*, 266–273.

Beech, J.R. (1980) Imaginal vs. perceptual scanning of a visual representation. *Percep. Mot. Skills, 50*, 367–370.

Beech, J.R. and Allport, D.A. (1975) Visualization of compound scenes. *Perception, 7*, 129–138.

Betts, G.H. (1909) *The Distribution and Functions of Mental Imagery*. New York, Columbia University Press.

Bower, G.H. (1972) Mental imagery and associative learning. In L. Gregg (ed.), *Cognition in Learning and Memory*. New York, Wiley

Cooper, L.A. (1975) Mental rotation of random two-dimensional shapes. *Cog. Psychol., 7*, 20–43.

Cooper, L.A. and Shepard, R.N. (1973) Chronometric studies of the rotation of mental images. In W.G. Chase (ed.), *Visual Information Processing*. New York, Academic Press.

diVesta, F.J., Ingersoll, G., and Sunshine, P. (1971) A factor analysis of imagery tests. *J. verb. Learn. verb. Behav., 10*, 471–479.

Egan, D.E. and Grimes-Farrow, D.D. (1982) Differences in mental representations spontaneously adopted for reasoning. *Mem. Cog., 10*, 297–307.

Ekstrom, R.B., French, J.W. and Harman, H.H. (1976) *Manual for Kit of Factor Referenced Tests*. Princeton, NJ, Educational Testing Service.

Ernest, C.H. (1977) Mental imagery and cognition: a critical review. *J. ment. Imagery, 1*, 181–216.

Farah, M.J. and Kosslyn, S.M. (1981) Structure and strategy in image generation. *Cog. Sci., 4*, 371–383.

Fechner, G. (1860) *Elements of Psychophysics*. New York, Holt, Rinehart, and Winston, 1966 (originally published 1860).

Finke, R.A. (1980) Levels of equivalence in imagery and perception. *Psychol. Rev., 86*, 113–132.

Finke, R.A. and Kosslyn, S.M. (1980) Mental imagery acuity in the peripheral visual field. *J. exp. Psychol. Hum. Pecep. Perf., 6*, 126–139.

Galton, F. (1883) *Inquiries into Human Faculty and its Development*. London, Macmillan.

Gordon, R.A. (1949) An investigation into some of the factors that favour the formation of stereotyped images. *Brit. J. Psychol., 39*, 156–167.

Johnson, S.C. (1967) Hierarchical clustering schemes. *Psychometrika, 32*, 241–254.

Kosslyn, S.M. (1973) Scanning visual images: some structural implications. *Percep. Psychophys., 14*, 90–94.

Kosslyn, S.M. (1975) Information representation in visual images. *Cog. Psychol., 7*, 341–370.

Kosslyn, S.M. (1978) Measuring the visual angle of the mind's eye. *Cog. Psychol., 10*, 356–389.

Kosslyn, S.M. (1980) *Image and Mind*. Cambridge, MA, Harvard University Press.

Kosslyn, S.M. (1981) The medium and the message in mental imagery. *Psychol. Rev., 88*, 46–66.

Kosslyn, S.M. (1983) Mental representation. In J.R. Anderson and S.M. Kosslyn (eds.), *Tutorials in Learning and Memory: Essays in Honor of Gordon H. Bower*. San Francisco, CA, W.H. Freeman.

Kosslyn, S.M., Ball, T.M. and Reiser, B.J. (1978) Visual images preserve metric spatial information: evidence from studies of image scanning. *J. exp. Psychol. Hum. Percep. Perf., 4*, 47–60.

Kosslyn, S.M., Berndt, R.S., and Poyle, T.J. (1984) Dissociations between imagery and language. Office of Naval Research Technical Report #5. Harvard University.

Kosslyn, S.M., Brunn, J.L., Cave, K.R. and Wallach, R.W. (1983a) *Components of mental imagery representation*. Office of Naval Research Technical Report, The Johns Hopkins University.

Kosslyn, S.M., Holtzman, J.D., Farah, M.J. and Gazzaniga, M.S. (In press) A computational theory of mental image generation: evidence from functional dissociations in split-brain patients. *J. exp. Psychol.: Gen.*

Kosslyn, S.M., Murphy, G.L., Bemesderfer, M.E. and Feinstein, K.J. (1977) Category and continuum in mental comparisons. *J. exp. Psychol. Gen., 106*, 341–375.

Kosslyn, S.M., Reiser, B.J., Farah, M.J. and Fliegel, S.L. (1983b) Generating visual images. *J. exp. Psychol. Gen..*

MacLeod, C.M., Hunt, E.B. and Mathews, N.N. (1978) Individual differences in the verification of sentence–picture relationships. *J. verb. Learn. verb. Behav., 5*, 493–508.

Marks, D.F. (1973) Visual imagery differences and eye movements in the recall of pictures. *Percep. Psychophys., 14*, 407–412.

Marks, D.F. (1977) Imagery and consciousness: a theoretical review from an individual differences perspective. *J. ment. Imagery, 1*, 275–290.

Marr, D. (1982) *Vision*. San Francisco, CA, W.H. Freeman.

Mathews, N.N., Hunt, E.B. and MacLeod, C.M. (1980) Strategy choice and strategy training in sentence–picture verification. *J. verb. Learn. verb. Behav., 19*, 531–548.

Paivio, A., Yuille, J.C. and Madigan, S. (1968) Concreteness, imagery, and meaningfulness values for 925 nouns. *J. exp. Psychol. Mono. Suppl., 76*.

Pinker, S. (1980) Mental imagery and the third dimension. *J. exp. Psychol.: Gen., 109*, 354–371.

Pinker, S. and Kosslyn, S.M. (1978) The representation and manipulation of three-dimensional space in mental images. *J. ment. Imagery, 2*, 69–84.

Pylyshyn, Z.W. (1981) The imagery debate: analogue media versus tacit knowledge. *Psychol. Rev., 87*, 16–45.

Richardson, A. (1969) *Mental Imagery*. New York: Springer.

Shepard, R.N. (1978) The mental image. *Amer. Psychol., 33*, 351–377.

Shepard and Cooper (1983). *Mental Images and their Transformations*. Cambridge, MA, MIT Press.

Sternberg, R.J. (1977) *Intelligence, Information Processing, and Analogical Reasoning: the Componential Analysis of Human Abilities*. Hillsdale, NJ, Lawrence Erlbaum Associates.

Shwartz, S.P. (1979) Studies of mental image rotation: implications for a computer simulation of visual imagery. Ph.D. Thesis, The Johns Hopkins University.

Weber, R.J. and Bach, M. (1969) Visual and speech imagery. *Brit. J. Psychol., 60*, 199–202.

White, K., Sheehan, P.W. and Ashton, R. (1977) Imagery assessment: a survey of self-report measures. *J. ment. Imagery, 1*, 145–170.

Witkin, H.A. (1964) Origins of cognitive style. In C. Sheerer (ed.), *Cognition: Theory, Research, Promise*. New York, Harper & Row.

Reference note

1. Pennington, N., and Kosslyn, S.M. (1981) The 'oblique effect' in mental imagery. Harvard University manuscript.

6

The neurological basis of mental imagery:
A componential analysis*

MARTHA J. FARAH

Carnegie-Mellon University

Abstract

The neurological literature contains numerous reports of loss of mental imagery following brain damage. This paper represents an attempt to interpret the patterns of deficits and preserved abilities in these reports in terms of a componential information-processing model of imagery. The principal result was a consistent pattern of deficit in a subset of patients, which could be attributed to a loss of the image generation component of imagery;examination of the lesion sites in this subset of patients implicated a region in the posterior left hemispheres as critical for the image generation process. The analysis also provided evidence that the long-term visual memories used in imagery are also used in recognition, and that dreaming and waking visual imagery share some underlying processes.

Cases of loss of visual imagery due to brain damage have been described in the neurological literature for decades. Despite the relatively long history of the study of this phenomenon, however, little progress has been made in understanding the neurological basis of visual imagery. This paper represents an attempt to synthesize what is now known about visual imagery in normal humans with the existing data on visual imagery deficits in brain-damaged humans, with the hope of shedding new light on both topics. In particular, the approach is to reinterpret the 'loss of imagery' literature in terms of a *theory* of imagery, making distinctions among the *components* of imagery ability that may be individually susceptible to brain damage. It will then be possible to look for the anatomical correlates of componentially-defined im-

*Preparation of this paper was supported by PHS grant 1F32 MH 08876-01 and by the MIT Center for Cognitive Science under a grant from the Alfred P. Sloan Foundation. The author thanks Neal Cohen, Lee Cranberg, William Estes, Howard Gardner, Mark Greenberg, Stephen Kosslyn, David Levine, R. Duncan Luce and Steven Pinker for helpful comments and suggestions on earlier drafts of this paper. Reprint requests should be sent to Martha J. Farah, Department of Psychology, Carnegie-Mellon University, Pittsburgh, PA 15213.

agery deficits, as well as ways in which the breakdown of imagery ability after brain damage constrains our theories of imagery in normal individuals.

A search of the literature yielded 37 descriptions of cases of loss of imagery published in English. Where anatomical data are available, the areas of the brain that are implicated as relevant to visual imagery are varied: parietal lobe, occipital lobe and temporal lobe damage have all been associated with loss or severe deficit of visual imagery ability, and neither hemisphere can be excluded. Some authors have attempted to generalize about the critical lesion sites. For example, Nielsen (1946) has stated that a loss of imagery may be used as a diagnostic *localizing sign* of damage to the inferior convex portion of area 19 of the occipital lobes (p. 270). Arbuse (1947) has proposed a left parietal basis for imagery, and more recently Bisiach and his colleagues (Bisiach and Luzzati, 1978; Bisiach et al., 1949) have demonstrated parietal involvement in the use of imagery. Humphrey and Zangwill's (1951) presentation of three cases of loss of dreaming and waking imagery is often cited as support for a right hemisphere locus for imagery, although the authors themselves asserted that "disorders of visual imagination appear liable to follow lesions on either side." Ehrlichman and Barrett (1983) cite many authors who assume that imagery is a function of the right hemisphere, but conclude that the evidence available does not support this assumption.

What are we to make of this lack of association between loss of imagery and damage to particular areas of the brain? Two possibilities suggest themselves. First, it is possible that imagery is not a 'faculty' of the brain, but merely a collection of epiphenomena which emerge when other memory and reasoning processes interact in particular ways, as has been argued by some psychologists (e.g. Pylyshyn, 1981). If this were the case, then damage to one or more of the interacting systems might or might not produce a manifest 'imagery deficit', depending upon the ability of the remaining systems to produce some of the alleged properties of imagery. This state of affairs would lead to just the complex and inconsistent pattern of data described in the last paragraph. An alternative possibility is that imagery is a faculty or, in Luria's (1973) terms, a "functional system" of the brain, and like language or perception it has an internal structure, the components of which have different physiological bases. If this were the case, then the inconsistencies would be only apparent, the result of our grouping together deficits in different components of visual imagery. A consistent picture would emerge if we were to look for the brain areas associated with these components individually. This second possibility may be thought of as a hypothesis: imagery is a faculty or system of the brain, made up of identifiable subsystems that each have a direct neurological instantiation.

In order to test this hypothesis using the published case reports of loss of visual imagery, and thereby to attempt to localize the components of the imagery system in the brain, two additional kinds of information are needed. First, we need a theory of visual imagery that specifies the components of the visual imagery system. Second, we need to know which of these components were destroyed in each of the case reports that form our data base.

A theory of visual imagery

Kosslyn (1980) has provided a comprehensive and well-supported componential theory of visual imagery in normal adults. For present purposes, only the most general features of the theory will be used, corresponding to the highest level 'parse' of the imagery system into different kinds of information-bearing *structures* and information-manipulating *processes*. The long-term visual memory structures store information about the appearances of objects. Like other long-term memory structures, we are not conscious of this information except when it is being accessed or otherwise manipulated by one of the processes specified by the theory. A second kind of structure, the 'visual buffer', is not itself information-bearing but is the medium in which images occur. The visual buffer has been found to have certain invariant properties such as visual angle and grain which are independent of the image that is 'displayed' in it. The spatial, pictorial information-bearing structure that we consciously experience as an image consists of patterns of activation in the visual buffer.

The *processes* postulated by Kosslyn include those that 'generate', 'inspect' and 'transform' the image in the visual buffer. The generation process (actually decomposable into component processes, which are not relevant here) creates the image in the visual buffer from information stored in long-term visual memory. The inspection process converts the patterns of activation in the visual buffer into organized percepts, identifying parts and relations within the image. For example, when we image a Star of David by mentally combining two triangles, it is the inspection process that allows us to find the embedded hexagon in the center. This process has not been modeled in detail by Kosslyn but presumably resembles the elementary pattern recognition processes that Ullman (this issue) has called "visual routines". Finally, there are processes that transform (e.g., rotate, translate) the image.

Given this analysis of the imagery system, we might expect to find cases of loss of imagery that correspond to losses of different structural or processing components of imagery. That is, a patient would be expected to have no imagery on introspection, and be unable to perform tasks requiring the consulting of an image, if any of the following components were destroyed by brain damage: the long-term visual memories, the visual buffer, the generation process, or the inspect process. Loss of image transformation processes would be expected to give rise to distinct deficits in visual/spatial thought processes, but not to the loss of imagery altogether.

What remains to be done in order to carry out a componential analysis of the imagery deficits reported in the literature is to find a way to infer from the descriptions of patients' performances in various tasks *which* component or components of the imagery system must have been damaged. This was accomplished by the use of 'task analyses' of the tasks reported in each case study. A task analysis is a theory of the cognitive processing required to carry out a task. As such, task analyses are clearly dependent on a general theory of cognitive processing: the general theory specifies what components are available for performing a given task, how they will interact, and what their results will be.

There are six main kinds of task that are described in the case studies and are relevant to assessing imagery ability: question-answering tasks, introspection tasks, drawing and construction tasks, recognition tasks, and sensory and perceptual tasks. In order to write task analyses for these tasks, the processing components of the imagery model had to be augmented with some general (that is, non-imagery) components as described in the next section.

Additional theoretical assumptions

In order to model performance in all phases of the tasks included in the task analyses in this paper the following additional components were added to the basic Kosslyn model: a 'describe' component for question-answering tasks in which the contents of the visual buffer (either an internally generated image or a visually encoded percept) must be inspected and described, a 'copy' component for constructional tasks in which the contents of the visual buffer (either an internally generated image or a visually encoded percept) must be inspected and drawn or constructed, and a 'detect' component for simple visual perception tasks and imagery introspection tasks, in which the patterns of activation in the visual buffer need not be inspected (i.e., the structure or form of the pattern need not be processed) but the mere presence of activation must be detected. These additional components are obviously complex systems in their own right, and it may be misleading to refer to them as components. However, as will be seen shortly, care was taken to avoid making any inferences from the task analyses that could depend on the nature of these components; they function in the task analyses as place-holders for systems of non-imagery processing that are not directly relevant to assessing imagery ability.

In order to infer which component of imagery is damaged in each patient, it was also necessary to augment the imagery model with a visual encoding process that encodes stimuli into the visual buffer. Support for the claim that imagery and perception share a common visual buffer comes from findings of interactions between images and percepts in the visual buffer (Farah, 1985; Finke and Schmidt, 1977, 1978; Finke and Shepard, In press) and from findings of many subtle, quantitative similarities between the visual buffer in imagery and in perception (Finke and Kosslyn, 1980; Finke and Kurtzman, 1981; Podgorny and Shepard, 1978).

Finally, a recognition process was added to the framework of the Kosslyn imagery theory. The standard approach to modelling visual recognition (e.g. Marr, 1982; Selfridge and Neisser, 1960) was use: after a percept has been encoded into the visual buffer and inspected, it is translated into the format of the long-term visual memories and compared with those memories. Recognition consists of a match between the representation derived from the input and one of the long-term visual memories. In order to infer which component of imagery is damaged in each patient, it was necessary to assume initially that the long-term visual memories used in image generation are the same memories that are used in visual recognition. Although this assumption seems extremely reasonable on the grounds of parsimony, the only way to justify the assumption is by testing it. This was done by examining cases of *content-specific* imagery deficits, that is, cases in which the patient could visualize some kinds of objects but not others. If the long-term memories of the imagery system are also the basis for object recognition, then we would expect parallel content-specific recognition deficits in these patients. To anticipate the results of the analysis of the case reports, there were six cases of content-specific agnosia in which imagery ability was examined, and in four of these imagery for both recognizable and unrecognizable categories of stimuli was tested. All four of these cases displayed a parallel imagery deficit.

Figure 1 shows the complete theory from which the task analyses will be derived. From Kosslyn's theory come (1) the *long-term visual memories* of the appearance of objects, (2) the *visual buffer*, the short-term memory medium in which images occur, (3) the *generation* process, which takes the information about the appearance of objects stored as deep images and creates a surface image, a spatial distribution of activation in the visual buffer, and (4) the *inspection* process, which organizes and transmits the information displayed in the visual buffer to other cognitive systems.

Added to the imagery structures and processes are (1) sensory processes that *encode* stimuli into the visual buffer and *detect* activation in the visual buffer, (2) recognition processes that *match* the inspected contents of the visual buffer with long-term visual memories, (3) visual to verbal translation

Figure 1.   *The general model of perception and imagery from which task analyses were derived. Patterns of activation are formed in the visual buffer either by an image generation process (from long term memories) or a perceptual encoding process. The presence of activation in the visual buffer may simply be detected, or an inspection process may read out structured patterns of activation for further processing: description (in the case of question-answering tasks), copying (in the case of drawing or construction tasks) or matching with long term visual memories (in the case of recognition tasks).*

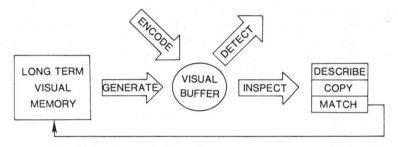

processes that *describe* the inspected contents of the visual buffer, and (4) visual to motor translation processes that *copy* the inspected contents of the visual buffer.

Tasks and task analyses

Figures 2–8 show the task analyses for each of the relevant tasks described in the case reports. These include the tasks deemed by the authors of the case reports to require imagery, as well as other tasks that are useful as controls for possible non-imagery deficits.

The task most commonly used to infer a loss of imagery is to ask patients to describe or answer questions about the visual appearance of objects. Of course, it is always conceivable that a patient could perform adequately on such a task without consulting an image but instead by consulting explicitly encoded facts about the object's appearance; however, there is evidence from laboratory studies with normal humans that for retrieving information about aspects of appearance not often explicitly discussed (e.g. whether George Washington had a beard) and particularly spatial, relational information (e.g. whether the entrance to one's house is in the center or off to one side of the front) imagery is used (Eddy and Glass, 1981; Kosslyn and Jolicoeur, 1980). In most cases the authors of the case reports asked appropriately subtle questions. Some examples are: "Did George Washington have a beard?" (Brownell *et al.*, 1984), "What color are the stars on the American flag?" (Brownell *et al.*, 1984; Boyle and Nielsen, 1954), "Describe the exterior of your home." (Brain, 1954; Levine, 1978; Nielsen, 1946). In a few cases, the questions did not meet the criteria of requests for subtle relational and non-explicitly coded information, for example: "What are the colors of a canary? The sky? Gass?" (Levine, 1978; Nielsen, 1946). Similarly, the ability of an architect or builder to describe familiar buildings such as his own home was not taken as evidence for intact imagery because this information is likely to be explicitly encoded by such individuals (Brain, 1954, Case 1; Nielsen, 1946, p. 227). In these cases patients' answers were not used as evidence of imagery ability for the purpose of making inference to the damaged component. The task analysis for the question-answering task is shown in Fig. 2. An image must be generated from long-term memory into the visual buffer, inspected and described.

Many patients spontaneously reported a loss of imagery based on their own introspection. In this context introspection does not involve the reporting of *how* a given thought process seems to the thinker to be proceeding, but rather a self-report about the existence of the thought process or, more accurately, the existence of a product of a thought process, a visual image. The task analysis for introspection is shown in Fig. 3. An image must be generated from long-term memory into the visual buffer, and its presence must be detected. Although the task analysis for introspection is very similar to the task analysis for question-answering, it should be noted that in introspection the patient is commenting more explicitly on his internal mental state than during question-answering, and there is therefore a greater chance of the patient's responses being affected by his or her naive theories about the mind. There are only three cases (Humphrey and Zangwill, 1955) in which any inferences rest on introspection alone.

Imagery deficits can also be detected in constructional tasks, either drawing a requested object or assembling it from parts such as sticks or blocks. As with question-answering and description from memory, not all drawing tasks require imagery; in particular, it is assumed that imagery is not needed to

Figure 2. *Task analysis for question-answering from memory.*

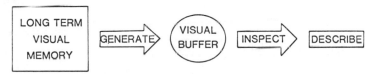

Figure 3. *Task analysis for 'introspection': the detection of imagery.*

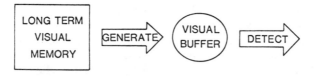

Figure 4. *Task analysis for drawing or constructing from memory.*

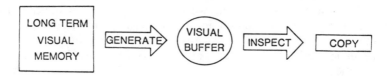

draw simple geometric shapes such as a circle or schematic cannonical forms such as a human stick figure. For constructional tasks, Fig. 4 shows the required structures and processes. An image must be generated from long-term memory into the visual buffer, inspected and copied.

Four further tasks are relevant to inferring the component of imagery ability that has been damaged. They are copying tasks, recognition tasks, perceptual tasks, and sensory tasks. In most cases in which a patient was asked to draw or construct something from memory, he or she was also asked to copy (from a visible model) either the same subject or a subject of comparable familiarity and complexity. Knowledge of a patient's performance in this task is clearly helpful in interpreting his or her performance at drawing or constructing from memory. The task analysis for copying a visible model is shown in Fig. 5 and consists of encoding the model into the visual buffer, inspecting it and copying it.

Figure 5. *Task analysis for drawing or constructing from a visible model.*

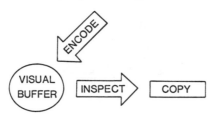

Finally, a patient's ability to perceive and recognize objects can be helpful in inferring which component of the visual imagery system has been damaged. Testing sensory, perceptual and object recognition ability is a standard part of any neurological examination following brain damage. Visual agnosia is the inability to recognize an object by sight alone, in the absence of any elementary perceptual or general intellectual impairment. To be diagnosed an 'associative visual agnosic', a patient must meet several requirements. He or she must have adequate sensory processes for encoding stimuli, and also have the ability to perceive stimuli as organized wholes (i.e., not have an 'apperceptive' visual agnosia, also called simultanagnosia or 'gestalt deficit'). The patient must be be generally alert, be able to identify objects by touch, sound, or other non-visual modalities, and yet be unable to identify the same objects by sight. The patient need not be able to name an object to demonstrate his or her recognition of it; simply indicating its function either verbally ot motorically is adequate to rule out agnosia. Associative agnosia is thus a specific failure to associate a perceptual representation with a long-term memory representation. The task analyses for sensory, perceptual and recognition tasks are shown in Figs. 6–8. To demonstrate that he or she can see, a patient must be able to encode a stimulus into the visual buffer, and detect its presence (Fig. 6). To demonstrate complete perceptual abilities, a patient must be able to encode an object into the visual buffer and produce a recognizable description of it (Fig. 7), for example by providing the colors, shapes, or names of objects or pictures. The ability to copy a stimulus from a model (Fig. 5) also is sometimes taken by neurologists as evidence for intact perceptual abilities. To demonstrate that he or she can recognize objects, a patient must be able to encode the object into the visual buffer, and match it with a long-term memory representation (Fig. 8).

The reliability with which the descriptions of tasks described in the case reports could be classified into the categories of tasks represented in Figs.

Figure 6.   *Task analysis for detection of visual stimuli.*

Figure 7.   *Task analysis for description of visual stimuli.*

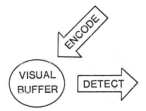

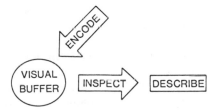

Figure 8.   *Task analysis for recognition of visual stimuli.*

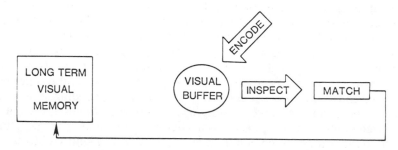

2–8 was tested by having a second reader perform the classifications independently. The second reader was shown the task analyses of Figs. 2–8 and given
copies of the 37 case reports, with instructions to identify occurrences of the
seven tasks in the case reports. The reader was an undergraduate psychology
major who did not know the results of the original analysis. She also knew
virtually nothing about neuroanatomy, ruling out the possibility of her grouping together tasks performed similarly by patients with similar lesions. The
two readers' classifications were largely in agreement; specific differences are
discussed in the next section.

Inferences using task analyses

Once the task analyses have been constructed, the damaged imagery components can be inferred. If a patient cannot perform a task, then one or more of
the cognitive components required for that task must be damaged. We can
narrow down the candidate components by noting which of those same components are required by the tasks that the patient *can* perform. This is because
if a patient can perform a task, then it is likely that all of the cognitive
components required by that task are intact. Therefore, we can infer that a
component is damaged if it is the only component in the task analysis of a
failed task that does not also occur in the task analysis of a successfully
performed task.

   To summarize the differences between the second reader's classifications
and my own original classifications, the second reader's were somewhat more
inclusive than mine, resulting in more cases having been inferred to be cases
of loss of imagery based on her classifications (27) than based on mine (25).
For the 24 cases inferred to be cases of imagery deficit on the basis of both
readers' task classifications, the inferences to the particular component of
imagery that was damaged were always the same. Therefore, I will only

report 'compromise' inferences, which resulted from a discussion between the two readers after the classifications were completed.

Cases classified as lacking evidence of imagery deficit are displayed in Table 1. The most common reason that cases were put into this category was that the original author of the report has simply stated that a patient had an imagery deficit without describing any of the behavioral evidence that presumably had led him to that conclusion.

Table 1.   *Cases for which an imagery deficit could not be inferred. For each case the primary topic of the case report, the etiology and the general anatomical area of cortical damage are listed*

Case	Topic	Etiology	Lesion site
Arbuse (1947)	Gerstmann's syndrome	Neoplasm	Left parieto-occipital
Brown (1972) Case 11	Apperceptive visual agnosia	Anoxia	Bilateral posterior
Brown (1972) Case 12	Apperceptive visual agnosia	Cerebrovascular accident?	Bilateral posterior
Holmes (1945) p. 359 (cited as loss of imagery by Critchley, 1953)	Color agnosia	Cerebrovascular accident	Left occipital
Nielsen (1946) p. 203 (cited as loss of imagery, 1955)	Visual agnosia	Cerebrovascular accident	Right occipital
Nielsen (1946) p. 230 (cited as loss of imagery, 1955)	Gerstmann's syndrome	Cerebrovascular accident	Left parieto-occipital
Nielsen (1955) Case 7	Loss of imagery	Neoplasm	Left occipital
Nielsen (1955) postscript Case 1	Loss of imagery and dreaming	Neoplasm	Left occipital
Nielsen (1955) postscript Case 2	Loss of imagery and dreaming	Neoplasm	Left occipital
Wilbrand (1887) (described by Nielsen, 1955)	Loss of imagery	Cerebrovascular accident	Left posterior

Inferring the damaged component of imagery

Among the 27 patients classified as having impaired imagery systems, there are three distinct patterns of abilities and deficits that emerge, from which we may infer damage to different components of the visual imagery system.

Generation process deficit

Eight patients display the following pattern of abilities and deficits, illustrated in Fig. 9. Figure 9a illustrates the performance of the patients of Brownell *et al.* (1984), Lyman, *et al.* (1938), and Nielsen (1946, pp. 200, 227), who were unable to answer questions requiring imagery, although they did possess the ability to answer similar questions about visible stimuli and could recognize visually presented stimuli. The patients of Brain (1954, Cases 1 and 2) displayed this same basic pattern of deficits, but with some unusual additional features. Whereas Case 1, a construction supervisor, was no longer able to visualize plans or elevations at work, Brain reports that the patient was able to give a satisfactory description of "an object he could not visualize, e.g., his own house." Case 2 showed an inability to describe familiar objects or answer questions involving imagery only when his eyes were closed; with eyes open his performance inexplicably improved. Figure 9b illustrates the performance of the patients of Lyman *et al.* (1938) and Spalding and Zangwill (1950), who were unable to draw common objects from meory, although they were able to copy comparable or identical objects and recognize visually presented objects. Figure 9c illustrates the performance of the patients of Brain (1954, Cases 1 and 2), Humphrey and Zangwill (1951, Case 3), and Spalding and Zangwill (1951) who were unable to detect any imagery on introspection, although they were aware of being able to see. In each section of Fig. 9 the only component of the failed tasks that does not occur in the successful tasks is the image generation process. Therefore, in these patients the generation process is likely to be damaged.

When the eight cases inferred to have damage to the image generation process are considered as a separate group, a trend in lesion sites emerges, shown in Table 2. The two cases in the image generation process group that provide detailed anatomical data from surgery (Lyman *et al.*, 1938) or autopsy (Nielsen, 1946, p. 227) show tumors in the left parieto-occipital area, although in both cases signs of increased intracranial pressure were noted, implying possible pressure effects on the functioning of tissue distant from the tumors. Nielsen's case also had a left thalamic tumor. The remaining six cases provide varying amounts of information on lesion site. Spalding and Zangwill's (1950) patient was wounded by a penetrating missile, whose point

Figure 9. *Inferring an image generation process deficit. Solid outline indicates that a component is ruled out as the reason for the patients' failure in the imagery tasks by virtue of appearing in the analysis of a successfully performed task.*

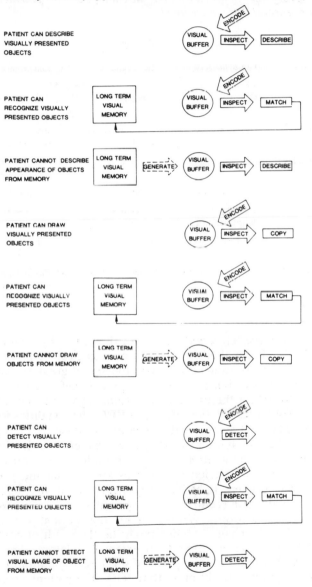

Table 2.   *Cases inferred to have an image generation process deficit. For each case the primary topic of the case report, the etiology and the general anatomical area of cortical damage are listed*

Case	Topic	Etiology	Lesion site
Brain (1951) Case 1	Loss of imagery	Head injury	Left posterior
Brain (1951) Case 2	Loss of imagery	Head injury	?
Brownell *et al.* (1984)	Loss of imagery	Cerebrovascular accident	Bilateral parietal (greater on right), left frontal
Humphrey and Zangwill (1951) Case 3	Loss of dreaming	Penetrating head wound	Right posterior parietal (left handed)
Lyman *et al.* (1938)	Alexia and agraphia	Neoplasm	Left parieto-occipital
Nielsen (1946) p. 200	Topographic disorientation	Cerebrovascular accident	Left posterior
Nielsen (1946) p. 227	Gerstmann's syndrome	Neoplasm	Left parietal and occipital
Spalding and Zangwill (1950)	Loss of 'number form'	Penetrating head wound	Bilateral, greatest in left parieto-occipital

of entry was between the left angular gyrus of the parietal lobe and area 19 of the occipital lobe. From skull X-rays and neurological signs, the authors assert that the left parieto-occipital area was the site of greatest damage. Of the remaining five cases of image generation process deficit shown in Table 2, there are two for which the available localizing signs indicate a left posterior focus of pathology (left parieto-occipital EEG abnormalities for Brain's (1954) head-injured Case 1 and clinical presentation indicating a left posterior cerebral artery stroke for Nielsen's (1946 p. 200) patient). In Brain's (1954) second case a physical examination provided no information on lesion site and further tests were not carried out. It was known that the patient had fallen and sustained a severe right fronto-vertical head injury, suggesting a probable right frontal lesion (coup) and, one might speculate, a possible left posterior lesion (contra-coup). Writing about this patient earlier, Brain (1950) proposed that the imagery deficit might be the result of contra-coup. The patient of Brownell *et al.* (1984) had extensive bilateral damage from several strokes, with a written description of a CT scan mentioning involvement of both parietal lobes (right more than left). The patient's records also included mention of possible left anterior damage on the basis of the patient's dysphasia. Finally, the third case of Humphrey and Zangwill (1951) had sustained a posterior right parietal lesion from a penetrating missile (shown in skull X-rays), but two factors suggest that this patient had reversed hemispheric dominance. He was a left-hander and, more importantly, his unilateral right-hemisphere damage left him dysphasic. Thus, this patient follows the trend for posterior dominant hemisphere damage.

It is clear that the quality of the localizing information and the nature of the lesions themselves (size and etiology) in these cases cannot support an inference to a critical lesion site in any individual case. The claim that the left posterior region contains critical structures for image generation is based on the trend observed across cases, *viz.*, in the seven cases with localizing information, six have predominantly or exclusively posterior dominant hemisphere damage.

For the sake of examining the trend towards left posterior damage found in these cases of image generation deficit, we can return to the *non-agnosic* cases of Table 1, in which the authors had claimed that the patients had lost imagery, but did not provide the information needed to infer a loss of imagery using task analyses. If these patients had indeed lost imagery, then their lack of an agnosia implies that they were cases of image generation process deficit (by the process of elimination depicted in Fig. 9). These patients all had left posterior damage: Arbuse's (1947) patient had a left parieto-occipital tumor (with increased intracranial pressure), Nielsen's (1946, p. 230) patient had a stroke with lesions in the left posterior parietal and occipital lobes as well as a small lesion in the motor strip, the case of Wilbrand described by Nielsen (1955) had a stroke with a right homonymous hemianopia as the only neurological sign, implying left posterior cerebral artery stroke, and Nielsen's (1955) Case 7 had what was described as a "small" tumor in the left occipital lobe. There are two additional cases of loss of imagery reported in a postscript to Nielsen's (1955) paper, with no mention of agnosia. Assuming that the presence of agnosia would have been mentioned, these patients are also likely to have had image generation deficits, and they, too, had left occipital tumors.

Long-term visual memory deficit

Thirteen patients display the following pattern, illustrated in Fig. 10. These patients are listed in Table 3. Figure 10a illustrates the performance of the patients of Albert, *et al.* (1975), Basso, *et al.* (1980), Beyn and Knyazeva (1962), Boyle and Nielsen (1954), Epstein (1979), Macrae and Trolle (1956), Nielsen (1946, p. 176), Ratcliff and Newcombe (1982), Shuttleworth *et al.*

(1982, Case 2), Taylor and Warrington (1971), Wapner *et al.* (1978), and Wilbrand (1887, translated by Critchley, 1953) who were unable to recognize visual stimuli and also unable to answer questions requiring imagery, although they were able to describe and answer questions about the appearance of visual stimuli. In other words, in addition to their imagery deficit these patients had an associative visual agnosia. Figure 10b illustrates another aspect of the performance of the patients of Albert *et al.* (1975), Beyn and Knyazeva (1962), Macrae and Trolle (1956), Ratcliff and Newcombe (1982), Shuttleworth *et al* (1982), Taylor and Warrington (1971) and Wapner *et al.* (1978), who, in addition to the disabilities already mentioned, were unable to draw objects from memory, although they were able to copy objects. Finally, Fig. 10c illustrates the performance of the patients of Basso *et al.* (1980), Humphrey and Zangwill (1951, Case 1), Macrae and Trolle (1956) and Shuttleworth *et al.* (1982), who, in addition to the above-mentioned recognition difficulties, were unable to detect their own imagery upon introspection, but were able to see.

From these patterns of performance we can conclude that either the long-term memories have been damaged or both the generation process and the matching process have been damaged. Several factors favor the inference that the long-term memories have been damaged. First, parsimony favors the interpretation that one component occurring in all and only failed tasks, is damaged, rather than the interpretation that a pair of components, each of which occurs in one failed task are damaged. Second, a distinguishing feature of this group is that several of the cases showed content-specific imagery deficits, as well as content-specific agnosias. This suggests that damage has been done to one of the representational, or information-bearing, components of the imagery system. Third, when a content-specific imagery deficit exists, it is paralleled by a content-specific recognition deficit affecting the same class of stimuli, which suggests that the same component is responsible for both the imagery and recognition deficit: Beyn and Knyazeva's (1962) patient was able to recognize only 3 of 16 common objects that he could not reportedly image, but could recognize 13 out of 16 common objects that he could image. Wapner *et al.*'s (1978) patient was also better at imaging those objects he could recognize, as inferred from his drawing performance. Although Shuttleworth *et al.*'s (1982) second patient was not tested on imagery other than for faces, she introspected that she could image anything but faces, and her recognition difficulties were primarily encountered with faces. Despite his claims that he had lost all imagery, including auditory and olfactory imagery, Basso *et al.*'s (1980) patient could draw and describe from memory as well as recognize most common objects, but failed when these same tasks involved geographical locales and performed only mediocrely

Figure 10. *Inferring a long term visual memory deficit. Solid outline indicates that a component is ruled out as the reason for the patients' failure in the imagery tasks by virtue of appearing in the analysis of a successfully performed task.*

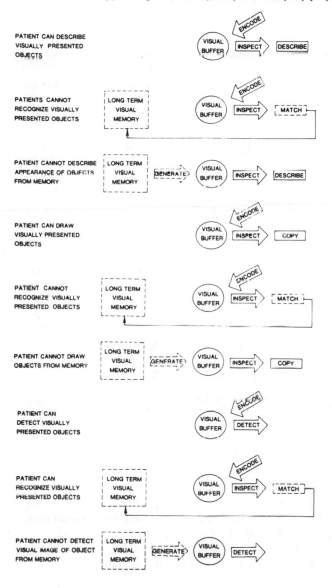

Table 3.   *Cases inferred to have a long term visual memory deficit. For each case the primary topic of the case report, the etiology and the general anatomical area of cortical damage are listed*

Case	Topic	Etiology	Lesion site
Albert *et al.* (1975)	Visual agnosia	Cerebrovascular accident?	Right anterior, bilateral posterior
Basso *et al.* (1980)	Loss of imagery	Cerebrovascular accident	Left temporal and occipital
Beyn and Kuyazeva (1962)	Prosopagnosia and visual object agnosia	Cerebrovascular accident	Bilateral posterior
Boyle and Nielsen (1954)	Visual agnosia	Neoplasm and surgical trauma	Bilateral occipital (greater on right)
Epstein (1979) Case 1	Loss of dreaming	Cerebrovascular accident	Left posterior (left handed)
Humphrey and Zangwill (1951) Case 1	Loss of dreaming	Penetrating head wound	Right parietal
Macrae and Trolle (1956)	Visual agnosia	Head injury	Bilateral temporal and parietal (greater on left)
Nielsen (1946) p. 176	Visual agnosia	Cerebrovascular accident	Right occipital, left temporal and parietal
Ratcliff and Newcombe (1982)	Visual agnosia	Cerebrovascular accident	Bilateral occipital, parietal, temporal (greater on right)
Shuttleworth, *et al.* (1982) Case 2	Prosopagnosia	Head injury	Bilateral posterior
Taylor and Warrington (1971)	Visual agnosia	Cortical atrophy	Diffuse (left more than right)
Wapner *et al.* (1978)	Visual agnosia	Cerebrovascular accident	Left temporal, bilateral occipital (greater on left) (left handed)
Wilbrand (1887, transl. Critchley, 1953)	Visual agnosia	Cerebrovascular accident	Bilateral posterior

when they involved faces. For these three reasons I am classifying the patients discussed in this section as having damaged long-term visual memories rather than as having a combination of damaged generation and match processes. However, this classification is supported by a less direct inference than the preceding classification of image generation deficit.

In all but three of the cases of loss of long-term visual memories, the damage was known to involve one or both occipital lobes, as shown in Table 3. (Humphrey and Zangwill's (1951) Case 1 had sustained a penetrating head wound from a metal fragment that entered in the right posterior parietal region, which might or might not have caused occipital damage. Macrae and Trolle's, (1956) patient had a closed head injury causing abnormal EEG in the temporal and parietal regions. The anatomical information in this case is very weak, and so we cannot conclude much from a lack of positive evidence for occipital damage. Taylor and Warrington's (1971) patient had diffuse atrophy with no focal damage.)

There is less anatomical regularity within the long-term visual memory group than within the generation process group; there is no clear trend here either in laterality or in region within the posterior lobes. This greater heterogeneity could reflect the necessity for a further componential analysis of long-term visual memory deficit. That is, perhaps different cognitive components of the long-term visual memories, having different anatomical locations, have been disrupted in different cases. Unfortunately, there are not enough data available on the specific nature of the imagery and recognition deficits in these cases to suggest what the different components might be.

In one case (Humphrey and Zangwill, 1951, Case 2) there is not enough information to decide whether the imagery deficit was due to loss of the generation process or loss of long-term visual memories. This case is shown in Table 4. Although agnosia or recognition difficulties are not mentioned in this case, the report refers to "some topographic and related visual memory loss" (p. 323). On the one hand, if this "visual memory loss" refers to recognition memory then this patient has the pattern of deficits and abilities that would place him among the long-term visual memory cases. On the other hand, if it refers to his inability to recall visual information, then this patient belongs in the image generation process group. We are not aided in our decision by the following two quotes from the patient, one of which suggests a complete, across-the-board loss of imagery, and the other of which suggests

Table 4.   *Case inferred to have either an image generation process deficit or a long term visual memory deficit*

Case	Topic	Etiology	Lesion site
Humphrey and Zangwill (1951) Case 2	Loss of dreaming	Penetrating head wound	Bilateral parieto-occipital (greater on left)

a partial and possibly content-specific imagery deficit: "I think only in words, never in pictures," and, "If someone says: 'Can you visualize what your home is like?' Well I can do that, but I can't visualize a lot of things, such as faces sometimes or places I've been to." This patient's brain damage was in the parieto-occipital regions of both hemispheres, predominantly the left.

Inspection process deficit

Five patients showed a pattern of abilities and deficits indicative of damage to the inspection process. Four of these patients (Adler, 1944; Brain, 1941; Brown, 1972, Case 13, also described in Benson and Greenberg, 1969; Levine, 1978) showed the pattern of abilities and deficits illustrated in Fig. 11, and the fifth patient (Nielsen, 1946, p. 188) showed the same pattern except that his drawing ability was not tested. These patients were each the subjects of detailed examinations by their physicians, with the following results. These patients are not blind, but have difficulty describing complex stimuli. Their performance on imagery question-answering tasks is poor, and their descriptions of the appearances of objects from memory is reported to be vague, sparse, and inaccurate. For the four patients whose drawing ability was tested, both their copies and their drawings from memory were sketchy, inaccurate and disorganized. In view of their perceptual deficits, it is not surprising that these patients also had difficulty recognizing objects.

These patients are so impaired that there are very few components that can be ruled out by virtue of occurring in a successfully performed task. Therefore, an inference can only be made on the basis of parsimony. The only component that occurs in all and only the failed tasks is the inspection component. The simplest alternative account of these patients' deficits requires that three cognitive components be damaged: long-term visual memories, copy, and describe. The relevance of parsimony may be questioned here, however, in view of these patients' rather extensive bilateral damage, from carbon monoxide poisoning (Adler, 1944; Brown, 1972, Case 13), infection (Brain, 1941), surgical trauma (Levine, 1978), or multiple strokes (Nielsen, 1946, p. 188).

Associated cognitive deficits

Imagery has been hypothesized to play an essential role in many kinds of thinking and problem-solving. One might therefore expect loss of imagery to be accompanied by other cognitive deficits. Although most of the patients described here had some other cognitive deficits, none of these deficits ap-

Figure 11. *Inferring an inspection process deficit. Solid outline indicates that a compo-nent is ruled out as the reason for the patients' failure in the imagery tasks by virtue of appearing in the analysis of a successfully performed task.*

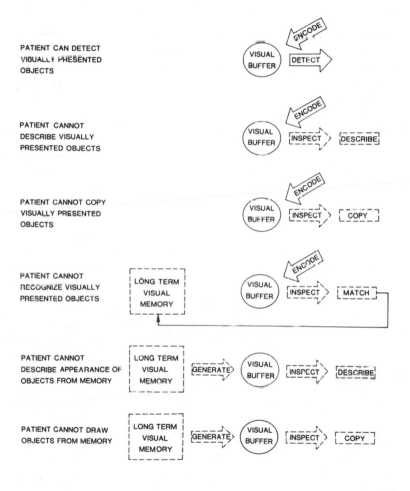

Table 5.   *Cases inferred to have an inspection process deficit. For each case the primary topic of the case report, the etiology and the general anatomical area of cortical damage are listed*

Case	Topic	Etiology	Lesion site
Adler (1944)	Visual agnosia	Anoxia	Diffuse (especially posterior)
Brain (1941)	Visual agnosia	Infection	Diffuse
Brown (1972) Case 13 (also described by Benson and Greenberg, 1969)	Visual agnosia	Anoxia	Diffuse (especially posterior)
Levine (1978)	Visual agnosia	Surgical trauma	Bilateral temporal, parietal and occipital (greater on right)
Nielsen (1946) p. 188	Simultanagnosia	Cerebrovascular accident	Bilateral parietal and occipital

peared consistently, either across all patients or within a single group of patients. Indeed, Brain (1954) expressed surprise at the general sparing of intellectual ability in his patients who had lost imagery ability. This lack of consequence may reflect the flexibility of human cognition, and the availability of alternative means of performing what might normally be imagery-mediated tasks, such as route-finding, mental arithmetic, or spelling aloud.

The only consistent functional associate of loss of imagery in these cases was loss of dreaming. Of the 17 cases of loss of imagery which included information about dreaming, all but 3 reported either a total loss of dreaming (Basso *et al.*, 1980; Boyle and Nielsen, 1954; Humphrey and Zangwill, 1951, Cases 2 and 3; Lyman *et al.*, 1938; Nielsen, 1955, postscript Cases 1 and 2), a dramatic reduction in dreaming (described by the patient as, e.g., "almost no dreams": Epstein, 1979, Case 1; Humphrey and Zangwill, 1951, Case 1; Wilbrand, 1887, transl. Critchley, 1953), or a selective loss of the visual component of dreaming (Adler, 1944; Brain, 1954, Case 1; Brown, 1972, Case 13; Macrae and Trolle, 1956). The exceptions to this trend for impairment of dreaming were Shuttleworth *et al.*'s (1982, Case 2) prosopagnosic patient, who maintained that she did experience visual elements in her dreams, Brain's (1941) apperceptive agnosic child, who was able to relate a dream involving black and white dogs (which suggests that visual elements were present in the dream), and Brown's (1972, Case 12) apperceptive agnosic who, while cortically blind, suffered from vivid nightmares. (The report of Brown's Case 12 did not make clear what the criteria were by which the patient was judged to have lost his imagery ability, leaving open the possibility that this patient had not actually lost imagery.) In order to decide whether these cases undermine the hypothesis that common structures and processes underlie dreaming and waking imagery we would want to know if the dreams of these patients, though present, have deficits that parallel the deficits of their waking imagery. For example, in the case of Shuttleworth *et al.'s* patient, the critical association or dissociation would not simply be between the presence of dreams and her waking imagery deficit, but between the presence of faces in her dreams and her waking imagery deficit, as this primarily involved faces. Although a selective deficit for dreaming of faces might seem a far-fetched idea, such a deficit has been described by Tzavaras (1967), in the context of prosopagnosia. Similarly, we would want to know whether Brain's patient could image a black dog as distinct from a white one while awake.

Cases of impaired dreaming with preserved waking imagery would naturally not be included in the present review of loss of imagery, but would nevertheless be relevant to assessing the strength of association between waking and dream imagery. Greenberg and Farah (in press) reviewed the loss of dreaming literature, including but not limited to the cases cited here, and found no cases of loss of dreaming in which loss of waking imagery was noted to be intact. Thus, there is a strong association between waking and dream imagery after brain damage, which suggests shared neural mechanisms for these two processes.

Summary and discussion of findings

Two general goals for this project were set out at the beginning of the paper: First, to use a componential analysis of imagery derived from studies of normal humans to understand the neurological phenomena of loss of imagery, and second, to use the results of this neurological study to illuminate the functioning of the intact imagery system. Most of the paper so far has focused on the first goal, by describing the componential model of imagery and the ways in which the different patterns of preserved abilities and deficits found in different cases can be interpreted in terms of the model: on the basis of the model we expected to find greater homogeneity within groups of patients sharing a deficit in the same underlying component than across different kinds of imagery deficits, and this expectation was borne out.

Patients with a deficit in the image generation process showed a consistent trend in lesion site, despite rather weak localizing information in many cases.

Most of the patients had most or all of their damage in the posterior left quadrant of the brain. The quality of the localizing information makes a more precise localization impossible at present. However, the most obvious and perhaps the most striking aspect of this relatively coarse-grained localization is its laterality. As Ehrlichman and Barrett (1983) have documented, there exists a widespread assumption that imagery is a right hemisphere function. However, in reviewing the neuropsychology literature on the laterality of imagery, they found that the data supporting the 'right hemisphere' hypothesis do not actually apply to image generation *per se*, but rather to various forms of so-called 'spatial ability' and higher visual perceptual processing.

The laterality of the image generation process identified here is in agreement with the outcome of a recent case study of a split-brain patient (Farah *et al.*, 1985). Whereas the disconnected left hemisphere could perform a task requiring image generation, the right hemisphere could not, despite its facility with all of the components of the imagery task except for image generation itself. Both hemispheres could classify briefly presented lower case letters as including or not including a long 'stem' (e.g. 't' and 'g' have long stems, 'a' and 'r' do not), and both could associate a briefly presented upper case letter with the corresponding lower case form. Their performances diverged sharply, however, in the corresponding imagery task: When given the upper case form of a letter as a cue to classify the lower case form as having ot not having a long stem, the left hemisphere continued to perform essentially perfectly, and the right hemisphere dropped to chance levels of performance.

The present project provides inductive evidence that if a patient has lost the ability to generate images then he or she will have left posterior damage. We do not yet know what proportion of patients with damage in this area will also have an image generation deficit. Although published reports of loss of imagery are rare compared with reports of other cognitive disabilities (e.g. linguistic, attentional), this measure may greatly underestimate the incidence of imagery disorders for two reasons. First, the critical area for image generation may be close to the posterior language centers of the left hemisphere. Thus, many patients with lesions in this area may be unable to communicate their loss of imagery. Second, patients are not as likely to complain to their doctors about a loss of imagery as they are about a loss of language or vision. In this vein, it is interesting to note that of the seventeen cases of loss of imagery in which the patient's occupation or hobby was reported, eight patients worked in architecture, building, carpentry, painting or set design, activities that demand visualization.

Although an anatomical locus for long-term visual memories was not found, there was a trend for parallel content-specific deficits in imagery and recognition, implying that the imagery system shares representations with perceptual processes in the brain, an intuitively appealing idea (e.g. see Hebb, 1968) for which little evidence exists.

This analysis of loss of imagery also has implications for our understanding of the intact imagery system in normal humans. The most obvious implica tions have already been mentioned. Neuropsychological evidence for the existence of an image generation process, distinct from the long-term visual memories themselves and from other recall processes, and a functional localization for that process. Other relevant findings include the associations between waking imagery and dreaming, and between content-specific imagery and recognition deficits, which suggest the existence of shared components for these pairs of seemingly disparate processes in the functional architecture of the normal brain.

At a more general level, the results of this project support the existence of an imagery system distinct from other memory and reasoning processes, with an internal structure corresponding to the components outlined in this paper. On a 'single code' account of imagery, such as Pylyshyn (1981) has put forward, imagery consists of recalling and manipulating information about the appearances of objects in a way that is not fundamentally different from recalling and manipulating information about other memory contents, such as historical facts, philosophical arguments, etc. If this were true, then one would not expect to find cases of selective loss of imagery ability any more than of selective loss of history or philosophy ability, and one would certainly not expect to find a separate brain area dedicated to one of these abilities.

The ability of the componential analysis of imagery used in this paper to interpret the loss of imagery literature also provides support for that particular analysis. Despite an occasional stray datum, for example the effect of opening the eyes on Brain's (1954) second patient, there is a substantial match between the observed patterns of performance on different tasks under different conditions and the kinds of patterns that are allowed assuming the present componential model. The situation could have been otherwise: for example, patients might have been described who had content-specific imagery deficits but no recognition deficits, or an isolated imagery deficit for remote but not recent memories. By and large the deficits and abilities reported did divide up along the lines that the model can account for. Therefore, although the case reports were interpreted *assuming* the model to be true, it is not entirely circular to consider the ability of the model to interpret these cases as supporting the model.

The last 15 years in cognitive psychology have seen enormous growth in our understanding of mental imagery. This progress has been made almost entirely within the theoretical confines of the information-processing paradigm, which eschews all concerns with neural 'hardware'. This paper represents an initial attempt to make contact between the theoretical constructs of cognitive theories of imagery and neurological phenomena. The results presented here are preliminary, and limited by the quality of the cognitive and neurological information available in the case reports. Nevertheless, they are grounds for optimism for future studies of imagery in neurological patients, using the experimental methodologies as well as the theoretical framework of current cognitive psychology.

References

Adler, A. (1944) Disintegration and restoration of optic recognition in visual agnosia. *Arch. Neurol. and Psychiat., 51*, 243–259.

Albert, M.L., Reches, A. and Silverberg, R. (1975) Associative visual agnosia without alexia. *Neurology, 25*, 322–326.

Arbuse, D.I. (1947) The Gerstmann syndrome: Case report and review of the literature. *J. Nerv. Ment. Dis., 105*, 359–371.

Basso, A., Bisiach, E. and Luzzatti, C. (1980) Loss of mental imagery: A case study. *Neuropsychologia, 8*, 435–442.

Benson, D.F. and Greenberg, J.P. (1969) Visual form agnosia. *Arch. Neurol., 20*, 82–89.

Beyn, E.S. and Knyazeva, G.R. (1962) The problem of prosopagnosia. *J. Neurol.. Neurosurg. Psychiat., 25*, 154–158.

Bisiach, E. and Luzzatti, C. (1978) Unilateral neglect of representational space. *Cortex, 14*, 129–133.

Bisiach, E., Luzzatti, C. and Persni, D. (1979) Unilateral neglect, representational schema and consciousness. *Brain, 102*, 609–618.

Boyle, J. and Nielsen, J.M. (1954) Visual agnosia and loss of recall: Report of case. *Bull. Los Angeles Neurol. Soc., 19*, 39–43.

Brain, R.W. (1954) Loss of visualization. *Proc. R. Soc. Med., 47*, 288–290.

Brain, R.W. (1950) The cerebral basis of consciousness. *Brain, 73*, 465–479.

Brain, R.W. (1941) Visual object agnosia with special reference to the Gestalt theory. *Brain, 64*, 43–62.

Brown, J.W. (1972) *Aphasia, Apraxia and Agnosia: Clinical and Theoretical Aspects*. Springfield, IL, Charles C. Thomas.

Brownell, H.H., Farah, M.J., Harley, J.P. and Kosslyn, S.M. (1984) Distinguishing imagistic and linguistic thought: A case report. Paper submitted for publication.

Critchley, M. (1953) *The Parietal Lobes*. London, Arnold.

Eddy, J.K. and Glass, A.L. (1981) Reading and listening to high and low imagery sentences. *J. verb. Learn. verb. Behav., 20*, 333–345.

Ehrlichman, H. and Barrett, J. (1983) Right hemispheric specialization for mental imagery: A review of the evidence. *Br. Cog., 2*, 39–52.

Epstein, A.W. (1979) Effect of certain cerebral diseases on dreaming. *Biol. Psychiat., 14*, 77–93.

Farah, M.J. (1985) Psychophysical evidence for a shared representational medium for visual images and percepts. *J. exp. Psychol. Gen., 114*, 91–103.

Farah, M.J., Gazzaniga, S.M., Holtzman, J.D. and Kosslyn, S.M. (1985) A left hemisphere basis for visual imagery. *Neuropsychologia, 23,* 115–118.

Finke, R.A. and Kosslyn, S.M. (1980) Mental imagery acuity in the peripheral visual field. *J. exp. Psychol.: Hum. Percep. Perf., 6,* 126–139.

Finke, R.A. and Kurtzman, H S. (1981) Area and contrast effects upon perceptual and imagery acuity. *J. exp. Psychol.: Hum. Percept. Perf., 7,* 825.

Finke, R.A. and Schmidt, M.J. (1977) Orientation-specific color aftereffects following imagination. *J. exp. Psychol.: Human. Percept. Perf., 3,* 599–606.

Finke, R.A. and Schmidt, M.J. (1978) The quantitative measurement of pattern representation in images using orientation-specific color aftereffects. *Percep. Psychophys., 23,* 515–520.

Finke, R.A. and Shepard, R.N. (In Press) Visual functions of mental imagery. In L. Kaufman and J. Thomas (eds.), *Handbook of Perception and Human Performance.* New York, John Wiley & Sons.

Greenberg, M.S. and Farah, M. J. (In press) The laterality of dreaming. *Brain and Cognition.*

Hebb, D.O. (1968) Concerning imagery. *Psychol. Rev., 75,* 466–477.

Holmes, G. (1944) The organization of the visual cortex in man. *Proc. R. Soc. Lond., 132,* 348–361.

Humphrey, M.E. and Zangwill, O.L. (1951) Cessation of dreaming after brain injury. *J. Neurol., Neurosurg. Psychiat., 14,* 322–325.

Kosslyn, S.M. and Jolicoeur, P. (1980) A theory-based approach to the study of individual differences in mental imagery. In R.E. Snow, P A. Federico and W.E. Montague (eds.) *Aptitude, Learning and Instruction: Cognitive Processes Analysis of Aptitude,* Vol. 1. Hillsdale, NJ, Erlbaum.

Kosslyn, S.M. and Shwartz, S.P. (1977) A simulation of visual imagery. *Cog. Sci., 1,* 265–295.

Kosslyn, S.M. (1980) *Image and Mind.* Cambridge, MA, Harvard University Press.

Levine, D.N. (1978) Prosopagnosia and visual object agnosia: A behavioral study. *Br. Lang., 5,* 341–365.

Luria, A.R. (1973) *The Working Brain: An Introduction to Neuropsychology.* Baltimore, Penguin.

Lyman, R.S., Kwan, S.T. and Chao, W.H. (1938) Left occipito-parietal brain tumor with observations on alexia and agraphia in Chinese and English. *Chinese Med. J., 54,* 491–516.

Macrae, D. and Trolle, E. (1956) The defect of function in visual agnosia. *Brain, 79,* 94–110.

Marr, D. (1982) *Vision.* San Francisco, W.H. Freemand & Co..

Nielsen, J.M. (1946) *Agnosia, Apraxia, Aphasia: Their Value in Cerebral Localization.* New York, Paul B. Hoeber.

Nielsen, J.M. (1955) Occipital lobes, dreams and psychosis. *J. nerv. ment. Dis., 121,* 30–32.

Podgorny, P. and Shepard, R.N. (1978) Functional representations common to visual perception and imagination. *J. exp. Psychol.: Hum. Percep. Perf., 4,* 21–35.

Pylyshyn, Z.W. (1981) The imagery debate: Analogue media versus tacit knowledge. *Psychol. Rev., 87,* 16–45.

Ratcliff, G. and Newcombe, F. (1982) Object recognition. In A.W. Ellis (ed.), *Normality and Pathology in Cognitive Functions.* New York, Academic Press.

Selfridge, O.G. and Neisser, U. (1960) Pattern recognition by machine. *Scient. Am,m 203,* 60–68.

Shulman, S.L., Remington, R.W. and McClean, M.C. (1979) Moving attention through visual space. *J. exp. Psychol.: Hum. Percep. Perf., 5,* 522–526.

Shuttleworth, E.C., Syring, V. and Allen, N. (1982) Further observations on the nature of prosopagnosia. *Br. Cog., 1,* 302–332.

Spalding, J.M.K. and Zangwill, O.L. (1950) Disturbance of number-form in a case of brain injury. *J. Neurol., Neurosurg. Psychiat., 13,* 24–29.

Taylor, A. and Warrington, E.K. (1971) Visual agnosia: A single case report. *Cortex, 7,* 152–161.

Triesman, A.M. and Gelade, G. (1980) A feature-integration theory of attention. *Cog. Psychol., 12,* 97–136.

Tzavaras, A. (1967) Contribution a l'etude de l'agnosie des physiognomies: Memoire pour le titre d'assistants etrangers. Paris, Faculte des Medicine de Paris, *1.*

Ullman, S. (1984) Visual Routines, *Cog., 18,* 97–159.

Wapner, W., Judd, T. and Gardner, H. (1978) Visual agnosia in an artist. *Cortex, 14,* 343–364.

Index

Italicized page numbers following names indicate reference entries.